Data Stewardship in Action

A roadmap to data value realization and measurable
business outcomes

Pui Shing Lee

Data Stewardship in Action

Group Product Manager: Niranjan Naikwadi

Publishing Product Manager: Tejashwini R

Book Project Manager: Kirti Pisat

Senior Editor: Vandita Grover

Technical Editor: Rahul Limbachiya

Copy Editor: Safis Editing

Proofreader: Safis Editing

Indexer: Manju Arasan

Production Designer: Jyoti Kadam

DevRel Marketing Coordinator: Vinishka Kalra

First published: January 2024

Production reference: 1250124

Published by Packt Publishing Ltd.

Grosvenor House

11 St Paul's Square

Birmingham

B3 1RB, UK.

ISBN 978-1-83763-659-4

www.packtpub.com

To my beloved wife, Annie, the beacon of my life who has always been my strongest pillar of support and my ceaseless source of inspiration. Your patience and love have been the guiding lights in my journey of writing this book.

To our precious newborn baby, Lok Yan, the newest spark of joy in our lives. Your arrival has filled our hearts with immense happiness and has given me renewed strength and motivation. Every word penned in these pages is a testament to the hope and dreams we hold for you. You are the future; the future is yours.

To my cherished family, who have stood by me through thick and thin, always encouraging me, believing in me, and cheering me on. Your unwavering faith in me has been my greatest strength. I am forever grateful for your love and support.

And lastly, to my three lovely fur babies, BallBall, Brownie, and Creamy. Your purrs and cuddles have been the best stress-relievers during the most challenging times of this journey. Your feline antics have brought joy and laughter to our home, making the process of writing this book a delightful experience.

This book is a product of all the unconditional love, support, and patience that you have generously given me. I dedicate it to you all, with my deepest gratitude and love. Thank you!

In memory of BallBall

– Pui Shing Lee

Foreword

I have over 30 years of experience in the data industry, from databases to artificial intelligence, and in recent years, I established the Data Literacy Association, with the goal of empowering users to effectively utilize data and leverage its business potential in their daily work and lives. This book on data stewardship is extremely timely. As more users incorporate data into their everyday routines and data becomes an integral part of their lives, it is crucial for them to understand the significance of data stewardship and implement it within their companies.

It's comparable to having a smart home equipped with intelligence, convenience, and personalized services. If you fail to secure the door and properly manage the security of your home devices while safeguarding your day-to-day data, disaster may strike one day. I urge you to read this book attentively and take action before it's too late. It's not just a book for technical and data professionals; it's also relevant to business leaders and executives, as well as anyone who uses data in their daily lives.

I extend my gratitude to the book author, Pui Shing Lee, for investing significant effort in writing this book and spending time to distill his invaluable experiences and presenting them in an easily understandable manner. Thanks for your contribution to the world of data literacy.

Dr. Toa Charm

Founding Chairman

Data Literacy Association

Contributors

About the author

Pui Shing Lee is a visionary leader with two decades' experience in FinTech, data, AI, and cloud across Europe, the US, and APAC. He is a cloud solution strategist (Data & AI) at Microsoft. With a passion for deriving actionable insights from data, he provides comprehensive solutions for customers' journeys, ensuring tangible business outcomes.

Shing holds industry-leading certifications including DAMA CDMP and EDMC CDMC V1. His professional experience includes roles as chief data officer at Hang Seng Index, head of data governance at HKEX, and APAC director at IHS Markit. As the co-founder of the Data Literacy Association, Shing advocates for a culture-fit data strategy, self-service models, and automated governance on robust cloud platforms.

I want to thank the Packt team who have been very supportive. Vandita, Kirti, and Tejashwini, thanks for the coordination and guidance.

A heartfelt thank you to my friend Lance for being the reviewer; your insightful advice has elevated this book to its greatest potential.

I extend my deepest gratitude to Dr. Toa Charm for graciously writing the foreword of my book; your esteemed perspective has truly enhanced its value.

About the reviewers

Anthony A Afolabi is a principal consultant on major data management and governance engagements, with over 12 years of experience in the financial services, consulting, banking, and capital market sectors. He is deeply experienced in the implementation of design principles for banking applications, enterprise risk data architectures, and data warehouse solutions, planning, and mobilization, the execution of global programs, and operational risk management. He has been integral to the implementation of BCBS 239 at major banking groups, G-SIBs, and D-SIBs across Europe and North America, where he was responsible for both the end-to-end delivery and post-implementation assurance frameworks for the first, second, and third lines of defense.

Lance Yeung is the data governance lead at the **Hong Kong Science and Technology Parks Corporation (HKSTP)**, where he steers organizations from various sectors towards success in the digital economy. His strategic leadership ensures robust data integrity and compliance, which are vital for innovation in industries such as banking, insurance, logistics, transportation, healthcare, hospitality, and government. Lance's seasoned background includes impactful stints at the **Hong Kong Monetary Authority (HKMA)** and **Hong Kong Exchanges and Clearing Limited (HKEX)**. This multidimensional exposure equips him with insights to craft data governance frameworks and strategies that enable businesses to navigate and excel in a data-centric global marketplace.

Table of Contents

3

Getting Started with the Data Stewardship Program   35

Part 2: How to Become a Data Steward and Shine!

4

Developing a Comprehensive Data Management Strategy   53

5

People, Process, and Technology   73

6

Establishing a Data Governance Organization   103

7

Data Steward Roles and Responsibilities   125

11

Theory versus Real Life   211

12

Case Studies   229

Preface

In an age where data is often heralded as the new oil, the role of a data steward has become increasingly critical. As organizations navigate the complexities of digital transformation, the need for a comprehensive understanding of data stewardship is more pressing than ever. This book is a response to that need—a guide that demystifies the role of data stewards, equips aspiring professionals with actionable insights, and serves as a beacon for those who wish to master the art and science of data management.

The journey of writing this book began with a simple observation: while there is a wealth of information on data science, engineering, and analytics, there is a noticeable gap when it comes to the nuanced field of data stewardship. This gap is not just academic; it reflects a real-world disconnect that organizations grapple with daily. The role of a data steward is often misunderstood, undervalued, and yet, absolutely vital to the health and success of any data-driven enterprise.

This book aims to bridge that gap by providing a comprehensive and practical guide to the world of data stewardship. It is crafted for individuals who recognize the importance of data as a strategic asset and are seeking to either step into the role of a data steward or enhance their existing data management practices.

As you turn these pages, you will embark on a journey that begins with the alignment of business strategy to data strategy and culminates in the implementation of robust data stewardship programs. You will learn not just the theory but also the practicalities of managing data effectively. Each chapter is designed to be both informative and engaging, offering real-life examples, case studies, and best practices that have been tested and proven in the field. Moreover, this book recognizes the ever-evolving nature of technology. It delves into how emerging tools such as **Generative Pre-trained Transformer (GPT)** models can revolutionize data governance and stewardship, providing a glimpse into the future of data management.

The preface would be incomplete without acknowledging the collective wisdom that has shaped this book. Insights from industry experts, feedback from peers, and the experiences of those on the front lines of data stewardship have all contributed to its creation. This book is a testament to the power of collaboration and the shared vision of elevating the practice of data stewardship.

Who this book is for

This book is for individuals interested in the role of a data steward and seeking to advance in the field of data management. It targets existing data team members, chief data officers, chief digital officers, strategy managers, and newcomers to the field aiming to gain a deeper understanding of data stewardship responsibilities, best practices, and implementation strategies.

What this book covers

Chapter 1, *From Business Strategy to Data Strategy to Data Stewardship*, explores the transformation from business strategy to data strategy and, ultimately, to data stewardship, emphasizing skill development and execution practices for effective data management programs.

Chapter 2, *How Data Stewardship Can Help Your Organization*, explains data stewardship's role in enhancing competitive advantage by improving data accuracy, security, and management, leading to cost reduction and increased customer satisfaction.

Chapter 3, *Getting Started with the Data Stewardship Program*, guides you on starting a data stewardship program, highlighting stakeholder buy-in, key program elements, and strategies for addressing initial data management challenges.

Chapter 4, *Developing a Comprehensive Data Management Strategy*, takes you through creating a data management strategy, from assessing current states to defining future goals and executing governance, quality, and security plans.

Chapter 5, *People, Process, Technology*, delves into the interplay of people, processes, and technology in data stewardship, showing ROI and improving practices through automation and **artificial intelligence (AI)**.

Chapter 6, *Establishing a Data Governance Structure*, outlines the steps for establishing a data governance structure, fostering a data culture, and defining KPIs, and provides tools for creating and measuring a successful governance program.

Chapter 7, *Data Steward Roles and Responsibilities*, defines data steward roles, emphasizing data quality, access control, security, and compliance, equipping you with frameworks for effective data governance.

Chapter 8, *Effective Data Stewardship*, discusses principles of effective data stewardship, including data ownership, role assignment, accountability, and leveraging continuous training for a successful data governance roadmap.

Chapter 9, *Supercharge Data Governance and Stewardship with GPT*, explores using GPT for enhancing data governance and stewardship, automating management tasks, and ensuring data privacy, security, and the prevention of bias in AI applications.

Chapter 10, *Data Stewardship Best Practices*, shares best practices for data stewardship, aligning mindsets, upskilling teams, fostering accountability, and ownership, and integrating emerging technologies for effective data management programs.

Chapter 11, *Theory versus Real Life*, addresses the gap between theory and real-life data stewardship, emphasizing collaboration, continuous monitoring, and improvement for bridging this divide and ensuring program success.

Chapter 12, *Case Studies*, presents two case studies on effective data stewardship: the Bank of East Asia fosters a data-driven culture for operational efficiency, while Fencore's solution streamlines fund management, showcasing the practical impact of data strategies.

To get the most out of this book

We assume you have a basic understanding of data life cycle and process flow management in the context of enterprises. You should also be familiar with the basic data and cloud technology for data ingestion, transformation, and storage. Ideally, you should have experience in fostering a new working culture for an organization and a strong interest in extracting the utmost value from raw data.

To fully engage with the practical elements of this book, especially in chapters discussing the integration of AI in data stewardship, you may need to set up an OpenAI/Azure OpenAI account for access to GPT models.

Additionally, while not mandatory, registering with professional bodies such as the **EDM Council (EDMC)** or DAMA International could enhance your understanding and provide valuable resources aligned with the advanced topics covered in this book. These platforms offer a wealth of knowledge and community support that can complement your learning journey.

Conventions used

There are a number of text conventions used throughout this book.

Keyword: This indicates a new word or phrase when it is first introduced. Here is an example: "**Data stewardship** is the practice of managing data ethically and responsibly."

Italics: This is used to add emphasis to a sentence or add a figure, table, chapter, or other reference. Here is an example: "We have several key building blocks, as illustrated in *Figure 2.2* in *Chapter 2*."

Get in touch

Feedback from our readers is always welcome.

General feedback: If you have questions about any aspect of this book, email us at `customercare@packtpub.com` and mention the book title in the subject of your message.

Errata: Although we have taken every care to ensure the accuracy of our content, mistakes do happen. If you have found a mistake in this book, we would be grateful if you would report this to us. Please visit `www.packtpub.com/support/errata` and fill in the form. Visit `https://github.com/PacktPublishing/Data-Stewardship-in-Action` to refer to published errata for this book.

Piracy: If you come across any illegal copies of our works in any form on the internet, we would be grateful if you would provide us with the location address or website name. Please contact us at copyright@packtpub.com with a link to the material.

If you are interested in becoming an author: If there is a topic that you have expertise in and you are interested in either writing or contributing to a book, please visit authors.packtpub.com.

Share Your Thoughts

Once you've read *Data Stewardship in Action*, we'd love to hear your thoughts! Scan the QR code below to go straight to the Amazon review page for this book and share your feedback.

https://packt.link/r/1-837-63659-1

Your review is important to us and the tech community and will help us make sure we're delivering excellent quality content.

Download a free PDF copy of this book

Thanks for purchasing this book!

Do you like to read on the go but are unable to carry your print books everywhere?

Is your eBook purchase not compatible with the device of your choice?

Don't worry, now with every Packt book you get a DRM-free PDF version of that book at no cost.

Read anywhere, any place, on any device. Search, copy, and paste code from your favorite technical books directly into your application.

The perks don't stop there, you can get exclusive access to discounts, newsletters, and great free content in your inbox daily

Follow these simple steps to get the benefits:

1. Scan the QR code or visit the link below

https://packt.link/free-ebook/9781837636594

2. Submit your proof of purchase
3. That's it! We'll send your free PDF and other benefits to your email directly

Part 1:
Why Data Stewardship
and Why Me?

Here, you will begin the foundational journey of aligning your business strategy with data strategy and stewardship in the initial chapters of this insight-packed book. You will discover how to unlock the latent value of data, develop the required mindset and skillset, and transition seamlessly from strategic planning to execution. These chapters are crafted to guide you through the inception of data stewardship, demonstrating its organizational benefits and providing a practical roadmap to initiate a robust data stewardship program.

This part has the following chapters:

- *Chapter 1, From Business Strategy to Data Strategy to Data Stewardship*
- *Chapter 2, How Data Stewardship Can Help Your Organization*
- *Chapter 3, Getting Started with the Data Stewardship Program*

From Business Strategy to Data Strategy to Data Stewardship

"Data is the new oil"

"Data is the new currency"

"Data is the common language"

All these buzz-phrases fail to resonate when you are trying to secure a budget for data programs in a management meeting. Distracted stakeholders, lack of impact, and stagnating initiatives often become the norm as data quality issues mount and data compliance challenges multiply.

Everyone recognizes the need for a data-driven culture, yet nobody wants to own the responsibility. Conducting a lot of data workshops will not bring you closer to your objectives if data stewardship and strategy are not aligned with the business strategy.

The struggle is real and the cycle is repetitive – once you leave the organization after years of struggle, your successor restarts the data stewardship program, and the story replays.

Does this sound familiar to you?

As a data professional, it is unrealistic for you to expect other business functions to dedicate time to understanding data intricacies, just as you would not spend days learning about marketing, HR, or accounting.

The key question for your audience is the following: *What is in it for me?*

Consider redefining your data initiatives, including a data stewardship program, as a solution to practical problems: freeing up Friday nights spent on report consolidation, introducing efficient self-service data analytics tools, and offering potential bonuses tied to meeting data quality metrics.

Now we are talking.

Data stewardship is not limited to a data workshop or two. It's a direction, a mindset, and a problem-solving mechanism. In the first chapter, we'll emphasize the pivotal role of data stewardship in aligning data initiatives with business strategy and solving real business issues.

Then how does data stewardship relate to the business strategy?

Again, think from the C-level perspective – what is in it for the senior executives if they invest x amount of money and y amount of head counts into data stewardship initiatives?

So, what is data stewardship and why is it essential? We will explore these questions and a few more in this chapter.

In this chapter, we will discuss the following:

- Understanding the strategic, tactical, and operational value of data stewardship
- Unlocking business value with data stewardship
- Exploring the mindset and skillset gap
- Translating strategy into execution
- Decoding data governance, management, and stewardship

Understanding the strategic, tactical, and operational value of data stewardship

Data stewardship is the practice of managing data ethically and responsibly. Data stewards are responsible for ensuring that data is used in a way that respects the rights of individuals and meets the business objectives of the organization. Data stewardship requires a holistic approach to data management. It involves developing a data strategy that aligns with the organization's business strategy, establishing data governance policies and procedures, and designing data models and architectures that can support the implementation of an automated data operating model on the cloud. All of these only make sense if you can tie them to business objectives.

Now, we will look at how data stewardship is related to business strategy and how it can help businesses achieve their goals. We will also discuss how to develop a data strategy that aligns with the business strategy and how to identify the key stakeholders involved in the data stewardship process. Finally, we will discuss how to develop a data stewardship program that will help businesses unlock the value of their data.

Bridging the gap between data strategy and data operation

Data stewardship is not a tick-box exercise. It is a continuous refinement of your data operation to support your new business model. You need to tackle from strategic, tactical, and operational levels (*Figure 1.1*) to make it a sustainable program and ensure that it meets both short- and long-term business objectives horizontally and vertically:

- **Strategic**: It's designed with the entire organization in mind and begins with an organization's mission. This will also influence the culture within an organization.

- **Tactical**: It describes the series of plans to achieve the ambitions outlined in the strategy.

- **Operational**: It is highly specific with a measurable metric and usually couples with **standard operating procedures (SOPs)** to ensure the consistency of operation excellence.

Figure 1.1 shows how a high-level strategy gets broken down into mid-level tactical plans, and then finally into on-the-ground operations.

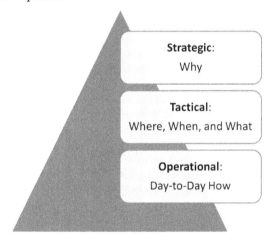

Figure 1.1 – An organizational view of data stewardship

It is a *business-friendly* way to visualize how things get done in a big organization.

Your organization's business strategy drives your data, AI, marketing, cybersecurity, and all other strategies. From there, specifically for data, you need the data governance and stewardship program to link up strategic and operational levels. Then you have the data operating model and related SOPs to make sure that data is utilized and protected in the right way in day-to-day activities.

Data stewardship is a core element of the tactical layer but it can also cover some of the of operational activities too. The key takeaway is you have to align the expected outcomes and prioritize the deliverables with the stakeholders along with relevant and measurable outcomes. You should make sure it can glue the high-level strategy and the ground-level execution together.

In the upcoming section, we will also talk about not just the three horizontal layers but also the vertical bonding so that team resources and outcomes are aligned.

Data stewardship is not another IT project that runs for 15 months and into a never-ending **user acceptance test** (**UAT**) of new software. Then, stakeholders do not even appreciate your team's effort when you think you have been going the extra mile. No one is happy in this case and it happens quite often in the corporate world. You do not want to run into this scenario.

Let's now discuss how data stewardship helps create more business value by translating strategy into operation.

Unlocking business value with data stewardship

Let's explore the importance of data stewardship in unlocking business value. Data stewardship can help your organization to make informed decisions based on trustworthy data. This is the cornerstone of all your data analytics and AI initiatives because data is the ultimate fuel.

Let's understand what a business strategy is and why it's relevant to data strategy and data governance.

Understanding business strategy

Let's zoom in on the concept of business strategy and how it is used to drive business outcomes. Since it is not a book about business strategy, we will just lightly touch on how a business strategy is developed.

A **business strategy** is a plan of action that outlines how a business will achieve its goals and objectives. It involves setting objectives, identifying resources, analyzing the competitive environment, and creating a plan of action to reach the desired outcome. The strategy should be tailored to the company's unique strengths and weaknesses and should take into account the external environment, such as customer needs, competitive pressures, and market trends.

Here are the steps to help create an effective business strategy:

1. To understand how your organization's business executives develop a business strategy, you need to identify your organization's goals and objectives. These should be **SMART**:

    *   **Specific**: Your objective should clearly state what you or the team needs to achieve. For example, you can set a target to boost the quarterly sales revenue by 15% by introducing new data-driven marketing strategies.

    *   **Measurable**: You must have a quantitative way of measuring what you have effectively achieved. For example, improve your customer satisfaction score from 75% to 85% over the next six months by utilizing customer feedback data to improve your services.

- **Achievable**: Your objective must be possible to achieve and you should secure the resources required to achieve it. Assessing the achievability of an objective necessitates a thorough evaluation of available resources, including finances, personnel, your team's expertise, time, technology, and past experience with similar objectives. Say you want to mitigate data breach risks in your company. This could be achieved by implementing a robust data encryption protocol within the next three months, utilizing the expertise of your in-house data security team.

- **Relevant**: A goal is relevant to your organization's objectives when it aligns with the broader vision, mission, and strategic direction of the company. It should contribute to the advancement of key business priorities, whether that's expanding market share, increasing revenue, or improving operational efficiency. For example, a the sales manager, increase cross-selling opportunities by 20% over the next quarter by leveraging customer purchase data.

- **Time-bound**: Data stewardship is a continuous operation but you still need to set start and end times to achieve the objective for each milestone. For example, launch a data-driven customer feedback system by the end of Q1 to proactively address customer issues and improve overall satisfaction.

2. These examples illustrate how data stewardship can contribute toward business strategy and broader organizational goals such as revenue growth, customer satisfaction, and risk management.

3. Once the goals and objectives have been established, the next step is to analyze the competitive environment. This involves researching the industry, understanding the competitive landscape, and identifying opportunities and threats.

4. The next step is to identify the resources needed to achieve the goals and objectives. This includes financial resources, human resources, and technological resources:

- **Financial resources**: These are the funds required to achieve your goals. For example, if your objective is to implement a new data management system, you need to consider costs such as software purchases or subscriptions, hardware upgrades, and potential training costs for staff. Budgeting accurately for these expenses is vital to ensure financial feasibility.

- **Human resources**: This refers to the personnel needed to carry out tasks. If your goal is to improve data quality, you'll likely need data analysts, data scientists, and possibly data stewards. Assess the current team's capabilities and determine whether additional hiring or training is needed. Also, consider the time commitment required from each team member.

- **Technological resources**: These are the tools and systems needed to achieve your objectives. If your aim is to increase data security, you may need to invest in advanced encryption software or a secure data storage system. Evaluate the current technological infrastructure and identify what upgrades or additions are necessary.

5. Once the resources have been identified, the next step is to create a plan of action. This involves setting milestones, establishing timelines, and outlining the steps that need to be taken to reach the desired outcome. For example, if your goal is to implement a new data governance framework, the milestones could be the following:

    I.   Completing audit – by the end of Q1

    II.   Designing framework – by the end of Q2

    III. Training staff – throughout Q3

    IV.   Implementing framework – by the end of Q4

    V.   Reviewing framework – by Q1 the following year

6. Finally, the strategy should be monitored and evaluated to ensure that it is achieving the desired results. This includes tracking progress, making adjustments as needed, and ensuring that the strategy is aligned with the company's goals and objectives. Along the journey, communication with stakeholders is critical. Let's say the strategy is to implement a new data management system. Progress can be tracked by monitoring system setup and integration stages, staff training completion, and the successful migration of data into the new system.

Let me now introduce you to the concept of data strategy and how it is used to support a business strategy. We will look at the different components of a data strategy, such as data architecture, data governance, and data stewardship.

Understanding data strategy

Data is a strategic asset that organizations must manage strategically. By recognizing its value, we can leverage data to gain competitive advantages and drive growth.

Data strategy is the process of developing a plan to leverage data and analytics to achieve business objectives. It involves understanding the data needs of the organization, assessing the current data landscape, and creating a plan to acquire, manage, and use data to drive business decisions.

Data strategy is used to support a business strategy by providing insights into customer needs, competitive pressures, and market trends. By leveraging data and analytics, organizations can gain a better understanding of their customers, their competitors, and their industry. This helps them to make more informed decisions and create strategies that are tailored to their unique needs. It also helps organizations to identify opportunities and risks. By understanding the data landscape, organizations can identify areas of opportunity and potential risks. This helps them to create strategies that are more likely to succeed and to avoid potential pitfalls.

With a good data strategy, organizations create more efficient and effective processes. By leveraging data and analytics, organizations can streamline processes, reduce costs, and increase efficiency. This helps them to create strategies that are more cost-effective and efficient.

From strategy to operation, you need data stewardship to glue people, processes, and technology together. This is where business strategy, data strategy, and data stewardship align and collaborate to ensure the quality, availability, security, and usability of data across the organization as a day-to-day operation.

Having explored the importance of a well-defined data strategy and its alignment with business objectives, we now step into the practical aspect of this journey. In the next section, we will discuss how to transform your data strategy from a conceptual framework into a functional, day-to-day operation that drives organizational efficiency and effectiveness.

Operationalizing your data strategy via data stewardship

Data stewardship being a key component of any successful business and data strategy helps businesses unlock the value of their data by ensuring that data is accurate, secure, and accessible. Carefully crafted data stewardship helps businesses gain insights into their customers, markets, and operations that can help them make better decisions supported by quality data and achieve their business goals in a compliant way. Data stewards are the key actors who oversee and coordinate the data life cycle, from collection to analysis to dissemination.

Data stewardship is closely linked to business strategy. To develop a successful data stewardship program, a business must first understand its business strategy and how data can help it achieve its goals. This requires the business to identify its key stakeholders, such as customers, suppliers, and employees, and understand its needs and objectives. It also requires the business to understand its current data assets and how they can be used to meet its goals. The other direction is to gather a list of burning pain points and tackle them one by one. We will discuss the use of a prioritization matrix in the upcoming chapters to help you identify the low-hanging fruit to get stakeholders' buy-in, and also pinpoint the long-term strategic data initiatives for your organization's sustainable success.

Once a business has identified its stakeholders and data assets, it can develop a data strategy that aligns with its business strategy. This data strategy should include objectives, such as increasing customer satisfaction, improving operational efficiency, and reducing costs. It should also include a plan for how to use data to achieve these objectives. This will also drive the scope of your data collection and cleaning requirements. Beware that we do not want to boil the ocean. It is not realistic to clean every data cell from your data sources. More importantly, the ROI is low and it is just not worth the effort. Instead, you should develop the definition of **critical data elements** (**CDEs**) for your organization. Focusing on CDE, which may be 10-20% of your total data assets, can resolve 80% of your organization's data pain points. We will get into the details of CDE in the next few chapters.

Finally, a business must develop a data stewardship program that will help it achieve its data strategy objectives. This program should include policies and procedures for data governance, data quality, and data security. It should also include a roadmap for how to implement the program and measure its success so that you can report it in a business-friendly format to your stakeholders.

By developing a data stewardship program that aligns with its business strategy, a business can unlock the value of its data and achieve its goals.

To ensure that data is managed ethically, we must adhere to the principles of fairness, transparency, and privacy. These principles are essential for building trust and safeguarding the integrity of data, enabling us to unlock its true potential.

So now, finally, stakeholders understand how data stewardship is relevant to the overall business.

Often, we focus too much on the data skillset enablement and overlook the importance of aligning the right data mindset.

Let's now talk about mindset and skillset.

Exploring the mindset and skillset gap

Mindset is the direction; skillset is your muscle.

With the right direction and strong muscles, you are capable of doing the right things in the right way.

Data stewardship is a critical component of any successful business and data strategy. It requires a combination of the right mindset and the right skillset to ensure that data is managed and used effectively. In this section, we will explore the importance of having the right mindset and skillset when it comes to data stewardship.

The right mindset is essential to data stewardship. It is important to understand the value of data stewardship and how it can help the organization achieve its goals. This means having an understanding of the importance of data governance, data quality, and data security. It also means being able to identify the right data sources and datasets to use and understanding the impact of data on the organization. One of the most important elements in the data mindset is asking the right question. Having the perfect solution to the wrong question does not seem right at all. With the data mindset, we should ask ourselves and others: can we make an informed decision based on data and not (just) instinct?

How about a skillset for data stewardship?

Well, data storytelling skill is remarkably important. It includes having the ability to analyze data, visualize data, and secure data. It also includes understanding the technologies and tools used to manage data, such as data warehouses, data lakes, and data marts. Finally, it includes having the ability to develop and implement a data stewardship program, including setting up a data governance team and creating a data governance roadmap. With the right tooling and upskilling, data users should be able to drive insights from the data in a consistent and future-proof way.

Mindset and skillset are the two cornerstones of data stewardship. To ensure that data stewardship is successful, organizations must invest in measurable upskilling programs to guarantee that their data stewards have the necessary skills and knowledge. This includes providing training on data analysis, data visualization, data security, and data privacy. It also includes providing guidance on best practices for data governance, data quality, and data security.

By having the right mindset and skillset, an organization can ensure that its data stewards are well-equipped to develop and maintain a successful data stewardship program. This will enable it to achieve its business goals and objectives while ensuring that its data is managed and used effectively.

With all these solid foundations in place, let us explore how to execute data stewardship as a consistent data operating model.

Upon understanding the significance of the right mindset and skillset for effective data stewardship, we are now well-equipped to take the next step. We will discuss how to transform your set of plans into actionable steps, ensuring that your data stewardship efforts become a seamless part of your organization's operational model.

Translating strategy into execution

In this section, we will explore the process of transforming a business strategy into a data strategy and then into data stewardship. We will provide you with an understanding of how to create a feedback loop between business strategy and data stewardship to ensure continuous improvement.

Executing a data strategy involves putting the plan into action. This involves implementing the data collection and management processes, developing the analytics and reporting tools, and creating the necessary infrastructure to support the data strategy.

The following subsections list the steps to execute a data strategy, common challenges faced, and recommendations to tackle those challenges.

Data collection

The first step in executing a data strategy is to collect the necessary data. Again, do not boil the ocean, and try to use the concept of CDE to scale down the complexity when you start a pilot. This involves setting up the data scoping process, such as setting up data collection systems, developing data pipelines, and creating data warehouses.

The key challenge in collecting data is data silos. A **data silo** is a repository of fixed data that remains under the control of one department and is isolated from the rest of the organization, leading to a lack of transparency, collaboration, and overall efficiency. Data silos can hinder the ability to derive meaningful insights from the data and create barriers to effective data management and governance.

To overcome this, we should deploy a data catalog, which is a structured collection of data assets, equipped with metadata, descriptions, and data lineage. The cataloging process helps in organizing and making sense of large volumes of data. This offers two benefits:

- **Enhancing transparency**: By creating a central point of access for all data assets, data cataloging reduces the opacity caused by data silos. All users can view the data sources and understand their purpose, thus promoting transparency.

- **Facilitating collaboration**: Data cataloging enables different departments to access and share data, facilitating collaboration. This cross-functional accessibility breaks down the barriers of data silos and encourages a data-driven culture.

Data governance framework

After the data is collected, the next step is to manage the data. This involves developing data governance policies, setting up data quality processes, and creating data security protocols.

One of the key challenges in implementing a data governance framework is aligning business goals with IT capabilities. Often, there is a disconnect between what the business side of an organization wants to achieve with data and what the IT department can realistically deliver. This misalignment can lead to ineffective data governance, with policies and procedures that do not support the organization's objectives.

To overcome the challenge of aligning business goals with IT capabilities, we should establish clear lines of communication between these two entities by doing the following:

- **Involving both sides in planning**: Both the business and IT departments should be involved in the planning stages of the data governance framework. This helps to ensure that the framework supports both business objectives and technical feasibility.

- **Regular meetings and updates**: Regular meetings and updates between the business and IT departments can help to keep everyone on the same page and facilitate the alignment of goals.

- **Training and education**: Providing the necessary training and education can help both sides understand each other's perspectives better, leading to more effective collaboration.

- **Implementing a data governance council**: Establishing a data governance council or committee that includes representatives from both sides can help in making decisions that align with both business and IT needs.

Analytics and reporting tools

Once we have access to data, we need to develop the analytics and reporting tools to derive insights. This involves creating dashboards, developing algorithms, and creating data visualizations.

Once the analytics and reporting tools are in place, we should then create the necessary infrastructure to support the data strategy. This includes setting up data warehouses, creating and developing data lakes.

Here, the predominant challenge is dealing with the complexity and volume of data. As the scale of data increases, its complexity also grows, making it challenging to manage and analyze. The vast amount of data generated from various sources can be overwhelming, and if not managed properly, it can lead to inefficiencies and inaccuracies in reporting and analytics.

Hence, we need a future big data platform, among others that are listed as follows:

- **Big data platforms**: Big data platforms on the cloud can efficiently process and analyze large volumes of data. They are designed to handle the scale and complexity of big data.

- **Data processing automation**: Automating data processing tasks can significantly reduce the time spent on data preparation and increase efficiency. Machine learning algorithms can be particularly useful for this.

- **Data visualization tools**: Utilizing data visualization tools can help to simplify complex data and make it more understandable. Tools such as Tableau, Power BI, and QlikView can provide interactive visualizations that make it easier to extract insights from the data.

Tracking progress

Last but not least, the data strategy should be monitored and evaluated to ensure that it is achieving the desired results. This includes tracking progress, making adjustments as needed, and ensuring that the data strategy is aligned with the company's goals and objectives.

Measuring the success of the data strategy is one of the challenges you may encounter. It can be difficult to quantify the impact of a data strategy and to determine whether it is delivering the expected benefits. This is especially true if the organization does not have clear metrics or **key performance indicators** (**KPIs**) to evaluate the effectiveness of the data strategy.

We should align on the desired outcome of a future state. Clearly defined KPIs that align with the organization's goals and objectives can provide a tangible way to measure the success of the data strategy. These could include metrics related to data quality, data usage, data governance, or business outcomes. Conducting regular reviews of the data strategy can help to identify any areas that need improvement and ensure that the strategy continues to align with the organization's goals.

Data governance is the foundation of effective data management. It ensures that data is aligned with organizational goals and objectives, enabling better decision-making and mitigating risks. Through data governance, organizations can create policies and procedures to ensure data is secure, accurate, and compliant with regulations. Data governance also helps organizations maximize the value of their data by ensuring it is properly used and shared.

Let's not forget about the feedback loop. Data initiatives should be aligned with the business strategy such that data operations are efficient and effective. With the feedback loop, you can better understand the gap and adjust your implementation.

Data governance, data management, and data stewardship. Confusing enough?

Let's demystify them one by one in the next section.

Decoding data governance, management, and stewardship

Are data governance and data management different? What roles do data stewards play? You might have several questions at this point. Let's define these terms to help you understand the key differences and relationships between them.

Data governance is the comprehensive management of the availability, usability, integrity, and security of the data employed in an enterprise. It involves establishing methods, policies, and procedures to ensure the data is well-managed throughout its life cycle.

Consider a large multinational bank. In this context, data governance involves setting up robust policies and procedures to ensure the safety and accuracy of financial data. The bank needs to establish clear rules about who can access the data, how it can be used, and how it should be secured. These rules are enforced through a combination of technologies, processes, and people. The bank also needs to ensure that its data governance policies comply with global financial regulations to avoid penalties.

On the other hand, **data management** is the practice of collecting, storing, and using data efficiently, effectively, and in a cost-efficient manner. It involves the development and execution of architectures, policies, practices, and procedures that properly manage the full data life cycle needs of an enterprise.

Let's take an example of an e-commerce company. This company collects a lot of data about customers, such as their browsing history, purchase history, and feedback. Data management in this context involves storing this data in a structured and logical manner, such as in a database, so that it can be easily retrieved when needed. It also involves ensuring that the data is accurate and up-to-date and that it can be accessed quickly and securely. The company might use data management software to help with this process.

Lastly, data stewardship focuses on managing and supervising the data assets of an organization to ensure consistent access to high-quality data for business users. It is also the implementation of data governance policies. It would facilitate the data analytics capabilities for the organization, but data stewardship is not data analytics.

For instance, consider a hospital. In this context, a data steward might be responsible for ensuring the integrity and confidentiality of patient records. They would oversee the collection and storage of data, ensuring that it is entered correctly, stored securely, and used appropriately. They would also coordinate with various teams, such as IT and legal, to ensure that the hospital's data practices comply with health information regulations.

While data governance sets the policy and strategy framework for managing data, data management is about executing those policies and strategies in a technical sense. Data stewardship, on the other hand, is the hands-on operation that ensures daily adherence to data governance policies and the upkeep of data management practices.

Data stewards wear different hats

Data stewardship within a data governance framework is an irreplaceable role. Data stewards are responsible for the management and fitness of data elements – both the content and metadata. They work hand-in-hand with data governance teams, ensuring policies and guidelines are adhered to while maintaining the quality and security of data.

For instance, in a large pharmaceutical company, data stewards might be responsible for ensuring the integrity and confidentiality of clinical trial data. They would work within the data governance framework, abiding by industry regulations and company policies. Their role might involve coordinating with various teams, such as IT and legal, to ensure data is correctly classified, stored, and used.

Comparing data stewardship in data governance and SMEs

While the core principles of data stewardship remain the same, the role can differ significantly between that of a comprehensive data governance framework and (**small and medium-sized enterprises (SMEs)**).

In a large organization, data stewardship is often a dedicated role within a robust data governance structure. For example, in a multinational bank, data stewards would work to ensure the consistency, quality, and security of vast amounts of financial data. They would follow a detailed governance framework, which might involve complex data classification systems and rigorous compliance checks.

Contrastingly, in an SME, the role of a data steward could be part of someone's broader job description. For example, in a small tech start-up, a product manager might take on the role of a data steward, ensuring that user data from the company's app is handled correctly. Given the smaller scale and lower complexity, data stewardship in an SME might be less formalized and more intertwined with other business operations.

Exploring opportunities for data stewards in data quality and data governance

Regardless of the context, data stewards have a unique opportunity to enhance data quality and strengthen data governance. By overseeing data collection, storage, and usage practices, data stewards can directly impact the reliability and integrity of data.

For example, in a mid-sized e-commerce company, a data steward could initiate a project to clean up customer data. This might involve standardizing address formats, removing duplicate entries, and validating email addresses. This would not only improve the quality of the data but also optimize marketing efforts, leading to better customer targeting and higher conversion rates.

Similarly, a data steward in a hospital could work on enhancing the data governance around patient records. They could implement stricter access controls and audit trails, ensuring data privacy and compliance with health information regulations.

In both data governance and SME contexts, effective data stewardship can lead to improved decision-making, better regulatory compliance, and increased operational efficiency. It can also foster a data-driven culture, encouraging all employees to value and properly utilize data.

Summary

In conclusion our exploration of the journey from business strategy to data strategy to data stewardship, it is evident that a comprehensive approach to data management is required, one that fully aligns with the organization's overarching business strategy. It's the business strategy that sets the course for the data strategy, ultimately determining how data should be managed, used, and protected.

Implementing this strategy necessitates the establishment of robust data governance policies and procedures, which are brought to life through the right combination of people, processes, and technology. The execution of a data strategy is a multi-faceted process involving the collection and management of data, the development of analytical and reporting tools, and the creation of a sturdy and flexible data infrastructure.

Data stewardship plays a crucial role in this journey, acting as the key to unlocking the true value of data. However, realizing data value requires more than just the right tools and processes; it requires the right mindset and skillset to manage and use data effectively.

In the next chapter, we will dive deep to see how data stewardship can help your organization advance its success and become a data-driven organization.

How Data Stewardship Can Help Your Organization

Data stewardship is an essential component of any organization's data management strategy. It is a critical part of ensuring that data is accurate, secure, and accessible. It involves managing and overseeing all aspects of the data life cycle, from creation, collection, preparation, and usage to data storage and deletion. Data stewardship holds significant importance for an organization as it leverages data as a valuable resource and asset to help achieve strategic goals and objectives. It contributes to enhancing the quality, reliability, and consistency of data throughout the organization. Furthermore, it assures compliance with data regulations, policies, and standards, safeguarding the data against unauthorized access, misuse, or loss. Lastly, data stewardship plays a vital role in fostering a data-driven culture, empowering data users and consumers, thereby enhancing the overall efficiency of the organization.

In this chapter, we will discuss how data stewardship can help your organization. We will also cover these topics:

- Defining data stewardship
- Using business cases for storytelling and value realization
- Creating a competitive edge with data stewardship

Defining data stewardship

Data stewardship is the practice of managing and protecting data to ensure it is accurate, secure, and accessible. It involves the development of policies and procedures to ensure data is properly managed and used in accordance with legal and ethical standards.

According to the **Data Management Association (DAMA)** (www.dama.org), one of the goals of data stewardship is that employees can have a mutual data conversation and make decisions without the need for someone to show them the path. The *data governance committee* in an organization can focus more on education and communication to spread data culture and knowledge among employees to have consensus and fruitful conversations about their data. Later on, we will also use the guidelines from the **Enterprise Data Management (EDM)** Council (www.edmcouncil.org) to illustrate the best practices of data stewardship and governance.

Let's drill down to the key pillars of data stewardship and the key activities of a data steward.

The work scope of a data steward

Before we explore various tasks and activities a data steward performs, we need to understand their high-level work scope and the four key pillars that drive data stewardship (*Figure 2.1*):

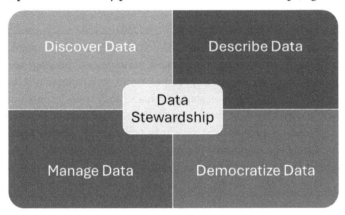

Figure 2.1 – Four key pillars of data stewardship

Let's discuss what these four pillars encompass:

- **Discover data**: Identifying an end-to-end data estate through connected data involves understanding the different sources of data within an organization, how they interact, and how they can be used to create a comprehensive view of the data estate.

  For example, a data steward might identify that a customer database, an order processing system, and a customer feedback system are all connected and can be used to create a comprehensive view of the customer journey.

- **Describe data**: Understanding data through applied business context involves understanding the business context of the data and how it can be used to inform decision-making.

  For example, a data steward might analyze customer data to understand customer preferences and behavior, which can then be used to inform marketing and product development decisions.

- **Manage data**: Managing data at scale to improve business outcomes involves understanding the data management processes and tools that can be used to ensure data quality and accuracy. For example, a data steward might implement data quality checks, data validation processes, and data cleansing tools to ensure that the data is accurate and up to date.

- **Democratize data**: This is the most difficult part, simply because it is about culture. It is about a new and better way of working, and not many people embrace changes easily in a working environment. Responsibly democratizing data to end users in adherence to data policies involves understanding the different ways in which data can be shared with end users in a secure and compliant manner.

  For example, a data steward might implement data access controls, data encryption, and data masking to ensure that data is shared securely and in compliance with data privacy regulations.

In the realm of data stewardship, a **data program** can be seen as a comprehensive umbrella under which numerous aspects of data management are coordinated and overseen. It is a strategic initiative that encapsulates the policies, procedures, and practices necessary for the systematic handling of an organization's data. This includes everything from data quality assurance to data privacy and security measures. The significance of a data program to data stewardship cannot be overstated. Essentially, it provides the framework and guidelines that data stewards follow to ensure that data is being used responsibly, efficiently, and in a way that aligns with the organization's objectives. By having a well-defined data program, data stewards can better maintain the data's integrity, safeguard its confidentiality, assure of its availability, and ensure its compliance with legal and regulatory requirements. Hence, the data program serves as the backbone of effective data stewardship.

We will now define the two key elements of any data program and communication with stakeholders, **data mindset** and **data skillset**.

A data mindset is an attitude and approach that values data as a strategic asset and leverages it for decision-making and problem-solving. This is considered a soft skill and data culture.

A data skillset is the ability and knowledge to collect, analyze, manage, and communicate data effectively and ethically. This is considered a hard skill and technical know-how.

To build a robust data stewardship program, both the data mindset and data skillset are fundamental. The data mindset, often regarded as a soft skill or data culture, is a pivotal aspect in shaping the organization's attitude toward data. It encourages the view of data as a strategic asset and promotes its utilization in decision-making and problem-solving. This mindset needs to permeate all levels of an organization, fostering an environment where the data's value is recognized and its potential is maximized.

Meanwhile, the data skillset, which embodies the hard skills or technical know-how, is equally critical. It involves the ability to collect, analyze, manage, and communicate data effectively and ethically. These skills ensure that the data is handled correctly and used responsibly, optimizing its benefits while minimizing risks.

So, how do we apply both a data mindset and a data skillset in real life?

In application, the data mindset should guide the development of the data stewardship program, establishing overarching goals and principles. It sets the tone for how data will be governed, valued, and utilized within the organization. On the other hand, the data skillset should dictate the practical execution of the program. It provides the technical means to implement the principles set forth by the data mindset, enabling the organization to manage its data assets efficiently and effectively. Ultimately, the harmonious application of both the data mindset and data skillset in a data stewardship program leads to enhanced data governance and superior data management.

In *Chapter 1, From Business Strategy to Data Strategy to Data Stewardship,* we discussed some building blocks for your data stewardship program, and here is how we can categorize them into the buckets of mindset and skillset.

Here's a categorization of the data stewardship program building blocks:

Building blocks of a data stewardship program	Data mindset	Data skillset
Establishing a data and data governance strategy	X	
Developing a data governance charter, policies, and procedures	X	X
Implementing data governance tools		X

Table 2.1 – Categorizing building blocks of a data stewardship program in mindset and skillset buckets

Usually, people tend to focus too much on the data skillset and underestimate the importance of a data mindset. We should strike a balance and make sure both data mindset and skillset are covered in the data stewardship roadmap.

Striking the right balance between a data mindset and a data skillset can indeed be a challenging task, but it is vital for successful data stewardship. Both aspects are equally important and should be developed concurrently.

One way to achieve this is to first foster a data-driven culture within the organization. This involves promoting the understanding that data is a strategic asset and that it can drive decision-making and problem-solving. This cultural shift helps to instill a data mindset across all levels of the organization, ensuring that everyone values and appreciates the importance of data.

Next, focus on training and development to enhance data skills. This can include workshops, seminars, or courses that cover data collection, analysis, management, and communication. It is important to ensure that these technical skills are not just confined to the IT department but are disseminated across the organization. This helps to develop a workforce that is not only data-aware but also data-competent. You can explore web pages of independent data associations such as the **Data Literacy Association (DaLa)** (`www.dalahk.org`).

Finally, encourage a symbiotic relationship between the data mindset and data skillset. The data mindset should guide the application of data skills, ensuring that data is used ethically and effectively. Conversely, a strong data skillset can help to reinforce the data mindset by demonstrating the practical benefits and potential of data.

By cultivating both a strong data mindset and a robust data skillset, you can ensure your organization's data stewardship program is both effective and sustainable.

Delving into the heart of data governance, we now explore the pivotal role of a data steward, the key player entrusted with the responsibility of managing, protecting, and enhancing the value of an organization's data assets. Let's look into the roles and responsibilities of a data steward.

Understanding the role of a data steward

The roles and responsibilities of a data steward vary depending on the organization, but typically include the following:

- **Developing and implementing data governance policies and procedures**: This encompasses the establishment of standards related to data quality, security, and accessibility, along with the formulation of a data governance blueprint under the leadership of the **chief data officer (CDO)** or data governance committee. It is also incumbent upon data stewards to verify that the implemented policies and procedures are congruent with the organization's business goals and strategic plans, as well as compliant with external regulations and industry benchmarks.

- **Monitoring data quality and even implementing a master data management (MDM) framework so that the organization can have a trustworthy single source of truth (SSOT)**: This includes measuring and reporting on the accuracy, completeness, consistency, timeliness, validity, and uniqueness of data throughout the organization, in addition to pinpointing and rectifying any data quality issues. It is also the responsibility of data stewards to put into place an MDM framework that delineates the processes, roles, and technologies for the creation, maintenance, and distribution of master data.

- **Master data represents the fundamental data that is utilized and shared by various business sectors and systems**. By maintaining an SSOT for master data, the organization can guarantee the reliability, consistency, and authority of data across diverse **business units (BUs)**. Ultimately, it fosters trust in data.

- **Ensuring data privacy so that data is used in accordance with legal and ethical standards**: Adherence to laws and regulations is of paramount importance to all businesses. This encompasses the gathering, processing, storage, dissemination, and disposal of personal or confidential data. It is the duty of data stewards to guarantee that data is used for its designated purpose and that the rights and preferences of data subjects are upheld. Additionally, data stewards need to put in place data privacy policies and procedures that detail methods of data collection, consent, anonymization, encryption, masking, or deletion.

- **Enforcing data security so that data is secure and protected from unauthorized access and misuse**: Implementing suitable measures and protections to avert data breaches, leaks, thefts, or losses is paramount. Data stewards must guarantee regular data backups and the establishment of **disaster recovery** (**DR**) strategies. They are also tasked with enforcing data security policies and procedures that lay out a methodology for data access, authentication, authorization, auditing, and encryption.

- **Creating and maintaining data dictionaries and data models**: Recording explanations, attributes, relations, origins, formats, and applications of data elements throughout the organization is required. Data stewards also need to develop and uphold data models that display the logical and physical configuration of data within databases or systems. Data dictionaries and data models are integral in standardizing data interpretation and representation across the organization, thereby promoting data integration, analysis, and communication.

- **Training and educating staff on data stewardship**: Promoting understanding and developing capabilities regarding the significance, worth, and advantages of data stewardship among employees across all organizational levels is crucial. Data stewards should offer training and education on superior practices, tools, techniques, and methodologies for efficient and responsible data management and usage. Moreover, data stewards must nurture an environment of data literacy and empowerment among staff.

- **Providing guidance and support on data-related projects**: Cooperating with project teams or business divisions to establish the scope, goals, requirements, deliverables, risks, and benefits of data-centric projects is essential. Data stewards also need to offer direction and support concerning the design, development, testing, implementation, upkeep, or assessment of data-related solutions or systems. Additionally, data stewards must ensure that data-focused projects adhere to set data governance policies and procedures.

- **Identifying and resolving data-related issues**: For example, **data incident management** (**data IM**) and **root cause analysis** (**RCA**). This involves actively observing and identifying any irregularities or issues related to data quality, security, privacy, or availability. Data IM serves as a guideline for handling any type of data incident, ensuring all stakeholders have a unified approach to the management and reporting of such incidents. Data stewards have the responsibility to address any problems by performing an RCA, applying **corrective actions** (**CAs**), or escalating these issues to the relevant authorities if necessary. In addition, data stewards must promptly document any issues or incidents that occur.

As we delve further into the realm of data stewardship, it is crucial to understand the various roles that contribute to this practice. Specifically, we'll be exploring three key types of data stewards – business data stewards, technical data stewards, and operational data stewards – to understand their unique responsibilities and contributions in the data governance ecosystem.

Types of data stewards

Now that we've learned about the duties of data stewards, let's explore the different types of data stewards and their corresponding focus areas with examples:

	Responsibility	Example
Business data steward	Understanding the business needs and requirements of the data domain or subject area	A sales domain data steward is responsible for the use and maintenance of the data related to sales activities, such as customer accounts, leads, opportunities, contracts, and revenue.
Technical data steward	Implementing solutions and tools for managing the data domain or subject area	A technical data steward is responsible for the design, development, and maintenance of the data warehouse that stores and integrates data from various sources for reporting and analysis purposes. Often, this role is in the technical team.
Operational data steward	Executing the day-to-day tasks for maintaining the data domain or subject area	An operational data steward is responsible for checking, monitoring, measuring, and reporting on data quality issues and anomalies and taking CAs to resolve them.

Table 2.2 – Types of data stewards and their expertise

So, what is the expectation from the corporation on data stewards? Let's check out some measurable **key performance indicators** (**KPIs**) or metrics for a data stewardship program:

- **Data compliance**: The level of adherence to data governance and compliance regulations throughout the data life cycle. Data compliance is important to avoid fines, reputational damage, customer dissatisfaction, and legal risks. In the broader context of data stewardship, the role of data stewards is integral to upholding data compliance. Data stewards are entrusted with the responsibility of ensuring that data management practices within the organization align with established data governance policies and compliance regulations. Some data compliance KPIs or metrics include the following:

  - **Regulatory adherence**: Gauge the degree to which the organization aligns with data privacy rules and regulations, including but not limited to the **General Data Protection Regulation** (**GDPR**) or the **California Consumer Privacy Act** (**CCPA**)

- **Effectiveness of access controls**: Assess the efficiency of access controls in protecting data and permitting access solely to authorized individuals

- **Compliance expense per issue**: Calculate the average cost of resolving a compliance issue, such as a data breach or a violation

- **Data quality**: The improvement in data quality metrics, such as accuracy, completeness, consistency, credibility, and timeliness. Data quality is important to support decision-making, reporting, analytics, and business processes. Data stewards are essentially the custodians of data quality. They constantly monitor the state of data within the organization to ensure that it is accurate, complete, consistent, credible, and timely. Some data quality KPIs or metrics include the following:

  - **Mean time to issue discovery**: Measure the average time it takes to identify a data quality issue, such as a missing value or an incorrect format

  - **Composite data quality score**: Measure the overall score by using key metrics such as accuracy and completeness to quantify the level of data quality for your organization

  You can refer to *Chapter 7, Data Steward Roles and Responsibilities,* to learn how we measure and improve data quality.

- **Data issue resolution**: This measures how effectively the organization handles and resolves data-related problems, such as errors, inconsistencies, conflicts, or gaps. Data issue resolution is important to maintain data quality, trust, and usability. Data stewards are the front-line defenders when it comes to spotting and resolving data issues. They are responsible for identifying and rectifying any inaccuracies, inconsistencies, conflicts, or gaps in the data. Some data issue resolution KPIs or metrics include the following:

  - **Number of data issues reported**: Count the number of data issues that are reported by users, systems, or audits

  - **Number of data issues resolved**: Count the number of data issues that are resolved by data stewards or other responsible parties

  - **Data issue resolution rate**: Calculate the percentage of data issues that are resolved within a given time frame or target

- **Data security**: This measures how well the organization protects its data from unauthorized access, use, modification, or disclosure. Data security is important to ensure data confidentiality, integrity, and availability. Data stewards act as the protectors of an organization's data assets. They are responsible for implementing and maintaining security measures that prevent unauthorized access to data. Some data security KPIs or metrics include the following:

  - **Data breach frequency**: Count the number of data breaches that occur within a given period or scope

- **Data breach severity**: Measure the impact of data breaches on the organization, such as the number of records compromised, the cost of remediation, or the legal liability

- **Data security compliance**: Measure the organization's compliance with data security standards and best practices, such as encryption, backup, or authentication

- **Subject area monitoring**: This measures how well the organization monitors and manages the data within a specific subject area, such as customer, product, or finance. Subject area monitoring is important to ensure data relevance, consistency, and alignment with business needs. Data stewards are responsible for monitoring specific subject areas, ensuring the data within these areas is relevant, consistent, and aligned with the organization's needs. Some subject area monitoring KPIs or metrics include the following:

  - **Data coverage**: Measure the percentage of data elements that are defined, documented, and governed within a subject area

  - **Data usage**: Measure the frequency and volume of data access, update, and analysis within a subject area

  - **Data value**: Measure the contribution of data to business outcomes, such as customer retention, product innovation, or revenue growth within a subject area

- **Training completion rate**: This refers to how well the organization educates and trains its employees on data governance and data stewardship concepts, principles, and practices. The training completion rate is important to increase data literacy, awareness, and competency across the organization. Data stewards act as educators and mentors within the organization. They are responsible for creating awareness about the importance of data governance and stewardship and imparting the necessary knowledge and skills to employees. Some training completion rate KPIs or metrics include the following:

  - **Training enrollment**: Count the number of employees who enroll in data governance and data stewardship training courses or programs

  - **Training completion**: Count the number of employees who complete data governance and data stewardship training courses or programs

  - **Training effectiveness**: Measure the impact of data governance and data stewardship training on employees' knowledge, skills, and behavior

- **Employee engagement**: This measures how well the organization engages and motivates its employees to participate in data governance and data stewardship activities, such as defining, documenting, cleansing, enriching, or sharing data. Employee engagement is important to foster a data-driven culture, collaboration, and ownership across the organization. Data stewards serve as the catalysts for employee engagement in data governance and stewardship activities. They play a pivotal role in fostering a culture where each employee recognizes their role in data governance and feels empowered to participate in data stewardship activities. Some employee engagement KPIs or metrics include the following:

  - **Employee satisfaction**: Measure the level of satisfaction that employees have with data governance and data stewardship policies, processes, and tools

  - **Employee feedback**: Collect and analyze feedback that employees provide on data governance and data stewardship issues, challenges, or opportunities

  - **Employee recognition**: Acknowledge and reward employees who demonstrate exemplary performance or contribution to data governance and data stewardship initiatives

- **Growth in data monetization**: This refers to how well the organization leverages its data assets to generate new or additional revenue streams, such as by creating new products or services, enhancing existing offerings, or selling data to external parties. Growth in data monetization is important to demonstrate the business value of data governance and data stewardship efforts. Data stewards are the gatekeepers of an organization's data assets and play a crucial role in unlocking their monetary potential. They ensure that the data is accurate, reliable, and readily available for use, which are prerequisites for effective data monetization. Some growth-in-data monetization KPIs or metrics include the following:

  - **Data revenue**: Measure the amount of revenue that is generated from data products or services, such as subscriptions, API licenses, or fees

  - **Data profitability**: Measure the amount of profit that is generated from data products or services, after deducting the costs of production, distribution, and maintenance

  - **Data ROI**: Calculate the **return on investment** (**ROI**) that is achieved from data products or services, by comparing the revenue and profit with the initial investment.

Comparing strategic data stewardship with a standard operating procedure

Data stewardship, in its broadest sense, is a strategic approach that encompasses the overall management, organization, and utilization of data within an enterprise. This strategic perspective of data stewardship is vital for the organization to maintain the quality, integrity, and security of its data, and to ensure its effective use in driving business decisions and outcomes.

On the other hand, data stewardship does contain some **standard operating procedures** (SOPs). When seen in this light, data stewardship is reduced to a series of procedures and tasks performed by specific roles within the organization, often the data stewards themselves. These tasks may include data cleansing, data validation, data classification, and maintaining data dictionaries, among others.

However, it's crucial to understand that data stewardship goes beyond just these operational tasks. While these procedures are a key part of data stewardship, they are merely the mechanical aspects of a broader strategic approach.

For instance, consider an e-commerce company looking to enhance its customer experience. As an SOP, data stewards might be tasked with cleansing and validating customer data, ensuring its accuracy for further analysis. They might also classify the data into various categories for easier access and utilization. However, this is just the operational facet of data stewardship.

From a strategic viewpoint, data stewardship in this scenario could involve setting up a system for continuous data quality improvement, defining policies for data access and usage, and identifying key data elements that can provide insights into customer behavior. It might also involve collaborating with various BUs to understand their data needs, ensuring that the data supports strategic decision-making and contributes to enhancing customer experience.

Therefore, while the SOPs form the groundwork for data stewardship, they should not be mistaken for the entire scope of this role. A comprehensive data stewardship program should seamlessly blend these operational tasks with a strategic approach that aligns data management with the organization's broader business objectives. It is this strategic approach that truly unlocks the value of data and enables organizations to leverage it as a competitive advantage.

One of the ways to demonstrate the benefits and impact of data stewardship is to use business cases for storytelling and value realization. In the following section, we will explore how to create and present compelling business cases that showcase the challenges, solutions, outcomes, and lessons learned from data stewardship initiatives.

Using business cases for storytelling and value realization

In *Chapter 1*, we learned how the business strategy should drive the data strategy, which is the lighthouse for your data stewardship program. How exactly are business strategy, data strategy, and use cases relevant to the data value realization?

Data value realization is one of the key business objectives of the data stewardship program.

It is the process of extracting tangible benefits from data, and it is closely linked to business strategy, data strategy, and use cases. These elements are interrelated and shape how an organization uses its data to achieve its strategic objectives:

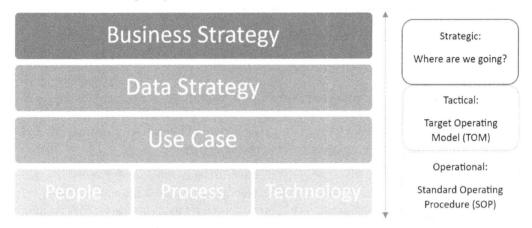

Figure 2.2 – Key building blocks for your data strategy, tactics, and operations

The business strategy outlines the overall goals and direction of the organization. It serves as a roadmap for what the organization wants to achieve and how it plans to do it. The data strategy, on the other hand, is a subset of the business strategy and defines how data will be used to support and achieve the objectives outlined in the business strategy.

The strategic direction provided by the business and data strategies drive the tactical implementation, which is operationalized by the **target operating model** (**TOM**). The TOM outlines how the organization's resources – people, processes, and technology – should be organized and utilized to implement the data strategy effectively.

The SOP mandates the day-to-day data operations. It provides detailed instructions on how data-related tasks should be carried out to ensure consistency, efficiency, and compliance with data governance policies.

What is a use case, then?

A business use case is a document and a process that describes the rationale, benefits, costs, and risks of a proposed project or initiative. A business use case for data stewardship is a way to justify the need, value, and impact of implementing a data stewardship program in your organization. It is essentially a story that illustrates how data can be used to solve a problem or seize an opportunity. Use cases help bring the data strategy to life by providing practical, relatable examples of how data can be used to drive value. They serve as a bridge between the strategic vision and the tactical implementation.

Why do we need to define a use case for data? Defining a business use case can help you to do the following:

- Communicate the vision, goals, and objectives of the data stewardship program to the stakeholders, such as senior management, data owners, data users, and data consumers.

- Secure the buy-in and support from senior leadership and stakeholders. Business cases can demonstrate the alignment of data stewardship with the organization's vision, mission, strategy, and goals. They can also justify the investment and resources needed for data stewardship.

- Identify and quantify expected outcomes and benefits of the data stewardship program, such as improved data quality, enhanced data security, increased data compliance, and optimized data usage.

- Estimate and compare the costs and resources required for the data stewardship program, such as staff, training, tools, and infrastructure.

- Assess and mitigate potential risks and challenges of the data stewardship program, such as resistance to change, lack of skills, or technical issues.

To accurately demonstrate the value of data management, practitioners must develop business cases and a value realization framework that includes metrics, measures, and KPIs for each business case.

What is a value realization framework?

A data value realization framework helps to measure the impact of how your organization applies enterprise data to facilitate business decisions, improve operational efficiency, and enhance processes. For example, data monetization is one form of data value realization. Some other examples include selling data and data API licensing.

The **Cloud Data Management Capabilities** (**CDMC**) data value realization framework is displayed here:

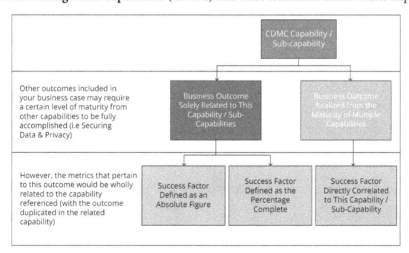

Figure 2.3 – CDMC data value realization framework (www.edmcouncil.org/frameworks/cdmc)

Your **data value realization framework** should include expected business outcomes that are already defined in the organization's business, data, and cloud strategies. The precision of the outcome estimates should be documented, as well as the risks associated with not achieving the targeted outcomes. Additionally, stakeholders should be identified and held responsible for achieving the targets.

With the business cases as your story and measurable business impact as your scorecard, you are on the right track in the data journey! By using business cases for storytelling and value realization, you can make your data stewardship program more compelling, engaging, and persuasive to your stakeholders. You can also use business cases to monitor and evaluate the performance and progress of your data stewardship program over time.

Moving forward, we will deep dive into the compelling concept of how data stewardship gives you a *competitive edge*, exploring how effective data stewardship can serve as a strategic differentiator, propelling your organization ahead in today's data-driven business landscape.

Creating a competitive edge with data stewardship

Data stewardship is not only a responsibility, but also an opportunity.

Data stewardship is also not just about data operation; it can be the competitive edge for an organization. Data stewardship is not a one-off project but a continuous process that requires constant adaptation and improvement. To maintain your competitive edge, you need to keep up with the changing data landscape, such as new data sources, technologies, regulations, and standards. You also need to foster a data-driven culture in your organization, where data stewards are empowered and supported by senior management and other stakeholders. By enabling these areas, your organization can stay ahead of the curve:

- **Operation excellence**

  This is about fostering a culture of continuous improvement across all aspects of the business while employees are empowered to make a change. Operation excellence is important to achieve a competitive advantage, optimize resource utilization, and foster innovation. Here's how to achieve it:

  - Embrace the self-service model by responsibly enabling data consumers across an organization to discover and access data in compliance with data policies, without involving the IT team.

  - Enable organizations to eliminate the brass tacks of manual data governance and management operations with policy-driven and **machine learning/artificial intelligence (ML/AI)**-powered intelligent and cost performance-optimized automation.

  - Increase innovation and agility by fostering a data-driven culture that encourages collaboration, experimentation, and learning from data, freeing up engineering and operations personnel to focus on more value-added tasks.

- **Better decision-making**:

This is the process of choosing the best course of action among multiple alternatives based on relevant information, criteria, and objectives. Better decision-making is important to achieve desired outcomes, avoid errors or risks, increase efficiency and effectiveness, and improve performance. Here are some examples:

  - **Generate actionable insights and intelligence to enable data owners and data stewards to manage and operate a fiscally responsible data estate**: This is important because data owners and data stewards need to have a clear understanding of the costs, benefits, and performance of their data assets, as well as the opportunities and risks associated with them. By generating actionable insights and intelligence, they can make informed decisions on how to optimize, prioritize, and govern their data estate. We can accomplish this by using data analytics and reporting tools that can provide data owners and data stewards with relevant metrics, dashboards, and alerts on their data estate. These tools can help them monitor the quality, usage, value, and compliance of their data assets, as well as identify issues, trends, or anomalies that require attention or action.

  - **Reduce costs and risks by avoiding data errors, duplication, inconsistency, and compliance issues that can result in fines, penalties, or reputational damage**: This is important because data errors, duplication, inconsistency, and compliance issues can have negative impacts on the organization's operations, performance, and reputation. They can lead to inaccurate or incomplete information, wasted resources, poor customer service, regulatory violations, or legal liabilities. We can accomplish this by implementing data quality and governance processes and standards that can ensure the accuracy, completeness, consistency, and compliance of data assets. These processes and standards can include data validation, cleansing, enrichment, deduplication, standardization, classification, security, privacy, and retention.

  - **Create new value and opportunities by leveraging data as a strategic asset that can generate insights, improve processes, and create new products or services**: We can accomplish this by using data analytics and **business intelligence** (**BI**) tools that can help the organization discover, analyze, visualize, and communicate the insights derived from the data assets. These tools can help the organization identify patterns, trends, correlations, or causations that can reveal new opportunities or solutions for improving processes or creating new products or services.

- **Increased customer satisfaction**:

This is the degree to which customers are satisfied with the products or services they receive from an organization. Increased customer satisfaction is important to retain existing customers, attract new customers, enhance loyalty and advocacy, and improve profitability. Some examples of how to improve customer satisfaction include the following:

- **Soliciting customer feedback and measuring customer satisfaction** using tools such as surveys, ratings, reviews, or **net promoter scores** (**NPSs**)

- **Understanding the needs and expectations of customers** by using user feedback data and delivering personalized products or services that meet or exceed them

- **Acting on customer feedback and implementing improvements** or innovations based on customer insights

There are other benefits of data stewardship:

- **Improved data quality**: Data stewardship helps ensure that data is accurate and up to date. This helps organizations make better decisions and improve their operations. Poor data quality can lead to errors, inefficiencies, missed opportunities, and reputational damage.

  For example, a bank can use data stewardship to improve its data quality by doing the following:

  - Establishing data quality standards and policies that define the expectations and requirements for data quality

  - Implementing a **data quality management system** (**DQMS**) that validates, cleanses, enriches, and standardizes the data from various sources, such as customer accounts, transactions, credit scores, and market data

  - Educating and training colleagues on the importance of data quality and how to follow data quality standards and policies

- **Improved data security**: Data stewardship helps protect data from unauthorized access and misuse. This helps organizations protect their data and ensure it is used in accordance with legal and ethical standards. Data breaches can result in financial losses, legal liabilities, customer dissatisfaction, and competitive disadvantage.

  For example, a healthcare provider can use data stewardship to improve its data security by doing the following:

  - Defining data security dimensions and metrics that are relevant for its compliance requirements, such as confidentiality, accountability, and the ability to audit

  - Implementing a **data security management system** (**DSMS**) that encrypts, masks, anonymizes, backs up, audits, and monitors data from various sources, such as patient records, medical images, lab results, and billing information

  - Detecting and responding to data security incidents and threats by assigning roles and responsibilities for data owners, custodians, and stewards who can investigate and fix problems

- **Improved data accessibility**: Data stewardship helps ensure that data is accessible to those who need it. This helps organizations make better use of their data and make more informed decisions. Data accessibility is essential for organizations to make better use of their data assets, gain insights, and create value. Lack of data accessibility can lead to wasted time, resources, and opportunities.

For example, a retailer can use data stewardship to improve its data accessibility by doing the following:

- Defining data accessibility dimensions and metrics that are relevant to its business objectives, such as the average time taken to find the data asset

- Implementing a data accessibility management system that catalogs, indexes, classifies, documents, and shares data from various sources, such as product inventory, sales transactions, customer feedback, and market trends

- Enabling and facilitating data discovery, analysis, visualization, and collaboration by providing user-friendly interfaces, dashboards, reports, and applications that allow users to explore and interact with the data

By having a comprehensive data governance program in place, organizations can ensure that their data is accurate, up to date, and secure. This allows them to make informed decisions based on reliable data, which can lead to improved customer satisfaction and reduced costs. Additionally, data stewardship can help organizations identify areas for improvement and develop strategies to optimize their data management processes to achieve better business results. Data stewardship can further advance your organization's success to the next level.

Summary

Data stewardship is crucial for organizations to ensure accurate, secure, and accessible data. It involves developing policies and procedures to manage data in accordance with legal and ethical standards. The key pillars of data stewardship include discovering, describing, managing, and democratizing data. Data stewardship requires both a data mindset and a data skillset to support both cultural and technical change for the organization.

Building a data stewardship program involves establishing a data governance strategy, developing policies and procedures, and implementing data governance tools. The role of a data steward includes developing and implementing data governance policies, monitoring data quality, ensuring data privacy and security, creating and maintaining data dictionaries, and resolving data-related issues. Measurable KPIs for data stewardship programs include data compliance, data quality, data issue resolution, and growth in data monetization. Business cases can be used to showcase the value and impact of data stewardship and secure buy-in from stakeholders. Last but not least, data stewardship can provide a competitive edge by enabling operational excellence, better decision-making, increased customer satisfaction, improved data quality, data security, and data accessibility.

As we proceed to the next chapter, we will unlock the initial steps of launching your data stewardship program, providing a comprehensive guide on how to effectively kickstart this essential initiative in your organization.

3

Getting Started with the Data Stewardship Program

As data becomes an increasingly valuable asset to organizations, it is essential to have a robust data governance framework in place. We begin this chapter by understanding the current data maturity level and setting the success criteria of the data stewardship program. Then, we will discuss the importance of gaining buy-in from stakeholders and understanding their needs and expectations. This is crucial as it helps ensure that the data stewardship program aligns with the organization's business objectives. Next, we will learn how to identify and prioritize data pain points to begin the data stewardship journey. Finally, we will discuss how we assess the current data maturity and the data capability gap analysis.

This chapter aims to provide a clear and concise guide on how to kick-start your data stewardship program. In this chapter, we will cover the following:

- Defining the origin and destination
- Getting buy-in of data stewardship from stakeholders
- Building a prioritization matrix
- Assessing data maturity
- Building the foundation of your data stewardship program

Defining the origin and destination of your data stewardship program

There are three essential questions that are universal to all kinds of planning and can address any problem statement.

In the context of data stewardship, consider the following:

- Where are you now?

  - Describe the current state of your organization's data assets, such as their quality, accessibility, usability, safety, and trustworthiness

  - Document the challenges that you face in managing and overseeing the data life cycle, such as data silos, inconsistencies, errors, breaches, or compliance issues

  - Use statistics to illustrate the problems or opportunities that arise from your data stewardship practices

- Where do you want to go?

  - Outline the vision or goals that you have for improving your data stewardship capabilities, such as enhancing data quality and security

  - Specify the benefits or outcomes that you expect to achieve from your data stewardship initiatives, such as better decision-making, customer satisfaction, operational efficiency, innovation, or competitive advantage

  - Use benchmarks to demonstrate the desired state or standards that you aim for

- How do you get there?

  - Propose the strategies or actions that you plan to take to implement or improve your data stewardship processes, such as defining roles and responsibilities, establishing policies and procedures, adopting tools and technologies, or providing training and education

  - Explain the rationale or evidence that supports your chosen approaches, such as alignment with business objectives, compliance with regulations, or proven results from other organizations

  - Use stages to organize your implementation plan or roadmap

Three questions. As simple as that.

OK. I know. It's not that simple.

If you have started working on a data stewardship program, then you may have heard about the *three questions* approach a lot from your external consultants.

They may charge you a hefty 3,000 USD per day and they may put things together on a slide deck after a series of interviews with stakeholders and market research. All your time and effort are only worth it if you can translate the slide deck into an operating model with a feedback loop.

Defining the origin and destination of your data stewardship program is important. It is much more than conducting interviews, filling in questionnaires, and making slide decks.

How can we translate data strategy into a tactical and then an operational level? We have several key building blocks, as illustrated in *Figure 2.2* in *Chapter 2, How Data Stewardship Can Help Your Organization*. In this context, we explained how we drive data strategy from business strategy and also the power of storytelling via a use case. Before we walk through the people, process, and technology in the next few chapters, we will first take a look into the preparation work – getting buy-in of data stewardship from stakeholders.

Getting buy-in of data stewardship from stakeholders

Before we can get to the data operating model, let's make sure we gain the buy-in from stakeholders.

Have you heard that the average duration of a **chief data officer** (**CDO**) at the same company is three years?

CDOs are the ones who initialize transformations to create master data, improve data quality, and trace data lineage. Why do CDOs usually not stay in the company for more than three years? Because they are not able to get the buy-in from stakeholders on the business value of data programs.

As a result, data and data programs are seen as a cost, funding gets stopped, and the CDO gets fired.

Despite the importance of the CDO role and data stewardship, they are set up to fail if there is poor buy-in from stakeholders.

Securing the approval and support of stakeholders is a crucial step in the process of data stewardship. The journey toward an effective data operating model necessitates the active engagement and cooperation of all key players. In this context, stakeholders are not mere spectators, but active participants and contributors to the process.

The importance of stakeholder buy-in lies in several key areas. Firstly, it ensures a shared understanding and commitment toward data governance objectives. This collective agreement is vital in driving the necessary actions and decisions to achieve the established goals.

Secondly, stakeholder buy-in fosters a sense of ownership and responsibility among key players. When stakeholders are actively involved and invested in the process, they are more likely to take responsibility for their roles and contribute effectively toward data management tasks.

Lastly, securing stakeholder buy-in helps to mitigate potential resistance to change. By involving stakeholders early in the process and gaining their support, it becomes easier to navigate through potential challenges and overcome obstacles.

Here are some key steps to getting buy-in from stakeholders for your data stewardship program:

1. **Identify the stakeholders and build relationships with them**: This includes understanding their roles, responsibilities, and goals. Once you have identified the stakeholders, you can begin to build relationships with them by having regular meetings and discussing their needs and objectives. This will help you understand their perspective and build trust.

2. **Create a compelling business case**: This includes demonstrating the value of data stewardship and the potential return on investment. You should be able to show how data stewardship can help the organization achieve its goals and objectives. This will help stakeholders understand the importance of data stewardship and why it is worth investing in. You can refer to *Chapter 2* to revisit how to create a compelling use case.

3. **Align the common interest and agree on the priority and roadmap**: Once you have identified the stakeholders and created a compelling business case, you need to align the common interests and agree on the priority and roadmap with the CDO and **data steering committee (DSC)**. This includes setting goals and objectives, developing a timeline, and determining the resources and budget needed to achieve the goals. This will help ensure that everyone is on the same page and that the data stewardship program is successful.

4. **Secure the funding and resources**: Then you need to secure the funding and resources needed to implement the data stewardship program. This includes developing a budget and securing the necessary resources. To maintain momentum and trust, you need to report the resource utilization and present the phased deliverables to stakeholders regularly.

After we align the common interest and get the buy-in of data stewardship from stakeholders, including but not limited to heads of departments, CTOs, CDOs, and DSCs, we start getting requests from multiple business units for different data projects such as acquiring new data sources, improving data quality, and so on.

Then, how should we prioritize the data use cases in the pipeline? We need to have a systematic approach to gather pain points and define a prioritization matrix, which we will discuss in the next section.

Building a prioritization matrix

Collecting data pain points from stakeholders is an essential part of the data management and governance process. This engagement with stakeholders allows organizations to pinpoint issues, challenges, and inefficiencies within the current data system.

Gathering data pain points can help to prioritize actions and resources. Not all data issues can be tackled at once, and understanding the most pressing pain points can guide an organization in prioritizing its efforts.

Here are the steps required to gather pain points about data operation from stakeholders:

1. **Engage with the business units**: The most effective method to identify challenges is to encourage direct communication from multiple business units – for example, conducting questionnaires and focus group interviews. This approach will enable you to accumulate insights from diverse viewpoints, nurturing a well-rounded understanding of the data landscape.

2. **Ask your sales and marketing team**: It is crucial to actively involve these groups as they frequently manage tasks at the forefront, interacting directly with data-related activities. Their immediate experience can offer a valuable understanding of prevailing data administration issues. They are a rich source of insights into the challenges your customers face.

3. **Listen to user feedback**: Collect feedback from users of your products or services, upstream and downstream vendors, and external business partners. This feedback can be gathered through customer support channels, social media, or other feedback mechanisms. Do not forget to combine the feedback from your teammates in steps 1 and 2 as well.

4. **Conduct user research**: Conduct user research to uncover the nature of your internal and external users' pain points. This can be done through usability testing, user interviews, or other research methods.

5. **Synthesize and prioritize the research**: Once you have collected data from multiple sources, synthesize it into a single list of pain points, then make use of some of the following prioritization matrices.

After gathering a list of pain points, we need to deploy a transparent approach to prioritization. We usually call it the prioritization matrix. Why do we need the **prioritization matrix**?

Firstly, resources – time, personnel, and finances – are often limited. It is not feasible to address all the pain points at once. A prioritization matrix helps identify the most critical issues that need immediate attention based on their impact and feasibility.

Secondly, the matrix helps strike a balance between the organization's strategic objectives and the immediate needs of stakeholders. By considering factors such as the value of the use case to the business, the effort required to implement it, and its urgency, the matrix ensures a balanced and effective approach to data governance.

Last but not least, a prioritization matrix can help manage stakeholder expectations. By transparently communicating what will be addressed and in what order, stakeholders can have a clear understanding of the process, thereby reducing potential frustration or confusion. Prioritization should involve stakeholders from multiple divisions to ensure interests are aligned. Once the order of priority of use cases is defined by the DSC, we should document the decision and share it with stakeholders to uphold transparent and open communication.

We will now discuss some common approaches to prioritization. The first one is the impact-effort matrix.

The impact-effort matrix

The **impact-effort matrix** is one of the most simple and widely used matrices. By following the scoring and ordering, one can identify the quick wins and major projects, which can bring tangible value to the table.

The impact-effort matrix is a useful tool for prioritizing tasks or use cases based on their potential impact and the effort required to implement them. It helps to visualize and decide which initiatives to pursue first.

Figure 3.1 depicts the typical outcome of the impact-effort matrix:

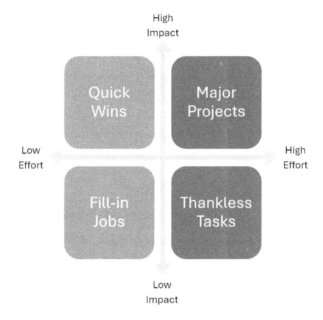

Figure 3.1 – Outcome of the impact-effort matrix

Here is how you can score and order use cases:

1. **Identify the criteria**: Start by defining what *impact* and *effort* mean within the context of your project. The impact could refer to potential benefits such as cost savings, improved customer satisfaction, or increased efficiency. Effort might encompass factors such as time, resources, or complexity.

2. **Score the use cases**: Assign a numerical value to each use case for both impact and effort. This could be on a scale of 1-10, for example, with 1 being the lowest and 10 being the highest. The scoring should be done based on agreed-upon criteria and should ideally involve the input of key stakeholders from multiple business units to ensure varied perspectives.

3. **Plot the matrix**: Draw a two-dimensional matrix with *effort* on the *x* axis and *impact* on the *y* axis. Each use case is then plotted on this matrix based on its scores.

4. **Order the use cases**: Use cases in the high-impact, low-effort quadrant are the *quick wins* and should be prioritized first. These initiatives will provide high value with relatively little effort. Next come the tasks in the high-impact, high-effort quadrant. These are major projects that need careful planning but will yield significant benefits. The low-impact, low-effort tasks (for instance, *Fill-in Jobs*) can be considered next, while those in the low-impact, high-effort quadrant (*Thankless Tasks*) should ideally be considered last or even avoided, as they require substantial resources but offer minimal benefits.

5. **Review and adjust**: Scoring and ordering is not a one-time process. As the project progresses, new information may emerge, requiring you to adjust your scores and reorder your priorities.

Having explored the intricacies of the impact-effort matrix in use case prioritization, let's now transition into understanding another highly effective prioritization tool – the RICE method.

The RICE method

RICE stands for **reach**, **impact**, **confidence**, and **effort**.

RICE is an influential prioritization technique employed in data governance and many other programs. This method provides a structured approach to decision-making by quantifying each project's potential value against its associated costs. The RICE method can be instrumental in creating a cost-effective and purpose-built data governance program. Take a look at *Figure 3.2*, the *Reach* and *Impact* components help you understand the potential benefits and scale of influence of each governance project, ensuring that your efforts are directed toward initiatives that can drive maximum value. *Confidence* allows you to gauge the reliability of your estimates, helping mitigate risk. The *Effort* component keeps costs in check by highlighting the amount of work required for each project, enabling you to allocate resources wisely. This multi-dimensional analysis facilitates informed and balanced project prioritization decisions.

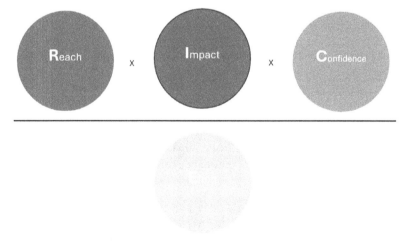

Figure 3.2 – Formula of the RICE method

Let's now discuss how the different elements illustrated in *Figure 3.2* help you prioritize your data governance use cases:

- **Reach**: This refers to the number of people or units that will be affected by the decision or action over a given period. In the context of data programs, it could be the number of departments or teams that will benefit from a data governance initiative.

- **Impact**: This measures the potential effect of the action on each individual or unit. Impact could be measured on a Likert scale, such as 1 for minimal effect, 2 for moderate, and 3 for significant.

- **Confidence**: This factor rates your certainty about the other three parameters (reach, impact, and effort). It's a way to account for uncertainty in your estimates. Confidence is usually expressed as a percentage.

- **Effort**: This is the amount of effort we need to put in place. It could include time, resources, and complexity.

The RICE score is then calculated as follows:

Reach, impact, and confidence are the positive factors, divided by the effort (the negative factor).

The higher the RICE score, the higher the priority of a use case.

Let's consider an example of a data governance initiative where an organization is contemplating several projects:

- Project A – Implementing a new data management tool
- Project B – Training staff on data privacy regulations
- Project C – Enhancing data security protocols

Now, let's compute the RICE score for each:

- **Reach**: For Project A, the new data management tool would impact all 5 departments in the company, so its reach is 5. For Project B, the training would only impact 2 departments directly, so its reach is 2. For Project C, enhancing data security would impact all employees in the company, spanning 7 departments, so its reach is 7.

- **Impact**: For Project A, the new tool would have a moderate impact on productivity, so we'll give it a score of 2. Project B has a significant impact on compliance, so its impact score is 3. Project C, despite its wide reach, might only have a minimal direct impact on daily operations, so its impact score is 1.

- **Confidence**: For Project A, the organization is quite sure of its impact and the effort required, so its confidence is 80%. For Project B, due to potential variability in how well the training is received, its confidence is 70%. For Project C, the organization is very confident about the outcomes, giving it a confidence level of 90%.

- **Effort**: For Project A, the implementation of the new tool will be a major undertaking, requiring significant time and resources, so its effort score is 5. Project B requires arranging a few training sessions, so its effort score is 2. Project C will require substantial resources for auditing and enhancing protocols, so its effort score is 4.

- Now, we calculate the respective RICE scores:

  - Project A: $(5 * 2 * 0.8) / 5 = 1.6$

  - Project B: $(2 * 3 * 0.7) / 2 = 2.1$

  - Project C: $(7 * 1 * 0.9) / 4 = 1.575$

Based on RICE scores, Project B, for staff training on data privacy regulations, should be the highest priority, followed by Project A, the implementation of a new data management tool, and then Project C, for enhancing data security protocols.

This example demonstrates how the RICE method can help an organization prioritize its projects based on quantifiable metrics, ensuring a balanced, transparent, and objective approach to decision-making in data governance initiatives.

After deep-diving into the impact-effort matrix and the RICE method for use case prioritization, it is time to transition our focus to another equally significant prioritization tool – MoSCoW analysis.

MoSCoW analysis

The **MoSCoW** method is an effective prioritization technique that classifies use cases or requirements into four categories *(Figure 3.3)*: Must Have, Should Have, Could Have, and Won't Have.

Here's an explanation of each component:

Must Have	Should Have	Could Have	Won't Have
• These are the non-negotiable tasks or requirements that are critical for the success of a project. Without these, the project will fail. • In a data program, this could include implementing essential data security measures or ensuring compliance with data privacy laws.	• These tasks are important but not critical for project launch or immediate success. They add significant value but if not addressed immediately, the project can still move forward. • For instance, this could be a nice-to-have feature in a data management tool that improves efficiency but is not necessary.	• These are the tasks or features that would be beneficial to have but are not necessary for the immediate success of the project. They are typically low-cost enhancements that don't affect the overall system if omitted. • An example might be additional data visualization tools that can support data analysis.	• These are the tasks or features that are least critical, may not provide enough value for the effort required, or are not feasible at the current time. • They are not planned for the current delivery time frame but could be considered in the future.

Figure 3.3 – Components of MoSCoW analysis

The MoSCoW method is particularly useful for data programs for several reasons:

Clarity and focus: It helps teams to focus on what's truly necessary for the project's success, ensuring critical elements are not overlooked

Resource allocation: It aids in distributing resources effectively by focusing efforts on the most necessary and value-adding tasks

Stakeholder management: It provides a clear communication tool for setting and managing stakeholder expectations

Flexibility: It allows for flexibility and adaptability in project management, as tasks can be moved between categories as circumstances change

By using the MoSCoW method, data programs can better prioritize their use cases, ensuring that the most critical and value-adding tasks are addressed first, thereby maximizing the effectiveness of the program.

Comparing different prioritization matrices

Each of the three prioritization methods – the impact-effort matrix, the RICE method, and MoSCoW analysis – has its own strengths and weaknesses, and its suitability can depend on the specific circumstances of a project. We will discuss each of them in *Table 3.1*:

Prioritization method	Advantage	Disadvantage	Best Used When
Impact-Effort Matrix	It is simple and easy to understand, making it great for quick decision-making. It provides a visual representation of tasks, facilitating discussions and consensus-building.	It can oversimplify complex decisions, as it only considers two factors (impact and effort). It may not account for uncertainties or dependencies between tasks.	You need to make quick decisions about a relatively small number of tasks or initiatives with clearly defined impacts and efforts.
RICE Method	It is a more comprehensive method that considers four factors, providing a more holistic view. It quantifies decision-making, making it more objective.	It can be more time-consuming and complex to implement. It requires detailed knowledge of each task to assign accurate scores.	You are dealing with complex projects with many tasks, and you have sufficient information to estimate reach, impact, confidence, and effort accurately.

Prioritization method	Advantage	Disadvantage	Best Used When
MoSCoW Analysis	It is simple and intuitive to all stakeholders and provides a clear categorization of tasks. It is flexible, allowing for changes in priorities as the project evolves.	It can be subjective, as the classification of tasks can depend on individual perspectives. It does not provide a quantitative ranking within categories.	You are working with diverse stakeholders and need a clear, shared understanding of priorities. It' s also helpful when you need flexibility to adapt to changing circumstances.

Table 3.1 – Comparing different prioritization matrices

In summary, the best approach depends on the specific needs of your project. For instance, if you are in the early stages of a project and need to quickly determine which tasks to tackle first, the impact-effort matrix may be the best fit. If you are dealing with a complex, long-term project with many tasks, the RICE method may be more suitable. If you are working with diverse stakeholders and need a flexible approach to manage changing priorities, MoSCoW analysis might be the most appropriate.

Assessing the maturity of your data is another important element of an effective data stewardship program, which we will discuss in the next section.

Assessing data maturity

Data maturity refers to the extent to which an organization can effectively and efficiently utilize its data. It encapsulates several facets, including data management, data governance, data quality, data integration, and the ability to derive insights and value from data. There are some well-recognized data maturity frameworks from the **Enterprise Data Management Council (EDMC)** (https://edmcouncil.org/) and **Data Management Association (DAMA)** (https://www.dama.org/).

You can refer to *Figure 4.5* in *Chapter 4, Developing a Comprehensive Data Management Strategy,* for the gap analysis of data maturity.

When you want to show the gap between the current and target state to the stakeholder, and when you want to keep track of the improvement in data maturity level for the organization, you need to know where you are now. That is why you need to have a data health check via a maturity assessment.

Why is a data maturity assessment vital to your organization? Here are the reasons and benefits:

Improved decision-making: A high level of data maturity means that an organization has reliable, high-quality data that can be used to drive decision-making. This can lead to more informed, accurate, and effective decisions.

Enhanced efficiency: An organization with mature data practices typically has well-defined processes for data collection, storage, management, and analysis. This can lead to improved efficiency and productivity, as less time is wasted on dealing with data-related issues.

Risk management: Keeping track of data maturity can help you to identify potential risks and issues, such as poor data quality or inadequate data security. This can enable proactive risk management and prevent costly issues down the line.

Competitive advantage: In today's data-driven world, the ability to effectively leverage data can provide a significant competitive advantage. Tracking data maturity can help an organization identify areas where it can improve its data capabilities and gain an edge over competitors. You can even benchmark your data governance program against industry best practices and standards, such as those of the CDMC, DAMA, and the Federal Data Strategy Data Governance Playbook (`https://resources.data.gov/assets/documents/fds-data-governance-playbook.pdf`).

Compliance: A high level of data maturity can also help to ensure compliance with data regulations, as it typically involves robust data governance and data protection measures.

In essence, monitoring data maturity allows an organization to understand its current data capabilities, identify areas for improvement, and make strategic decisions that enhance its ability to leverage data for business success.

Assess your organization's current data capabilities to understand its strengths, weaknesses, and gaps so that you can continually track the efficiency of your data governance initiatives over time and report on the business benefits. To bridge the identified gaps, we can formulate a plan as follows:

1. Choose a data governance maturity model that aligns with your organization's specific requirements and environment. Several data governance maturity models exist, such as the models proposed by the EDMC and DAMA.

2. The EDM Council is the international member-driven data and analytics association. It provides best practices, standards, and education to data and business professionals. Join the EDM Council (`https://edmcouncil.org/`) as a member to access the **Data Management Capability Assessment Model** (**DCAM**) framework and resources (`https://edmcouncil.org/frameworks/dcam/assessments/`).

3. Ensure your evaluation team participates in the DCAM framework training to gain a thorough comprehension of the fundamental principles, including the consistent application of the DCAM approach.

4. Conduct a self-assessment using the DCAM resources and survey spreadsheet to evaluate your data management program, capabilities, and dependencies:

   A. **Understanding DCAM**: Begin by gaining a comprehensive understanding of the DCAM model. The model includes eight core components – data strategy, data management, data architecture, technology architecture, data quality, data governance, data control environment, and analytics management.

B. **Download the resources**: From the EDMC's official website, download the DCAM resources and survey spreadsheet. The resources provide explanations of the eight components, while the spreadsheet allows you to assess your organization's data management capabilities.

C. **Conduct the assessment**: Assign a score or rating to each dimension and criterion of the data governance maturity model based on the data collected and analyzed. You can use a numerical scale, such as 1 (non-existent) to 5 (optimal), or a descriptive scale, such as basic, intermediate, advanced, or optimized. You can also use a color-coded system, such as red, yellow, green, or blue to indicate the level of maturity.

5. Compare your results with the benchmark report from the EDMC (`https://edmcouncil.org/innovation/research/benchmarks/`) or DAMA-Data Management Body of Knowledge (`https://www.dama.org/cpages/body-of-knowledge`) knowledge areas to identify strengths and gaps in your data management practices. Summarize and visualize the results of the data governance maturity assessment in a report or dashboard that highlights the strengths and weaknesses of your data governance program. You can use tables, charts, graphs, or heatmaps to present the results in an easy-to-understand way.

6. Create a roadmap for your data management and analytics program based on industry best practices and your organizational goals. You can prioritize actions based on their urgency, importance, feasibility, and cost-effectiveness. You can also assign roles and responsibilities to different people or teams to execute the actions. You may refer to *Chapters 4* and *12* for details.

7. Repeat the data governance maturity assessment periodically (for example, annually) to track the changes and improvements in your data governance program over time. You can compare the results of different assessments to measure your progress and performance.

8. Optionally, you can also engage one of the DCAM Authorized Partners to conduct an independent assessment and benchmarking of your data management and analytics program.

You can also refer to some other data organizations such as the Data Literacy Association (`https://dalahk.org`), and others for industry practices, best practices, and suggested controls.

After you have reviewed the data maturity level for your organization, let us walk through how to build and reinforce the foundation of your data stewardship program.

Building the foundation of your data stewardship program

Now that you've prioritized the data use cases and conducted the data maturity review, we will delve into the initial steps required to establish a successful data stewardship program. The success of such a program heavily relies on having the right people on board, hence our first focus will be on the recruitment of individuals with the appropriate mindset and skills to make up a formidable team. We will then explore the importance of defining the data scope from specific use cases. Subsequently, we will discuss the crucial role of a DSC, whose task is to oversee the entire program. Lastly, we will touch upon the significance of setting up quarterly, half-yearly, and annual plans for systematic progress tracking and adjustments. By comprehensively understanding these core elements, you will be well-equipped to build a robust foundation for your data stewardship program.

Let us zoom in on each core element, one by one:

- **Hiring the right people with the right mindset to form a winning team**: The team should be composed of individuals who are passionate about data, have strong technical skills, and understand the importance of data governance. It is also important to have team members who are able to collaborate with stakeholders, have excellent communication skills, and can work together to create a successful data stewardship program.

- **Determine the data scope from the use case**: This involves identifying the data sources, the types of data that will be used, and the purpose of the data. It is important to understand the data sources and the types of data that will be used in order to ensure that the data is of high quality and can be used for the intended purpose. You may even need to plan the cost of acquiring an alternative data source.

  Also, we should try to define the critical data elements from the whole dataset so that we can put more granular control and quality checks on those critical data elements.

- **Set up a DSC**: This committee should be composed of stakeholders from different departments, such as IT, finance, operations, and marketing. The committee should be responsible for setting the data governance policies and procedures, as well as overseeing the data stewardship program. Terms of reference should be agreed upon when the committee is established.

- **Quarterly, half-yearly, and annual plan**: You should create your own roadmap and deliverables for the quarter, mid-year, and end of the year.

  For example, during the first three months, the team should focus on setting up the data governance framework, such as policies and procedures. During the six-month period, the team should focus on implementing the data governance framework and establishing data quality metrics. During the twelve-month period, the team should focus on monitoring and maintaining the data governance framework.

Last but not least, when you think it makes sense and everyone should understand *garbage in, garbage out*, sadly, that doesn't happen in reality. Stakeholders from various backgrounds may not be able to appreciate the value of data when you start the data stewardship program. Put yourself into other's shoes. Whenever possible, please try to job-shadow various end-to-end positions in the data life cycle. You can even suggest that other teams job-shadow another team to better align the value proposition of the data program.

If you were the business user, what would make you think this was not another IT project that was going to fail? Make sure you have a solid answer before investing more time and energy.

Summary

Data stewardship is the keystone to enabling data governance in your organization. Data stewardship can help you to manage, use, and innovate with your data assets in a responsible and effective way. To start a data stewardship program, it is critical to first define your starting point and desired endpoint. This helps in outlining the program's journey. Next, securing the approval and support of key stakeholders is essential to the success of the program. To manage the tasks efficiently, a prioritization matrix is constructed to help in decision-making. Lastly, an assessment of data maturity is conducted to understand the organization's current data management capabilities, which in turn guides the progression of the stewardship program. Data stewardship is not a one-size-fits-all solution, but a tailored approach that depends on your organization's needs and context. You need to adapt and improve your data stewardship program over time to keep up with the changing data landscape and expectations. Data stewardship is not a destination, but a journey.

In the next chapter, we will talk about how to define the data management strategy so that you can deliver both short-term and long-term value to your organization via data programs.

Part 2:
How to Become a Data Steward and Shine!

Embark on a transformative journey through the intricate landscape of data management with *Chapters 4* to *9* of this insightful book. From crafting a robust data strategy to the nuanced roles of data stewards and harnessing the power of AI for governance, these chapters are designed to equip you with the skills needed to navigate the complexities of data stewardship effectively. Prepare to delve deep into practical frameworks, innovative technologies, and strategic insights that will supercharge your approach to data governance and stewardship.

This part has the following chapters:

- *Chapter 4, Developing a Comprehensive Data Management Strategy*
- *Chapter 5, People, Process, Technology*
- *Chapter 6, Establishing a Data Governance Structure*
- *Chapter 7, Data Steward Roles and Responsibilities*
- *Chapter 8, Effective Data Stewardship*
- *Chapter 9, Supercharge Data Governance and Stewardship with GPT*

4

Developing a Comprehensive Data Management Strategy

A data management strategy is crucial as it enables organizations to leverage their data as a valuable asset. It assists businesses in making informed decisions, improving operational efficiency, and driving business growth. Without a proper data management strategy, organizations run the risk of making decisions based on inaccurate, outdated, or irrelevant data. This could lead to financial losses, missed opportunities, and damage to their reputation. Furthermore, non-compliance with regulations related to data management can result in hefty fines and legal consequences.

A data management strategy addresses numerous challenges. Firstly, it ensures data quality by implementing processes to eliminate errors and inconsistencies in data. Secondly, it aids in data security, helping organizations protect sensitive information from breaches and cyberattacks. It also simplifies data integration, making it easier to combine data from different sources for analysis. Lastly, it supports regulatory compliance by establishing processes and controls that adhere to data protection laws and standards.

This chapter will provide readers with a comprehensive overview of how to develop a data management strategy. The chapter will begin with an introduction to the data maturity review, followed by setting the target state of your data stewardship program. This chapter will provide you with the knowledge and skills needed to create a comprehensive data management strategy.

We will cover the following key topics in this chapter:

- Assessing your current data environment and identifying areas for improvement
- Fulfilling the business and data strategy
- Introducing the people, process, and technology considerations
- Making the impact visible to your stakeholders

What is a data strategy?

A **data strategy** can be seen as the compass that directs an organization's use, management, and protection of its data. It is a holistic plan that not only determines how data will be handled but also how it will be strategically employed to meet business goals.

A data strategy is not just about managing data, but also about leveraging it as a strategic asset to generate insights, drive decision-making, and create value for the organization. In essence, it ensures that data is reliable, accessible, secure, and used effectively to support the organization's goals.

There are three elements involved when defining a data strategy, as depicted in *Figure 4.1*:

Figure 4.1 – Three considerations for your data strategy

Let's discuss these three considerations in detail:

- **Business value**: The primary purpose of a data strategy is to provide value to the business. This means that the strategy should align with the organization's objectives and goals. It should clearly define how data will be used to drive business outcomes, whether it's improving customer service, enhancing operational efficiency, or generating insights for decision-making. Considerations include identifying key business goals, defining metrics for success, and ensuring that data is accessible and usable for those who need it.

- **Risk control and compliance**: Data carries a significant amount of risk, especially considering aspects such as security breaches, data loss, or non-compliance with regulations. An effective data strategy must include robust risk control measures to protect data integrity and security. Compliance with data-related regulations, such as GDPR or CCPA, is also essential to avoid legal and financial penalties. Considerations include implementing data security measures, establishing data governance frameworks, and regularly auditing data practices to ensure compliance.

- **Operational excellence**: This pertains to the efficient and effective management of data operations. It involves establishing clear processes and standards for data collection, storage, processing, and usage. The goal is to ensure data operations are reliable, efficient, and able to deliver value to the organization. Considerations include investing in the right tools and technologies, training staff in data management best practices, and continuously monitoring and improving data operations.

Creating a mature data strategy is critical to your organization because it helps organizations effectively manage and leverage their data, leading to better decision-making, improved operational efficiency, risk mitigation, and value creation.

The following are some questions for your data governance team for self-reflection:

- Does the data management strategy effectively communicate the necessity for an independent enterprise data management program and secure a commitment from all levels of leadership and business units?

- Are the data management program's short-, medium-, and long-term goals well-defined and aligned with the organization's strategic priorities?

- Has the data management strategy outlined the key focus areas, resource allocation, operating model, and funding strategy required to successfully initiate and sustain the program?

So, how do we go about creating a comprehensive data strategy that addresses the preceding key considerations? Let's get started.

Assessing your current data environment for creating a data strategy – Where are you now?

I came across a discussion thread on Reddit (`https://www.reddit.com/r/dataengineering/comments/14e8nuu/what_is_the_best_way_to_optimize_5000_dashboards/`). Here the author wanted to understand how to go about BI Modernization if there are *5000 dashboards* thrown at you. Would the approach include gathering information on dashboards that got maximum hits, or check on data sources, how they are consumed and patterns on consumption?

What would you do if you were given this task?

Probably you should first ask why we need 5,000 dashboards. It does not make sense at all for most organizations. Maybe you should just shut down all 5,000 dashboards and then take a vacation. When you are back from holiday, see if your boss's boss comes to your desk with a solid dashboard use case. Then you have your fresh, new use case pipeline.

You need to clarify what exactly the problem statement is and understand the necessity of each data element in your organization. The example of 5,000 dashboards is a classic case of data overproduction and underutilization. Overloading with information can often lead to confusion and inefficiencies rather than providing clarity and value.

Assessing the current data environment and understanding the data maturity of your organization is a crucial step in refining your data strategy. It is important to evaluate whether the data you are accumulating and the way it is being processed is in alignment with your business objectives. This includes identifying redundant data, outdated systems, and ineffective data practices.

You need to ask why various data elements are needed in the context of the problem statement. It is crucial to clarify what our problem statement is. Why do we need 5,000 dashboards in the first place? Are there any duplicates of dashboards out of the 5,000 existing ones? And can we review whether all the reports are still relevant and required for the company?

Before you invest your time and energy, you should present a constructive challenge to the status quo by asking, are we moving in the right direction?

The term *status quo* refers to the existing state of affairs or the current situation within your organization, particularly in relation to its data management practices and data strategy. It encompasses the established norms, systems, and methods that your organization utilizes to handle its data. Challenging the status quo in this context means questioning the effectiveness of these existing data practices. Are they truly serving the organization's needs? Are they providing valuable, actionable insights? Or are they merely creating noise, as in the case of the 5,000 dashboards?

A data strategy is essentially the direction for all your data programs. If you go in the wrong direction, there is no way you can get to the destination, no matter how hard you try.

Once you understand the business strategy, you often realize there is a gap in the data capabilities of your organization. Thus you need to define a data strategy that can fill in the gap backed by use cases and measurable outcomes.

How do you identify the gap? You need to understand your current state and define the future state. The good news is you can learn from the industry's best practices for data maturity assessment and benchmarking.

In the next section we will discuss one of the popular frameworks – the **Cloud Data Management Capabilities(CDMC) framework** for data maturity assessment provided by the EDM Council (`https://edmcouncil.org/`).

Data maturity assessment

A **data maturity assessment** is a method that measures an organization's proficiency in managing, controlling, and making use of its data. It is a tool to understand the organization's current capabilities related to data and identify potential areas for enhancement.

Assessing data maturity is critical for several reasons. It provides a clear picture of the organization's current data practices, highlighting strengths and exposing weaknesses. By understanding their data maturity level, organizations can make informed decisions about where to invest resources for improvement. Moreover, it aids in the development of a strategic roadmap for advancing data practices, aligning them more closely with the organization's overall goals.

The data maturity assessment process includes several key steps:

1. **Defining the assessment criteria**: This involves identifying what components of data management need to be evaluated, such as the data lifecycle, data architecture, and data protection. You are recommended to refer to the CDMC framework coming up next.

2. **Evaluating the current state**: This step involves a thorough examination of the existing data practices within the organization. It requires an analysis of how data is gathered, stored, processed, and utilized, along with identifying any potential issues or gaps.

3. **Benchmarking against best practices**: Here, the organization's current practices are compared to industry standards or best practices. This comparison can highlight areas that need improvement and provide a benchmark for setting data maturity goals.

4. **Assessing organizational culture and skills**: This step evaluates the organization's data literacy and the cultural approach toward data usage. It seeks to understand whether employees comprehend the value of data and whether there is a culture of data-driven decision-making.

5. **Scoring the maturity level**: Based on the assessment, the organization's data maturity level is rated, often on a scale from *novice or not initiated* (where data is collected but not effectively utilized) to *expert or enhanced* (where data is strategically used for decision-making and innovation).

6. **Creating an action plan**: After identifying gaps and setting data maturity goals, an action plan is developed to enhance the organization's data practices. This could involve implementing new systems, improving data governance, or offering data literacy training.

The assessment model

Here are the stages of data capability and maturity from of the CDCM framework from EDMC (*Figure 4.2*).

Figure 4.2 – Stages of data capability and maturity

We can review the status in terms of three aspects at each stage:

- **Process**: Measures the extent to which the data management and analytics processes are established, structured, and repeatable
- **Evidence**: Identifies the business artifacts mandatory for audit against each capability statement
- **Engagement**: Ensures that the right stakeholders with appropriate levels of authority engage in the data management and analytics program

The leap from developmental capability to defined capability is the most difficult challenge. That is what we call the **crossing the capability chasm**.

Table 4.1 explains the expected outcome and performance at each stage of the curve:

Stage	Process	Evidence	Engagement
Not initiated: Capabilities are not being performed	Tactical	Ad hoc	Undefined
Conceptual: Capabilities are in their initial planning stages	Issues are under discussion	White-board planning	Data practitioners
Developmental: Capabilities are being developed	Policies, procedures, standards, roles, and accountabilities are being established	Ad-hoc meetings are underway	Stakeholders are identified
Defined: Capabilities are defined and formalized	Policies and standards exist; roles and responsibilities are being coordinated	Routines exist	Verified by stakeholders
Achieved: Capabilities are achieved and implemented	Policies and standards are implemented; proactive issue management	Capabilities are embedded into operations	Executive management authority with strategic investment funding
Enhanced: Capabilities are fully integrated into the operating culture of the organization	Automated with future-proof technology	Auditable	Aligned and implemented at all levels

Table 4.1 – Expected outcome in the data capability and maturity model

The key to data maturity assessment is to identify a gap. Working on a data maturity assessment usually requires a thorough understanding of the status quo of the organization. An assessment also requires a certain level of effort. This necessitates the early identification of a potential data champion or supporter. You may also choose a target organization to learn from when setting up your assessment. Let's say you are representing a government agency to plan their data strategy. You might want to select a target organization and follow the data model they employ to create a meaningful comparison.

The good news is you do not have to start from scratch to create a data maturity assessment framework!

The CDMC framework

Cloud Data Management Capabilities (**CDMC**) is a widely recognized framework from the EDM Council (`https://edmcouncil.org/frameworks/cdmc/`) to understand your organization's current data capabilities. CDMC started with a large bank, Morgan Stanley, and other large financial institutions recognizing, as they move a lot of sensitive data to the cloud, that cloud providers did not have a mature data control framework to apply. CDMC initially consisted of 300 professionals representing 100 firms in 2020 that formed a working group to contribute to the creation of CDMC. This included the world's major **cloud service providers** (**CSPs**) – Microsoft, AWS, Google Cloud, and IBM. CDMC was established because the industry struggled with the necessary regulatory engagements to help form legal and regulatory requirements.

You may want to refer to some of the industry best practices and six key areas of data maturity, as described by the CDMC framework (`https://edmcouncil.org/frameworks/cdmc/`) and depicted in *Figure 4.3*:

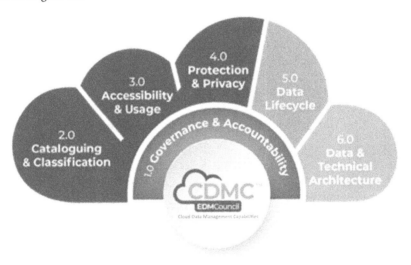

Figure 4.3 – The CDMC framework's key areas of data maturity (`https://app.smartsheet.com/b/form/6e2b0bf4a3024affb98daad174b08483`)

The benefits of using CDMC are manifold and have been realized by various organizations across a number of industries. For instance, a start-up looking to adopt cloud technology can use CDMC to assess its cloud readiness, identify gaps, and set priorities for its cloud adoption journey, much like a logistics company that used a CDMC Authorized Partner to streamline its transition to the cloud.

CDMC also helps to solidify the business case for cloud data management. A healthcare provider, for example, could use the framework to define and govern its business case for cloud data management, identifying opportunities for automation to enhance patient data processing.

CDMC ensures that a company's cloud strategy is built around best practices for migrating, creating, and managing data in the cloud. A financial institution might leverage CDMC to ensure its cloud strategy aligns with industry best practices, thereby enhancing data security and efficiency.

The robust guidance provided by CDMC, developed with the expertise of hundreds of cross-industry professionals, instills confidence in organizations. A manufacturing firm, for example, could gain confidence in its cloud data management approach, knowing it's based on sound advice from industry experts.

CDMC also supports measurable outcomes. An e-commerce company might use the CDMC framework to prioritize its cloud data goals, tracking progress and demonstrating measurable results in terms of improved data accessibility and usage.

Finally, CDMC helps ensure data protection and privacy, defining key controls for protecting data in the cloud. A multinational corporation with customers around the globe could use CDMC to meet data privacy requirements, thereby protecting customer information and building trust.

In the *Assessing data maturity* section of *Chapter 3*, we discussed the importance and benefits of conducting data maturity assessments. Then we also shared how we can bridge the gaps identified in the assessment. Now let's deep dive into the six key areas of the CDMC framework.

These six key areas to assess data maturity as identified by the CDMC are discussed as follows, in *Table 4.2*.

Key Area	Description
Governance & Accountability	This area involves setting up clear responsibilities and control mechanisms for data that is either migrated to or created in cloud environments. For instance, a financial services organization may establish a data governance board to ensure that data in the cloud adheres to regulatory requirements and internal policies.
Cataloguing & Classifications	Knowing what data you have in the cloud and the sensitivity level of each data asset is crucial. For example, a healthcare organization might develop a comprehensive data catalog that classifies data based on its sensitivity, such as personal health information, to ensure appropriate handling.
Accessibility & Usage	It is essential to monitor who accesses data and how it's used. An e-commerce company, for example, could implement data tracking tools to automate controls for data access, ensuring only authorized personnel can access specific data sets.

Key Area	Description
Protection & Privacy	Maintaining transparency, security, and protection levels is crucial, and tracking can help enforce these controls. A tech company handling user data, for instance, may use encryption and other protective measures to safeguard data, while also maintaining records to demonstrate compliance with data protection laws.
Data Lifecycle	It is important to manage data throughout its lifecycle, ensuring data assets are fit for use, and adhering to retention and archiving schedules. A government agency, for example, might implement lifecycle management controls to ensure data integrity and the timely disposal of outdated data.
Data & Technical Architecture	The design of your data architecture and the configuration of supporting technologies play a significant role in achieving business objectives. A multinational corporation, for instance, may design a robust data architecture that allows for efficient data flows between different business units, supporting decision-making and strategic goals.

Table 4.2 – Six key areas of CDMC to assess data maturity

When you define the **standard operating procedures** (**SOPs**) for the six key areas, you should look for ways to make it as automated as possible and embed the SOP workflow into the system. Here are some of the suggested key controls and automation for these six key areas to enable a strong data stewardship program:

- **Governance & Accountability**: In the area of governance and accountability, various controls and automation can be implemented to ensure efficient and secure data management:

  - For instance, it's essential to monitor data control compliance for all data assets that record sensitive information. This could be achieved through metrics and automated notifications, similar to how a bank might monitor compliance in handling customer financial data, alerting the relevant parties when anomalies or breaches are detected.

  - Moreover, for all sensitive data, it is important to identify the owner in the ownership field of a data catalog. If the ownership is not defined, it should be reported to a specified workflow. An example of this could be a hospital system where patient data is categorized and the ownership of each data set is clearly defined, ensuring accountability and proper management.

  - Additionally, it is crucial to maintain a record of authoritative data sources and provisioning points for all sensitive data assets. A large retail corporation, for example, could have a register that validates and tracks the sources of its customer data, ensuring its authenticity and reliability.

- Lastly, the movement of sensitive data across borders and its sovereignty must be recorded, auditable, and controlled according to a defined policy. For instance, an international tech company might have strict policies and tracking mechanisms in place to govern the trans-border movement of user data, adhering to regional data protection regulations and maintaining transparency.

- **Cataloguing & Classifications**: When it comes to cataloging and classification, there are key controls and automation techniques that can streamline and enhance data management:

  - Cataloging should be automated for all data when it is created or ingested, ensuring consistency across all environments. For example, a media streaming company could implement automated cataloging at the point of data creation, keeping track of vast amounts of user preference data across various platforms for a seamless user experience.

  - The classification of data should also be automated at the point of its creation or ingestion, and this process should be continuously active. This means that as soon as data enters the system, it is automatically classified based on predefined categories. A good example of this could be a cybersecurity firm that deals with a multitude of threat data. By automating classification, the firm can promptly identify and respond to various threat levels, ensuring quick action and efficient threat management.

- **Accessibility & Usage**: In the realm of accessibility and usage, specific controls and automation are crucial for managing sensitive data:

  - The entitlements and access to sensitive data should default to the creator and owner. This means that by default, the person who creates the data or is designated as its owner has the right to access it. Moreover, access to this sensitive data should be tracked. For instance, in a research institution dealing with sensitive experimental data, access controls could ensure that only designated researchers can access the data, and any access is duly logged for audit purposes.

  - All data-sharing agreements for sensitive data must identify how data will be used or consumed. This stipulates that any agreement to share sensitive data should clearly state why the data is being shared. A healthcare organization sharing patient data with a research institution, for example, would need to specify that the data is being shared for the purpose of medical research. This ensures transparency and adherence to data privacy regulations.

- **Protection & Privacy**: When it comes to protection and privacy, certain controls and automation techniques are essential:

  - It is imperative that suitable security controls are activated for sensitive data, and any evidence of such controls must be documented. For example, a financial institution dealing with sensitive customer financial data might employ advanced encryption techniques to protect the data, with evidence of these measures recorded for compliance and audit purposes.

- **Data Privacy Impact Assessments (DPIAs)** should be automatically initiated for all personal data, based on its jurisdiction. A DPIA evaluates the potential privacy risks when processing personal data, ensuring that appropriate measures are taken to mitigate these risks. For instance, a global e-commerce company dealing with personal customer data from various jurisdictions could automate DPIAs. This would ensure that any data-processing activities comply with the privacy laws of the respective jurisdictions, thereby protecting customer privacy and maintaining legal compliance.

- **Data Lifecycle**: In the context of the data lifecycle, implementing key controls and automation is crucial for effective data management:

  - Data quality measurement should be enabled for sensitive data, with metrics being distributed as soon as they are available. A telecommunications company, for example, could use automated data quality measures for its customer data, promptly distributing metrics to the relevant teams for immediate action or analysis.

  - Data retention, archiving, and purging need to be managed according to a predetermined retention schedule. This ensures that data is not kept longer than necessary, reducing storage costs and potential security risks. An example could be a legal firm that deals with sensitive client data. By adhering to a defined retention schedule, the firm can ensure that client data is securely archived for the required duration and purged when no longer needed, thereby maintaining data privacy and compliance with data protection laws.

- **Data & Technical Architecture**: In the domain of data and technical architecture, a couple of key controls and automation techniques stand out:

  - It is crucial that data lineage information is available for all sensitive data. Data lineage refers to the life cycle of data, including its origins, where it moves over time, and how it gets transformed. For example, a pharmaceutical company dealing with drug trial data would benefit from having clear data lineage, allowing for the traceability and validation of the data used in its research.

  - The cost metrics associated directly with data use, storage, and movement should be readily available in the catalog. This provides a clear understanding of the financial implications of data management. A cloud service provider, for instance, could provide a detailed breakdown of costs related to data usage, storage, and transfer in its catalog. This transparency can help customers manage their data more cost-effectively and make informed decisions about their data management strategies.

You may find more information about the fourteen key controls (`https://edmcouncil.org/frameworks/cdmc/14-key-controls/`) that represent the checklist of norms that should be automated to keep data compliant and safe.

You know where you are now, so let's define your destination; that is, how to fulfill your business and data strategy.

Fulfilling the business and data strategy – Where do you want to go?

If you were granted three wishes by a wizard for your data roadmap, what would you ask for?

To answer the question, you need to define what *good* looks like for your organization.

Now imagine you have to call the wizard via your stakeholders. Defining the good is the key to asking for the *apt* wishes from the wizard.

As you ask for the three wishes you have to convince your stakeholders that the three wishes are valid, measurable, and most importantly, relevant to the organization's goals.

So, what does it mean to stakeholders when the three wishes become true?

The three requirements for a good data roadmap are as follows:

- Formalized *data standards integrated* into modern engineering processes so that business users can trust the data with confidence. For example, during the data ingestion stage, an automated script could check whether incoming currency data adheres to the prescribed format and naming conventions, ensuring it uses USD rather than US.

- Systematic and *automated* data management controls, scanning, measurement, and access/authorization so that your organization can be agile enough to handle the future growth of data. You may refer to the preceding *Data maturity assessment* sub-section for the suggested key controls and automation.

- A single **enterprise data estate** engine for a company-wide inventory of data assets, metadata, a catalog, and data custodianship with *self-service data and analytics capabilities* so that non-technical users can realize the value of data much quicker.

In *Chapters 2* and *3*, you learned how to use business cases for story-telling and value realization to get stakeholders' buy-in for your data governance program. Now the stakeholders can feel that the benefits of unlocking data value are relevant to them.

Imagine you already have a nice ten-page data strategy and you got positive feedback about the 5-year data vision from the boardroom, but you still cannot move forward. Why? Because you cannot secure the funding and the stakeholders do not feel the data stewardship program is relevant to them.

Here is the challenge for you. Can you use simple language to explain the value added, time savings, and efficiency gains in the *pilot stage* (say, for the initial 3 to 6 months) and the *to-be stage* (with a horizon beyond 3 years)?

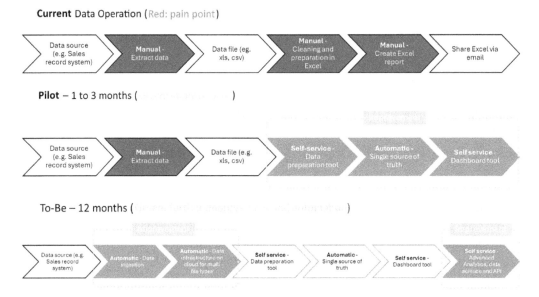

Figure 4.4 – Showing the business benefit when progressing to the pilot stage and on to the future state

Figure 4.4 is an example of how you can communicate and align the data roadmap with your stakeholders. This example showcases how you can demonstrate the progressive improvement that 12+ months of the data governance and modernization program will bring. Before you move on to the next stage, your stakeholders can see what pain points (in red) will be addressed and what improvements (in green) will be in place.

Now that you have prioritized the use cases, you can also tag the timeline for these use cases on the same diagram *(Figure 4.4)*. It is more than a data strategy document (that no one reads), it is a down-to-earth data roadmap.

Now the key question is: *What capabilities are required to enable the identified use cases?*

To address this, let's turn our attention to a practical tool that can help us understand our current situation and future goals better.

Spider web diagram

While the aforementioned CDMC framework is well established, feel free to fine-tune it to make it more relevant to your stakeholders. You can also contact the CDMC-authorized partners to help your organization conduct a detailed independent assessment. Personally, I prefer putting it in a **spider web diagram** to showcase the current position, to-be position, and the gap between the two in one simple diagram like the one shown in *Figure 4.5*:

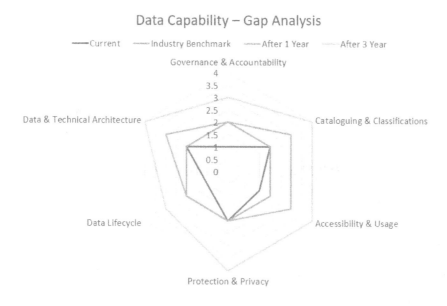

Figure 4.5 – Sample gap analysis for the data capabilities

That is my favorite way to tell the data story, align interests, and keep track of progress.

A spider web diagram, also known as a **radar chart**, is an excellent tool to visually display multi-dimensional data and can be effectively used for data capability assessments. The diagram typically consists of multiple axes, each representing a specific data capability, radiating from a central point like the strands of a spider's web.

As the first step, we can refer to the six key areas of the CDMC framework and use them as the six axes of the spider web.

Next, assess your organization's current level of proficiency in each of these capabilities. Plot these current state assessments on the corresponding axes of the diagram. Connecting these points will form a polygon that represents your organization's current data capability profile. Following the same method, assess and plot the desired future state, or 'to-be' state, for each capability on the same diagram. This will create a second polygon on the spider web diagram. You can also plot a polygon for industry peer benchmarking.

The gaps between the polygons for the current state and the *to-be* state visually represents the areas where improvements are needed. This gap analysis can help align stakeholders' interests by clearly showing where efforts and resources need to be directed.

All your data programs, be it a data stewardship program, self-service management reporting, or an AI forecasting solution, should be attached to this spider web diagram so that you can explain the business value to the stakeholders. You can also easily identify the gaps and then tailor the improvement plan when needed. As your data governance program progresses, you can periodically update the diagram to reflect the current state, providing a visual representation of progress over time. This can serve as a powerful communication tool to keep stakeholders informed and engaged in the data governance journey.

Having explored the utility of the spider web diagram in identifying gaps in data capabilities, we will now transition into the next crucial stage in our data governance journey. The upcoming section will delve into the strategic steps necessary to develop a robust data strategy and roadmap, examining the pivotal roles of people, processes, and technology in this endeavor.

Introducing the people, process, and technology – How do we get there?

After defining your starting point and your destination, how do you pave the way with the support of your data strategy?

Creating an effective data strategy is crucial for an enterprise to harness the full potential of its data, improve decision-making, and increase overall efficiency. *Table 4.3* lists the steps to develop a solid data strategy and roadmap for your organization:

Step	Milestone	Description
1	Define your business goal	The first step is to understand what you hope to achieve with your data. These goals should align with the overall business strategy. Whether it's improving customer service, streamlining operations, or gaining a competitive advantage, it's crucial to establish clear objectives.
2	Review your current data maturity level	As mentioned previously, you can conduct the review based on the CDMC framework or any other reference framework.
3	Define the target state for your organization's data maturity	Aligning the end game and its business outcome with your stakeholders.
4	Gap analysis and prioritization	By using the spider web diagram above, visualize the gap analysis result, prioritizing the use cases based on the approach introduced in *Chapter 3*.

Step	Milestone	Description
5	Establish and implement data governance	Establishment of rules, policies, and standards for data management. By using the right mix of people, processes, and technology, the whole data lifecycle can be standardized and automated to ensure the accuracy, consistency, and reliability of data.
6	Ensure data security and privacy	With growing concerns over data breaches, it's essential to have strong data security measures in place. This includes encryption, secure data storage, and access controls. Also, comply with data privacy regulations to protect the personal information of your customers.
7	Create a data culture	Encourage a culture that values data-driven decision-making. This requires training and educating employees about the importance of data and how to use it effectively.

Table 4.3 – Steps to create the data strategy and roadmap for your organization

Remember, a data strategy should serve as a roadmap that guides all data-related activities in an enterprise. It should be comprehensive, flexible, and aligned with the overall business strategy.

In *Chapter 5*, we will discuss how to choose the right people, process, and technology for your program, but in reality, *how to* is the least difficult part. The difficult part is getting an aligned view from the boardroom of the current and future states.

For example, imagine that end users (*people*) want to self-serve the data by connecting and creating datasets by themselves, you may need to re-engineer the business process (*process*). This may also require that the platform itself is low-code or no-code and future-proof (*technology*). The three aspects are orchestrated by the **target operating model** (**TOM**), which we will discuss in detail in *Chapters 5, 7,* and *8*.

As per my experience, I suggest you dream big but start small. Usually, data quality is one of the data horror stories that resonates with stakeholders. Beware that you do not want to boil the ocean – we will introduce the concept of **critical data element** in the forthcoming chapters. Other use cases include Customer 360, cross-sell and up-sell, profitability analysis, and of course, management reporting.

Having a data strategy is not enough; you need to maintain the momentum and keep the stakeholders informed about the progress so as to make your data stewardship program sustainable.

Making the impact visible to your stakeholders - Feedback loop to measure and report progress

Data stewardship is not a one-off exercise. Data stewardship is like your HR or Finance department. It exists for good reason. We need to foster a new culture of *fail fast and relearn fast*.

Before diving into the feedback loop mechanisms, it is essential to recognize the readiness to change within the organization. Change readiness is the ability to continuously initiate and respond to change in ways that create advantage, minimize risk, and sustain performance. It is an essential prerequisite to the successful implementation of data stewardship programs.

To evaluate the organization's readiness to change, consider the following factors:

- **Awareness of the need for change**: Ensure that there is a clear understanding across the organization of why change is necessary. This involves communicating the benefits and potential risks of not adapting to new data management strategies.

- **Desire to participate and support the change**: There must be a willingness among stakeholders to be part of the change. This can be fostered through engagement, education, and by addressing any concerns or resistance proactively.

- **Knowledge of how to change**: Provide sufficient training and resources to empower your team with the knowledge they need to implement new data stewardship practices.

- **Ability to implement the required skills and behaviors**: Assess whether the current skill sets and cultural behaviors support the change. If not, identify gaps and create a plan for skills development and behavioral adjustments.

- **Reinforcement to keep the change in place**: Establish mechanisms to ensure that the changes made are sustained over time. This includes recognizing and rewarding progress, as well as embedding new practices into the organizational culture.

By assessing these factors, the organization can determine its current state of change readiness and identify areas that need attention before moving forward with the data stewardship program. Integrating readiness to change into the feedback loop ensures that progress is not only measured and reported but also that the organization is agile and equipped to act upon the feedback received.

With the feedback loop, for example, in a monthly data stewardship town hall with the stakeholders from various departments, you should listen, review, and adjust the target operating model. Also, you should communicate the short-, mid-, and long-term aspects of the roadmap with all stakeholders to align the common interest and reprioritize use cases if needed.

Annual certification of trustworthy data sources, a list of critical data elements, and data quality metrics are also key as they enhance transparency, which creates trust among the end users.

Let's also not forget the communication and engagement model.

Engagement model

To better engage the stakeholders, "*do the right things in the right way with the agile mindset*".

To facilitate communication, we need the business, IT, and data governance teams to work together as a tribe. With a data culture that aligns with our organizational values and a target operating model fortified by people, processes, and technology, we can progressively launch a range of 'quick wins'. These are derived from the use cases that have been prioritized, fostering collaboration between the business, IT, and data governance teams, working together as a cohesive unit. All the stakeholders can adhere to the firm-wide data and business strategy, which will further advance the success.

The following visual representation (*Figure 4.6*) underscores the crucial collaboration between the business, IT, and data governance teams, which forms the backbone of any successful data governance program. The diagram depicts how these three entities engage, communicate, and work synergistically as one 'tribe'. This unified approach not only ensures seamless information flow but also facilitates effective decision-making and the execution of data strategies.

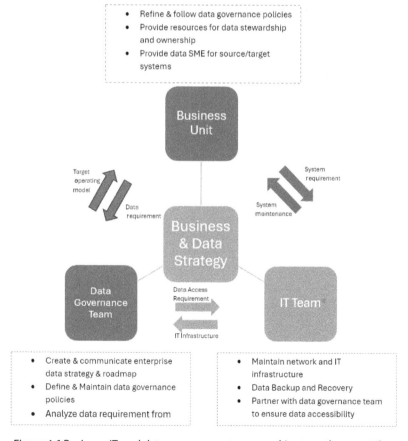

Figure 4.6 Business, IT, and data governance teams working together as a tribe

To make data stewardship a standardized day-to-day data operation, you need to have a target operation model, which we will be in the covering next chapter.

In conclusion, translating a data strategy into data operations requires careful planning and execution. It involves assigning roles and responsibilities, establishing controls, and implementing systems and processes that align with the data strategy. All of these should be supported by a transparent engagement model to enable different parties to work as one team. The goal is to ensure that data operations support the overall business objectives and comply with data governance standards.

Summary

In this chapter, we walked through the steps to develop a data management strategy. The chapter began with an introduction to the data maturity review and setting the target state of the data stewardship program. We then went into the details of people, process, and technology considerations and saw how to implement a feedback loop to measure and report progress.

We also highlighted the importance of translating strategy into execution and explained the benefits of using the CDMC framework as your starter kit. The chapter concludes by discussing the importance of aligning the data roadmap with your stakeholders.

As we turn the page to the next chapter, we will delve into the symbiotic relationship between people, processes, and technology, and how these components collectively cultivate a data culture within an organization.

5
People, Process, and Technology

Data stewardship is not the goal – it is the enabler for your organization to get to the desired data maturity level, reduce the business and regulatory risk, and drive measurable business value. In this pivotal chapter, we'll delve into the heart of data governance by exploring its key components: People, Process, Technology, Culture, and the **Target Operating Model (TOM)**.

The significance of these elements extends beyond their roles as collectively, they establish a robust, comprehensive data governance strategy. As per *Figure 2.2* in *Chapter 2*, you can see how People, Process, and Technology support the implementation of data use cases and fulfill business and data strategies. We'll begin with *People*, where we will delineate the roles and responsibilities, skills, and training required, as well as stakeholder engagement. When we cover *Process*, we will unpack the framework, data quality management, and the crucial aspects of compliance and risk management. Moving on to *Technology*, we will explore the data infrastructure, integration tools, and technologies that ensure data security and privacy. Moving on to *Culture*, we will discuss the strategies to cultivate a data-driven culture, overcome resistance, and measure cultural change. Lastly, regarding *the TOM*, we will guide you through the design, implementation, and evaluation of an effective operating model. By the end of this chapter, you will have a holistic understanding of how these elements intertwine to foster a successful data governance program.

In the next few sections, we will learn how to embed people, processes, and technology in the TOM that nurtures the data culture by covering these topics:

- Empowering people for an effective data stewardship program
- Standardizing processes to ensure consistent data operation
- Leveraging technology to fast-track your data journey
- Fostering the data culture
- Understanding the TOM – From strategy to operation

Empowering people for an effective data stewardship program

People form teams that evolve into culture.

An organized structure of people who have the proper skills is essential for the success of the data governance program. This structure is conceived and documented as part of the creation of the data governance charter.

You must establish the data steering committee, which contains senior stakeholders and decision-makers. They should be familiar with both the operation and strategic direction of the organization. The committee determines the high-level policies of the program and approves the procedures developed to carry out those policies:

- Align interest with stakeholders and make them own the data initiatives (for example, being the data owner, signing off the project success criteria, and so on).

- Upskill and continuous education to align the mindset and standard that work best for your organization. In terms of human resources, do not limit it to being full-time employees only; you can use part-time employees, contractors, and advisors when needed.

Roles and responsibilities

In this subsection, we will delve into the human aspect of data stewardship and governance, focusing specifically on the various roles within an organization that directly influence and control data management. It is crucial to understand that every role has distinctive responsibilities, requires unique skill sets, and is evaluated based on specific **key performance indicators** (**KPIs**).

The typical data roles in the organization are shown in *Table 5.1*:

Role	Responsibility	Skillset	KPI
Data steward	Responsible for the data quality of a dataset with predefined quality metrics Maintains the assigned list of critical data element	Strong understanding of data management principles and data quality standards Analytical skills and attention to detail Proficiency in data management tools	Data quality score Number of data issues resolved Timeliness of data delivery

Role	Responsibility	Skillset	KPI
Data owner	Accountable for data quality Reviews and approves data access Approves critical data elements	Strong decision-making skills Leadership skills	Timeliness of data access approval Health of critical data elements
Data producer	Systems or users that produce or collect data	Strong data collection and entry skills Strong understanding of various data sources	Number of data records produced Accuracy of data produced Timeliness of data production
Data consumer	Systems or users that use data	Understanding of how to interpret data Ability to apply data insights to real-world scenarios	Number of data-driven decisions made Impact of those decisions on business outcomes Level of data utilization
Data custodian	Responsible for maintaining data and access at the IT infrastructure level	Technical skills related to IT infrastructure, data storage, and access management	The number of data breaches prevented Data accessibility levels System uptime percentages
Data analyst	Researches and prepares data Creates a dashboard and report	Strong skills in data interpretation, statistical analysis, and reporting	The number of data insights provided Accuracy of reports Impact of their data analysis on decision-making

Role	Responsibility	Skillset	KPI
Data engineer	Data ingestion and transformation	Expertise in data modeling, **Extract, Transform, Load** (**ETL**) processes, and data warehousing	Number of data pipelines built and maintained Quality of data delivered for analysis

Table 5.1 – Roles and responsibilities of data roles in the organization

Skills and training

Data skills and training form the cornerstone of any successful data governance program. These skills encompass a broad range of abilities, from understanding and interpreting data to more complex competencies such as data analysis, data management, and data security. Training, on the other hand, refers to the ongoing process of equipping individuals with these skills and keeping them updated on the latest data-related trends and technologies.

The importance of data skills and training cannot be overstated. In an era where data-driven decision-making reigns supreme, these competencies enable organizations to make better, more informed decisions. Furthermore, they ensure that employees can effectively manage, protect, and utilize the organization's data resources.

However, equipping staff with data skills is not without its challenges. One of the key issues is the rapid pace at which data-related technologies and methodologies evolve. This makes it necessary for training to be an ongoing process. Additionally, organizations might face resistance from employees who are accustomed to traditional ways of working and are resistant to change.

To set up effective data skills and training, organizations should first identify the specific data skills that are relevant to their operations. Next, they should design or source training programs that cater to these needs. The training should be comprehensive, covering basic data literacy for all staff, as well as more advanced training for those in data-intensive roles. Furthermore, organizations should cultivate a culture that values continuous learning and encourages employees to update their skills regularly.

To set up a progressive and role-specific training pathway for multiple business units, it is essential to understand the specific data skills needed by each unit and role. Here is a step-by-step approach:

1. **Assessment**: Begin by assessing the current data skills within each business unit. This will help identify gaps and areas where training is needed. For instance, your marketing team might need training in data analysis to better understand customer behavior, while your HR team might need training in data privacy to manage employee data responsibly.

2. **Role-specific training paths**: Based on the assessment, create tailored training paths for each role. For instance, a data analyst might require advanced training in statistical analysis tools, while a project manager might need basic training in data interpretation and reporting.

3. **Progressive levels**: Each training path should have progressive levels, starting from foundational skills and moving toward more advanced competencies. For instance, an employee in the marketing team might start with basic data tooling, move to using data visualization tools, and eventually learn predictive analytics.

4. **Blended learning approaches**: Use a mix of learning methods to cater to different learning styles. This could include classroom sessions, online courses, hands-on workshops, and even on-the-job training.

5. **Continuous learning**: Encourage a culture of continuous learning. As data technologies evolve, ensure that employees update their skills by providing access to recent courses, seminars, and industry events.

6. **Evaluation and feedback**: Regularly assess the effectiveness of the training programs, and take feedback from employees to make necessary adjustments. This helps ensure that the training remains relevant and beneficial for the employees.

Let's consider an example of this approach. For a sales team member, the training pathway might start with understanding how to use CRM data to improve customer interactions. The next level might involve training on using advanced data analytics tools to predict sales trends. Finally, they might receive training in data governance regulations to ensure they handle customer data responsibly. Throughout this pathway, the training would be tailored to the specific needs and responsibilities of a sales role.

In terms of trends, there is a growing emphasis on *data democratization*, which involves making data accessible to non-technical staff. This requires training programs to be designed in a way that makes complex data concepts understandable to all employees, regardless of their technical background.

Stakeholder engagement

Stakeholder engagement is one of the most important components of successful data governance. It involves garnering support, fostering understanding, and ensuring active participation from all those who have a stake in the organization's data, ranging from top management to data users and providers.

The importance of stakeholder engagement in data governance stems from the fact that data impacts all areas of an organization. Engaging stakeholders ensures that everyone understands the value of data governance, their role in it, and the benefits it brings to their daily tasks and the organization at large. It also helps to address any concerns or resistance, thereby promoting acceptance and active participation.

However, stakeholder engagement comes with challenges from different dimensions. For example, varied understandings of data governance, resistance to change, and difficulty in demonstrating immediate value are some of the common obstacles.

To overcome these challenges, organizations can adopt the following step-by-step approach:

1. **Identify stakeholders**: First, identify all the stakeholders who have a stake in the organization's data. This could include executives, managers, data stewards, data users, data providers, and even external stakeholders such as customers and suppliers.

2. **Understand stakeholder needs and concerns**: Conduct interviews, surveys, or workshops to understand each stakeholder's needs, concerns, and perceptions about data governance. This will help tailor your engagement strategies.

3. **Develop a communication plan**: Create a communication plan that outlines what information will be communicated to stakeholders, when, and how. This could include regular updates about the data governance program, training sessions, and opportunities for stakeholders to provide feedback.

4. **Incorporate stakeholder input into decision-making processes**: Enable their participation in data governance councils, solicit their perspectives on data policies, or seek their feedback on proposed data governance measures.

5. **Showcase success stories**: Share success stories and demonstrate the value of data governance through tangible results. This could be through case studies, dashboards, or regular reports showcasing improvements in data quality, efficiency, or decision-making.

6. **Continuous engagement**: Engaging stakeholders is a continuous task. Keep them updated about data governance progress and consistently include them in decision-making. Ultimately, this will foster a sense of community and trust.

Demonstrating the return on investment (ROI) of a data stewardship program

When it comes to demonstrating the ROI of a data stewardship and governance program, it is important to highlight the tangible and intangible benefits. The ROI can be demonstrated through a framework that includes cost savings, increased efficiency, improved decision-making, risk mitigation, and enhanced customer satisfaction:

*   **Cost savings**: A well-executed data governance program can lead to significant cost savings. For instance, by improving data quality, an organization can reduce the costs associated with correcting errors and dealing with the consequences of inaccurate data. The man hours that have been saved can also be translated into an amount of dollars

*   For example, if the total man-hours saved from multiple departments is 1,000 hours per annum and the average hourly rate for your colleagues is 30 USD, then the cost saving from the data stewardship program is 30,000 USD per annum. Data stewards contribute to these savings by implementing data quality measures and continuously monitoring and improving data accuracy.

- **Increased efficiency**: Data governance can streamline data-related processes, leading to increased efficiency. For example, standardized data collection and processing procedures can save time and resources. Data stewards play a critical role here by establishing and enforcing these standardized procedures.

- **Improved decision-making**: High-quality, well-governed data can enhance decision-making by providing reliable and consistent insights. This can lead to better strategic decisions and improved business outcomes. As the custodians of data quality, data stewards contribute significantly to this aspect of ROI.

- **Risk mitigation**: Effective data governance can mitigate risks related to regulatory non-compliance, data breaches, and reputational damage. Data stewards help mitigate these risks by ensuring compliance with data-related regulations and implementing data security measures.

- **Enhanced customer satisfaction**: Better data governance can lead to improved customer experiences as it ensures accurate and consistent customer data. This can lead to more personalized customer interactions and higher customer satisfaction. Data stewards contribute to this by maintaining the integrity of customer data. In presenting the ROI to stakeholders, data stewards can provide examples and case studies that illustrate these benefits. They can also use metrics such as estimated cost savings, estimated avoided penalty fines, and customer satisfaction scores to demonstrate improvements in data quality, efficiency, and other areas. By doing so, they not only prove the value of the data governance program but also their crucial role in achieving these returns.

By doing so, organizations can ensure that their data governance program is well-understood, accepted, and actively supported by all stakeholders.

Now that we've learned about the importance of stakeholder engagement, let's steer our attention toward another fundamental pillar: standardizing processes.

Standardizing processes to ensure consistent data operation

In this section, we will deep dive into the necessity of uniform data operations and their profound impact on the overall data governance framework. The process of standardization ensures consistency, reliability, and accuracy in the way data is handled across the organization. As we navigate this section, we will explore the methods for implementing standard procedures and the benefits such an approach can yield in the realm of data governance.

Data governance framework

A **data governance framework** is a set of rules, policies, standards, and procedures that define how data is collected, stored, managed, used, and protected within an organization. It provides a structured approach to data governance, outlining responsibilities, decision-making processes, and the tools and technologies to be used.

The importance of a data governance framework lies in its ability to ensure data quality, integrity, security, and compliance. Setting clear guidelines helps organizations make better, data-driven decisions, reduces risks associated with data breaches or non-compliance, and enables efficient use of data.

In real life, data governance frameworks often fail due to various reasons. These may include a lack of top management support, inadequate understanding of data governance, resistance to change, and insufficient resources. Another common reason is the absence of a tailored approach – a one-size-fits-all framework may not work for every organization due to differences in data needs, organizational culture, and business objectives.

To establish a successful data governance framework, you can follow these steps to start your journey:

1. **Define objectives**: Understand what you want to achieve from data governance. This could be improving data quality, ensuring regulatory compliance, or enabling better decision-making.

2. **Identify stakeholders**: Identify all stakeholders involved in data governance and define their roles and responsibilities. This could include data owners, data stewards, data users, and senior management.

3. **Develop policies and procedures**: Create clear policies and procedures that cover all aspects of data governance. This could include data collection, storage, access, usage, quality control, security, and compliance procedures.

4. **Choose tools and technologies**: Decide on the tools and technologies that will be used for data governance. This could include data management systems, data quality tools, data security technologies, and data analytics tools.

5. **Implement the framework**: Implement the framework across the organization. This involves training staff, setting up necessary systems and processes, and integrating the framework into daily operations. You may refer to the framework from EDM Council (`https://edmcouncil.org/frameworks/dcam/#about`).

6. **Monitor and improve**: Consistently oversee the framework's efficiency and implement required modifications. This might include routine audits, feedback gatherings, and evaluations of data governance metrics.

By following these steps, organizations can establish a data governance framework that is tailored to their needs, accepted by all stakeholders, and capable of delivering the desired outcomes.

Critical data versus critical process

We need process governance to ensure consistent enforcement over the use of data in the whole data cycle. Again, we cannot boil the ocean. Usually, we go for the risk-based approach to identify the high-risk or high-value process. That is why we need to define and identify **Critical Data Elements (CDEs)**. CDE is a term that refers to a data element deemed vital for the successful operation of a business. These are essentially the most important pieces of information that an organization relies on for its decision-making processes, regulatory reporting, and risk management. CDEs often include data that is critical for the accuracy of financial reports, data that is necessary for compliance with laws and regulations, or data that is particularly sensitive and requires stringent controls for privacy and security reasons.

To identify a CDE effectively, you should also have a list of **Critical Data Processes (CDPs)**. CDP refers to the key activities or procedures involving data that are integral to the functioning and success of an organization. These processes can encompass a range of activities, such as data collection, processing, storage, distribution, and deletion. They are deemed *critical* due to their direct impact on the organization's ability to make informed decisions, maintain regulatory compliance, and manage risk.

Understanding and defining these critical data processes is a crucial step toward identifying CDEs. It provides a clearer picture of which pieces of data are most valuable or sensitive, and thus require a higher level of management and protection within the data governance framework. I recommend that your team identify the CDPs before defining CDEs.

Identifying critical business and data processes requires a thorough understanding of an organization's operational workflow and strategic objectives. Here are some criteria to consider:

- **Impact on business goals**: A process can be considered critical if it directly influences the achievement of the organization's key business objectives. For example, in a retail company, the process of inventory management could be critical because it directly affects sales and customer satisfaction.

- **Regulatory compliance**: Any process that involves data required for regulatory compliance is critical. For instance, in a healthcare organization, processes involving patient data handling are critical due to stringent healthcare privacy laws such as the **Health Insurance Portability and Accountability Act (HIPAA)**.

- **Risk management**: Processes that are vital for managing business risk are also critical. For example, in a financial institution, the process of credit risk assessment is crucial to prevent potential losses.

- **Dependency**: If other processes heavily depend on a particular process, it is likely to be critical. An example could be the data backup process in an IT company, which is vital for business continuity in case of data loss.

Do you still recall the Reddit story we mentioned in the *Assessing your current data environment for creating a data strategy – where are you now?* section in *Chapter 4*?

Probably one of the first few tasks we should do is disable the unused reports before you do any upgrade or migration. This implies we should not just assume the current process and use of data are still valid. We should challenge the status quo.

Do not just jump right in to automate the data process and implement data quality. Otherwise, you may just end up automating some unnecessary processes and producing some datasets that no one uses. It is ok if you leave the inefficient legacy processes untouched for various reasons but at least you have a mechanism to log and review later. For example, your organization may have multiple legacy systems operating in silos, making it difficult to share and integrate data across different departments. This may take a year or two to complete a data integration project.

Measuring for success

Measuring the success of a data governance program involves setting clear goals and defining metrics that align with these goals. Here's how you can measure effectiveness:

- **Define KPIs**: KPIs are quantifiable measures that are used to evaluate the success of an organization, employee, and so on in meeting objectives for performance. For a data governance program, KPIs could include data quality scores, the number of data issues resolved, compliance rate with data standards, and time taken to resolve data incidents.

- **Establish baselines**: To track progress, it is essential to establish baselines for your KPIs. This allows you to compare current performance against past performance and identify areas of improvement.

- **Monitor compliance**: Measure how well your organization adheres to data governance policies and regulations. This could involve tracking the number of data breaches, non-compliance incidents, or audit findings.

- **Evaluate data quality**: Measure the quality of data in terms of accuracy, completeness, consistency, and timeliness. This can be done using data quality tools that provide quantitative measures. You may refer to *Chapter 7* for details regarding data quality management.

- **Assess user engagement**: Track how well users are adopting the data governance practices. This could be measured through surveys, usage statistics of data governance tools, or feedback sessions.

- **Measure business impact**: Gauge how the data governance program is impacting business outcomes. This could be in terms of improved decision-making, increased operational efficiency, or reduced risk.

Remember, the goal of these measurements is not just to track progress but also to communicate the value of data governance to stakeholders. Therefore, the results should be presented in a clear, business-friendly manner that highlights the benefits and improvements brought by the data governance program. This can help you gain continued support and resources for the program, ensuring its ongoing success.

Data compliance and risk management

Compliance and risk management are crucial aspects of a data governance framework that focus on adhering to data-related regulations and mitigating risks associated with data handling.

Data compliance signifies conforming to applicable legal, regulatory, and standard benchmarks governing data management. For enterprises, this encompasses adherence to data privacy mandates such as the **General Data Protection Regulation (GDPR)** and sector-specific directives such as the **Payment Card Industry Data Security Standard (PCI DSS)** for entities processing card transactions.

Data risk management, on the other hand, involves identifying, assessing, and mitigating risks associated with data. In the realm of data governance, this could include risks such as data breaches, data loss, and non-compliance penalties. Effective data risk management requires a clear understanding of the organization's data landscape, the potential threats it faces, and the impact of these threats.

The procedures for ensuring compliance and managing risks include the following:

- **Regulatory awareness**: Regularly update knowledge on relevant data laws and regulations such as GDPR, CCPA, and HIPAA. This is crucial for understanding what is required for compliance.

- **Policy development**: Develop and implement clear data policies that are in line with the regulations. This could cover data collection, storage, access, usage, and disposal.

- **Data classification**: Classify data based on its sensitivity and the level of protection it requires. For example, personal customer data may be classified as highly sensitive and subject to strict access controls.

- **Risk assessment**: Regularly conduct risk assessments to identify potential data-related risks and their impact. This could include risks such as data breaches, data loss, and non-compliance with regulations.

- **Risk mitigation**: Define strategies to mitigate identified risks. This could include data encryption, access controls, backup and recovery strategies, and incident response plans.

- **Compliance monitoring**: Regularly examine data handling procedures to ensure compliance with regulations and the effectiveness of risk management strategies.

- **Training and awareness**: Conduct regular training and awareness sessions to ensure that all stakeholders understand the data policies, the importance of compliance, and their role in managing data-related risks.

Why are data compliance and risk management important to your organization?

Failure to manage compliance and risks properly can lead to severe consequences. For instance, non-compliance with regulations such as GDPR can result in hefty fines. A data breach due to inadequate risk management can lead to loss of sensitive data, reputational damage, loss of customer trust, and legal repercussions.

For example, a healthcare provider failing to secure patient data adequately could suffer a data breach, exposing sensitive patient information. This could result in legal action, fines under HIPAA, damage to the provider's reputation, and loss of patient trust. Therefore, effective compliance and risk management are not just regulatory requirements but also business imperatives.

Having established the importance of data compliance and risk management in safeguarding your organization's data integrity and trustworthiness, let's delve into the transformative role of technology.

Leveraging technology to fast-track your data journey

Technology is the enabler that allows people to carry out the right process in the most efficient way.

Leveraging technology can dramatically accelerate an organization's data journey. In this era of rapid digital transformation, the sheer volume and complexity of data can be overwhelming. Manual processes and traditional approaches often fall short when it comes to managing, processing, and deriving value from this vast sea of information. This is where technology steps in, providing the tools and platforms necessary to handle, analyze, and utilize data effectively and efficiently.

However, there is no one-size-fits-all solution. Here are some key considerations when you choose the technology you wish to use:

- **Automation**: This is a key factor in data governance as it can help streamline processes and reduce manual labor. Automation of data life cycle management can also help ensure data accuracy and integrity, as well as reduce the time and effort required to maintain data quality. Finally, automation can help ensure compliance with data privacy regulations, as well as provide real-time visibility into data usage and access

- **Choose a reliable cloud service provider**: You will likely need to use the cloud as a future-proof platform. The cloud service provider should offer secure data storage, encryption, and access controls. Look for providers that are compliant with relevant security standards and regulations, such as ISO 27001, HIPAA, and PCI DSS.

- **Protect data wherever it lives or travels**: Role-based access control (RBAC) is a method of managing and controlling access to resources within an organization based on the roles of individual users. It involves assigning permissions to specific roles in an organization and then associating users with appropriate roles. This ensures that only authorized personnel have access to specific resources, thereby enhancing security and operational efficiency.

- RBAC operates on the principle of least privilege, which means that users should only have the access necessary to perform their job functions and nothing more. This minimizes the potential for unauthorized or inadvertent access to sensitive information. For instance, let's consider a hospital management system. In such a system, different roles may include doctors, nurses, administrators, and patients. Each of these roles would require different access permissions:

  - Doctors would need access to patient medical histories, treatment plans, and possibly research data. However, they wouldn't need access to billing information or administrative records.

  - Nurses might need access to patient health records and medication schedules, but not necessarily to treatment plans or research data.

  - Administrators might require access to administrative records, billing information, and personnel data, but not to patient medical histories or treatment plans.

  - Patients would only need access to their own medical records and billing information.

- By implementing RBAC, the hospital can ensure that each user has access to the information necessary for their role, while sensitive data remains protected from unauthorized access. It also simplifies the task of managing user permissions as changes only need to be made at the role level, rather than for each user.

- Instead of just using encryption and RBAC to protect data that is at rest, you should also leverage the right technology with the right governance process to safeguard the data in use and in motion.

- **Enable self-service data analytics via data mesh architecture**: Data mesh architecture is a data domain-driven approach to data governance that focuses on providing users with the data they need when they need it. It is an architecture that allows data to be shared across multiple applications and services and enables users to access data from multiple sources securely and efficiently. It is designed to enable self-service data access and enable users to quickly access the data they need without having to wait for a centralized team to provide or approve it.

Data-as-a-product is a concept that focuses on making data available to users in a way that is easy to consume and understand. It involves making data available in a way that it is easily searchable and can be used to create meaningful insights.

Enabling self-service is a key element of your technology stack that focuses on making data available to users in a way that is easy to consume and understand. Upskilling your team is key here. To enable self-service, you need to have a well-designed data mesh architecture and create a data-as-a-product framework.

Self-service technologies empower users to access information, perform tasks, and make decisions without the need for assistance. Here are the tools and technologies that can enable self-service:

- **Business intelligence tools**: Applications such as Power BI, Tableau, and QlikView allow users to generate reports, visualize data, and extract insights without needing extensive technical expertise.

- **Data catalogs**: Tools such as Purview, Alation, and Collibra enable users to find, understand, and trust their data. They provide metadata management and data lineage capabilities, which enhance transparency and trust in data.

- **Data preparation tools**: Platforms such as DataFactory and Trifacta allow users to cleanse, structure, and enrich raw data, making it ready for analysis. These tools often feature intuitive user interfaces and pre-built functions, reducing the need for coding skills.

- **Self-service data analytics**: Tools such as Databricks and Alteryx enable users to build and execute data analysis workflows, fostering a culture of data-driven decision-making.

- **Data virtualization tools**: Tools such as Denodo or Power BI provide unified access to data from various sources, enabling users to access and analyze data without knowing its location or format.

- **Artificial intelligence and machine learning platforms**: Tools such as Azure Machine Learning Studio and DataRobot allow users to build and deploy machine learning models, which can automate decision-making and generate predictive insights.

Data infrastructure

Data infrastructure refers to the digital foundation that enables data collection, storage, processing, and analysis. It includes databases, data warehouses, servers, data management systems, and other technology tools used for handling data.

Understanding the importance of data infrastructure is key to comprehending its role in data governance. It provides the technical capabilities needed for effective data management, ensuring that data is accessible, secure, reliable, and usable. A robust data infrastructure can help organizations make data-driven decisions, improve operational efficiency, ensure regulatory compliance, and create value from their data.

The technical infrastructure required for effective data governance can vary depending on the organization's size, industry, and data needs. Nevertheless, it typically includes the pillar technologies shown in *Table 5.2*:

Technology	Description	Example Use Case	Tool
Databases, data warehouses, and data lake	Storing and processing structured and unstructured data	A telecom company might use a data lake to store vast amounts of raw call logs, a database for customer information, and a data warehouse for analyzed data.	Azure SQL and Synapse, Microsoft Fabric, AWS Redshift, and Google Cloud Big Query

Technology	Description	Example Use Case	Tool
Data security	Protect data from unauthorized access and breaches	A banking institution using encryption software and firewalls to safeguard customer's financial data	Azure Information Protection, Symantec Data Loss Prevention, and Microsoft Purview
Data quality	Maintaining and improving the quality of data	A retail business, for instance, might use a data quality tool to ensure the consistency of product information across multiple platforms.	Talend, S&P Global **Enterprise Data Management** (EDM), and Informatica
Data analytics	Analyzing data and extracting insights	An e-commerce company might use data analytics tools to identify buying trends and customer behavior	Databricks, Google Analytics, Azure Synapse, Microsoft Fabric, and Power BI
Cloud services	Scalable storage and computing power as the future-proof infrastructure	Allow users to access and process data from anywhere, at any time, at any scale	Microsoft Azure, AWS, and Google Cloud

Table 5.2 – Data technology pillars

Despite its importance, implementing a data infrastructure can pose several challenges. These include high setup and maintenance costs, complexity of data integration, ensuring data security, and maintaining data quality. Moreover, organizations may struggle with the rapid pace of technological change and the need to continuously update their infrastructure.

Addressing these challenges requires a strategic approach:

- **Planning and strategy**: Develop a clear strategy for your data infrastructure that aligns with your data governance goals and business objectives. This involves understanding the organization's data needs, identifying the necessary hardware and software components, and determining how these components will interact. A well-planned strategy ensures that the data infrastructure aligns with the organization's goals, supports its data workflows, and can scale with its growth.

- **Investment**: Ensure adequate investment in quality infrastructure and its maintenance. This includes the cost of hardware and software, as well as ongoing expenses such as maintenance, upgrades, and personnel training. It is crucial to allocate sufficient resources to this endeavor since a robust data infrastructure can significantly enhance the organization's ability to leverage data for decision-making, innovation, and competitive advantage.

- **Integration**: Use integration tools and practices to connect different components of the infrastructure and enable seamless data flow. It also minimizes data silos, which can hinder data accessibility and accuracy. Ultimately, you can make better business decisions with the support of data integration.

- **Security measures**: Deploy robust data security protocols, such as data encryption, access controls, and regular audits. The goal is to protect data from unauthorized access, corruption, or loss. It also includes practices such as regular security audits and disaster recovery planning. Effective security measures not only protect the organization from financial and reputational damage but also help ensure compliance with data protection regulations.

For example, a financial institution needs a robust data infrastructure to manage large volumes of transactional data, ensure regulatory compliance, and make data-driven decisions. However, integrating data from different sources can be a challenge. To address this, the institution can use data integration tools and practices to create a unified view of the data. It can also implement strong security measures to protect sensitive financial data.

Data integration

Data integration tools are software utilities that enable data to be merged from various sources into a cohesive, unified view. They can handle different data types, from structured to unstructured data, and can process data from various sources, such as databases, data warehouses, and cloud storage.

Data integration tools are pivotal in data governance for several reasons. They ensure data consistency, improve data accessibility, and facilitate data analysis. By integrating data from various sources, these tools enable organizations to have a comprehensive view of their data, thereby aiding in decision-making and strategic planning.

The trend in data integration is leaning toward real-time data integration and cloud-based solutions. Real-time data integration provides up-to-date, synchronized data, enabling more accurate and timely decision-making. Cloud-based solutions offer scalability, cost-effectiveness, and ease of implementation.

However, data integration does present challenges. These include dealing with data from disparate sources, handling large volumes of data, ensuring data quality, and maintaining data security during the integration process.

To address these challenges, we can consider the following solutions:

- **Data mapping**: Create a data map to understand where the data is coming from and how it relates to other datasets. This can help in handling data from disparate sources.

- **Scalability**: Choose data integration tools that can handle large volumes of data and scale as your data needs grow. For instance, Microsoft Fabric (`https://www.microsoft.com/en/microsoft-fabric`), when empowered by cloud infrastructure, can handle the increased data volume and complexity by allocating more resources as needed.

- **Data quality management**: Incorporate data quality management practices (you may refer to *Chapter 7, Data Steward Roles and Responsibilities*, for details) into the data integration process to ensure the accuracy and consistency of the integrated data.

- **Security measures**: Implement robust security measures to protect data during the integration process. This could include encryption, access controls, and secure data transfer protocols. For instance, a retail company might use data integration tools to merge customer data from its online store, physical stores (including handwritten information), and social media platforms. This can provide a comprehensive view of customer behavior and preferences, helping the company to tailor its marketing strategies. However, the company must ensure that the integrated data is accurate, consistent, and secure. It can do this by implementing data quality checks during the integration process and using secure data transfer protocols.

Data security and privacy technologies

Data security and privacy technologies refer to the tools, mechanisms, and strategies that are utilized to safeguard information from unauthorized access, breaches, or theft while ensuring its confidentiality and integrity. This discipline is not only about protecting raw data but also concerns the safe handling of personal and sensitive information.

The significance of these technologies is undeniable in the digital age. With the exponential growth in data collection and utilization, security vulnerabilities and privacy issues have surged. Data breaches can result in significant financial losses, harm to reputation, and penalties from regulatory bodies. Additionally, violations of privacy can lead to erosion of customer confidence and potential legal consequences.

Data security and privacy technologies can help organizations comply with regulatory requirements. Laws such as GDPR (https://eur-lex.europa.eu/eli/reg/2016/679) in Europe, the **California Consumer Privacy Act (CCPA)** (https://www.oag.ca.gov/privacy/ccpa) in the US, and **Personal Data Privacy Ordinance (PDPO)** (https://www.pcpd.org.hk/english/data_privacy_law/ordinance_at_a_Glance/ordinance.html) in Hong Kong mandate stringent data management and protection protocols. These technologies ensure data is handled securely and responsibly, with robust controls to prevent unauthorized access or data leaks.

For instance, technologies such as encryption and tokenization can protect sensitive data by converting it into unreadable formats, accessible only with specific decryption keys. Database activity monitoring tools can track and report suspicious activities, helping companies detect and respond to potential threats swiftly.

Data security and privacy technologies are now taking a more holistic and proactive approach. There is a growing emphasis on predictive analytics and machine learning to anticipate threats and breaches. For example, **User and Entity Behavior Analytics (UEBA)** is a type of security software that uses machine learning to detect anomalous behavior or usage patterns, flagging potential threats before they cause harm. Microsoft Sentinel offers UEBA features so that security analysts can respond proactively based on actionable intelligence.

Yet there are equally formidable challenges. The complexity and dynamism of the data landscape, coupled with the sophistication of cyber threats, make it difficult to maintain robust data security and privacy. Additionally, ensuring compliance with evolving data regulations across different regions can be complex and resource-intensive.

Take the case of a multinational corporation that needs to comply with different data regulations in multiple countries. A centralized data security and privacy technology solution can streamline compliance, but it requires significant investment and expertise to implement and maintain.

Investment strategy on technology for data stewardship

Investing in technology is not merely a matter of upgrading tools or software; it is a strategic move that can greatly enhance data stewardship capabilities. With the right technology, organizations can automate mundane tasks, improve data quality, ensure compliance, and unlock the true value of their data. It enables data stewards to focus on strategic initiatives, such as data analysis and governance policy development, rather than getting bogged down by routine data maintenance.

The first step in crafting an investment strategy is to identify the organization's technological needs. This involves a thorough assessment of how existing tools are serving the current data strategy and business objectives. It is essential to pinpoint gaps where technology can be leveraged to gain a competitive edge, improve efficiency, or reduce costs. This might include advanced analytics capabilities, enhanced data security measures, or more robust data integration solutions. You should also review and strike a balance between business strategy, data management needs, and regulatory requirements. In *Chapter 3, Getting Started with the Data Stewardship Program*, we showcased how we can prioritize the data and technology use cases based on multi-dimensional factors.

A meticulous cost-benefit analysis is vital before committing to any technology investment. You may refer to the *Demonstrating the return on investment (ROI) of a data stewardship program* section in this chapter for more information. This should encompass all direct costs, such as purchase prices and implementation fees, as well as indirect costs such as training and potential downtime during the transition. On the flip side, benefits must be quantified as much as possible. For example, automating data cleansing processes may reduce the need for manual intervention, thus saving on labor costs and reducing the likelihood of human error. The ROI can then be projected, considering these costs against the potential savings and revenue gains from improved data handling. When investing in technology, consider not just current needs but future growth as well. The chosen technology should be scalable, able to handle increasing volumes of data, and adaptable to evolving business needs without requiring constant overhauls. A scalable investment is more cost-effective in the long run as it reduces the need for frequent, disruptive upgrades.

Every investment carries risk, and technology is no exception. There is the risk of rapid obsolescence due to the fast pace of technological change, and the danger of vendor lock-in, where the organization becomes overly dependent on a single supplier. A thorough risk assessment should be conducted while considering factors such as the technology's life cycle, support, and maintenance terms, as well as the vendor's stability. Contingency plans should be put in place, such as ensuring the availability of alternative solutions or negotiating flexible contract terms with vendors. This article from Forbes may help you solidify your plan: `https://www.forbes.com/sites/forbestechcouncil/2021/03/30/understanding-the-potential-impact-of-vendor-lock-in-on-your-business/?sh=3260fa155455`.

Having examined the critical aspects of data infrastructure, integration, security, and investment strategy on technology, we'll shift our focus to an equally significant topic: fostering a data culture where data is valued, understood, and effectively utilized by everyone in the organization.

Fostering the data culture

A data culture refers to an organizational environment where decisions, strategies, and actions are guided by data insights rather than intuition or experience alone. This approach involves the widespread and effective use of data across all levels of an organization, promoting transparency, innovation, and evidence-based decision-making. All of these are reinforced by three elements: people, processes, and technology.

In fostering a data culture (*Figure 5.1*), the synergy of *People*, *Process*, and *Technology* plays a pivotal role in transforming data into actionable insights for the organization's growth and success:

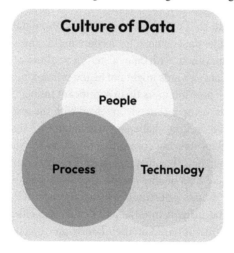

Figure 5.1 – People, Process, and Technology work together to facilitate data culture

As shown in *Figure 5.1*, People, Process, and Technology form the triad that collectively fosters and enhances an organization's data culture. After all, it is about data culture, and this is the competitive edge of your organization over the competitors. It starts with the right and aligned data mindset. Then, you have a data strategy that resonates with business strategy, supported by the people, process, and technology, guided by the data TOM and **standard operating procedure (SOP)**.

Now, the whole organization can see the value of data. Your teams move at the same frequency with the same pace in the same direction. You foster the self-service data culture with the support of data skill enablement.

Cultivating a data-driven culture

The importance of cultivating a data-driven culture cannot be overstated. Organizations that effectively leverage data can gain competitive advantages, improve operational efficiency, and enhance customer experiences. Moreover, a data-driven culture fosters a shared understanding and alignment across the organization, bridging departmental silos and promoting collaborative problem-solving.

Here are some plans for fostering a data-driven culture:

- **Leadership commitment**: Top-level executives should champion the importance of data, setting the tone for a data-driven mindset throughout the organization. For instance, leaders at Amazon mandate a Day 1 philosophy, which emphasizes the importance of data in decision-making.

- **Data literacy training**: Provide education and training to improve employees' ability to interpret, analyze, and use data effectively. You will see how The Bank of East Asia, Limited fosters a data-centric culture for its employees in *Chapter 12, Case Studies*.

- **Empowerment**: Enable all staff members to access and use data while ensuring proper data governance. This encourages data ownership, accountability, and innovation. At Spotify, teams are given autonomy to experiment with data, fostering a culture of innovation and data-driven decision-making. While data stewards might not be the primary decision-makers of a firm-wide data strategy, their unique position gives them significant influence over its establishment and refinement. Data stewards, being intimately involved with the organization's data, understand its nuances, potential value, and the challenges associated with managing it. They can provide valuable insights to the data steering committee into how the data can best be leveraged to support the organization's goals. For instance, data stewards can influence the data strategy by highlighting areas where data quality can be improved, suggesting methods to streamline data integration, or identifying opportunities for data usage that can drive innovation. They can provide on-the-ground insights into the practicality and effectiveness of the current data strategy, suggesting adjustments based on their hands-on experience.

- **Reward and recognize**: Acknowledge and reward the use of data in decision-making to reinforce its importance. This can be done through performance metrics, incentives, or recognition programs.

Overcoming resistance

Resistance to change, especially in the context of data governance initiatives, refers to the pushback or reluctance from individuals or groups within an organization when changes related to data governance are introduced. This resistance may stem from fear of the unknown, perceived loss of control, or lack of understanding about the benefits of data governance.

Overcoming resistance is crucial for the successful implementation of data governance initiatives. Without addressing this resistance, organizations may fail to fully realize the benefits of these initiatives, such as improved data quality, better decision-making, and compliance with data protection regulations.

You, as a data steward, can create a framework to address resistance that includes the following aspects:

- **Clear communication**: Communicate the purpose and benefits of the data governance initiative transparently and consistently. For example, in a healthcare organization implementing a new data governance policy, as a data steward, you can help explain how it will improve patient care and ensure compliance with health data regulations. By personalizing these messages to address the specific concerns or interests of various groups, data stewards can help reduce resistance to the initiative.

- **Enhance a sense of ownership to data stewardship**: Involve stakeholders from all levels in the planning and implementation process. For instance, a manufacturing company might form a cross-functional team comprising representatives from various departments and mentored by a data steward to drive its data governance initiative. This inclusive approach can foster a sense of ownership, encouraging stakeholders to support the initiative rather than resist it.

- **Tailor-made training and support**: Offer training to help employees understand the new systems or processes. Provide ongoing support to address concerns and difficulties. If employees do not understand how to use new systems or follow new processes, they may resist these changes. As a data steward, you can arrange for training sessions that help employees understand and adapt to these changes. A retail company, for example, might offer workshops to train staff on a new data management system.

- **Incremental implementation**: Implement changes gradually to avoid overwhelming staff. As a data steward, instead of introducing all changes at once, you could plan for a phased implementation. This might involve piloting the data governance initiative in one department, gathering feedback and reporting to the data steering committee, making necessary adjustments, and then rolling it out to more departments. This incremental approach allows the organization to learn from each phase, making the initiative more likely to succeed and less likely to be met with resistance.

Challenges in overcoming resistance may include entrenched cultural norms, lack of awareness or understanding, and fear of change.

So, what are the actionable items for data stewards to foster the data culture and over-resistance? Here are some recommendations:

- **Encourage data-driven decision-making**: Data stewards can organize regular training sessions to improve data literacy across the organization. This will help employees understand the value of data and how to use it effectively in their roles. Advocate for the use of data in decision-making processes at all levels of the organization. Provide examples of how data can lead to better outcomes.

- **Foster open and regular communication**: Encourage teams to share their data challenges and successes in a monthly data meetup. This can help spread best practices and foster a sense of collective ownership over the organization's data.

- **Standardize guidelines and procedures**: As experts in data governance, data stewards can help develop clear guidelines and procedures that alleviate fears and concerns about the changes. They can ensure these guidelines are comprehensive, practical, and easy to understand. They can also provide examples or case studies to demonstrate how these procedures work in practice, making the changes less abstract and more tangible.

Overcoming resistance is a vital part of any data governance initiative. By proactively addressing resistance, organizations can accelerate the adoption of these initiatives, leading to improved data quality, better decision-making, and regulatory compliance.

Measuring cultural change

Measuring cultural change involves gauging the shift in attitudes, behaviors, and values within an organization, particularly concerning data governance. It's about determining the extent to which the organization has embraced a data-driven culture.

The importance of measuring cultural change lies in its capacity to provide insights into the success of data governance initiatives. It helps identify areas of progress, resistance, and opportunities for improvement, enabling organizations to adjust their strategies accordingly.

To measure the change in culture toward data governance, several indicators can be considered:

- **Data literacy levels**: This measures the ability of staff to understand, analyze, and use data effectively. The metric for measurement can be the number of employees who have completed data literacy training. For example, an increase in the number of employees completing data literacy training could indicate positive cultural change.

- **Data usage**: This assesses the extent to which data is used in decision-making. We can record the number of decisions that are made using data-derived insights. For instance, an increase in the number of decisions backed by data insights could signify a shift toward a data-driven culture.

- **Data sharing**: This measures the extent of cross-functional collaboration and data sharing. We may use the frequency of cross-departmental data sharing as a metric. An increase in cross-departmental data sharing could indicate a breakdown of data silos, signaling a positive cultural shift.

- **Data quality**: This assesses the level of accuracy, consistency, and completeness of data. Tracking the number of data quality issues over time can serve as a metric. Improvements in data quality can indicate a greater appreciation for data governance.

- **Feedback and surveys**: Employee feedback and surveys can provide insights into attitudes toward data governance. The amount of positive feedback can be one of the metrics. For example, an increase in positive responses to questions about the value of data governance could denote a cultural shift.

However, it can be difficult to quantify attitudes and behaviors, and changes may occur gradually over time. To address these challenges, organizations should do the following:

- **Set clear and measurable objectives for cultural change**: The challenge of quantifying attitudes and behaviors can be mitigated by setting clear and measurable objectives for cultural change. This provides a benchmark against which progress can be measured. For example, a data steward can help define an objective such as "Increase the percentage of decisions supported by data from 60% to 80% within a year."

- **Use a combination of quantitative and qualitative methods**: Gradual changes in culture may not be immediately apparent through quantitative measures. Therefore, a combination of quantitative and qualitative methods can be used to provide a comprehensive view of cultural change. For instance, a data steward can implement quantitative measures such as tracking the number of employees who complete data training, while also incorporating qualitative measures such as conducting surveys or interviews to understand employee attitudes towards data usage and governance. This combination allows for a holistic understanding of the organization's data culture.

- **Regularly review and adjust measurement methods**: As changes in data culture often occur gradually, it is vital to regularly review and adjust measurement methods to ensure they remain relevant and effective. For example, a data steward can conduct quarterly reviews of the set objectives and measurement methods. If an objective such as "Increase data sharing between departments by 30%" is consistently not being met, the data steward can investigate the reasons, make necessary adjustments, and set a new, more attainable objective. Regular reviews ensure the measurement methods accurately reflect the ongoing cultural changes within the organization.

All in all, measuring cultural change is a vital aspect of implementing data governance initiatives. By tracking progress and identifying areas for improvement, organizations can better foster a culture that values and utilizes data effectively.

What's more? Hmm...

Let's try to tie the year-end bonus with the KPI of the data governance program.

Make it relevant to the stakeholders.

Having navigated the path of fostering a data culture, overcoming resistance to change, and measuring the success of data cultural change, we'll now turn our attention to another important aspect of data governance: the TOM. In the next section, we will unravel the concept of the TOM, its strategic importance, and how it effectively bridges the gap between strategy and operation in the realm of data governance.

Understanding the TOM – From strategy to operation

In the pursuit of effective data governance, the interconnected elements of people, processes, technology, and culture must be harmoniously aligned. This alignment is achieved through a well-defined TOM.

The implementation, execution, and assessment of the TOM is typically carried out by the organization's data steering committee and chief data officer, with the aid of various stakeholders from different departments. This includes IT, operations, finance, and others who understand the organization's strategic goals. However, among these, data stewards play a pivotal role in the success of the TOM.

In the context of the TOM, the role of a data steward can be broken down as follows:

- **Defining data processes**: Data stewards outline the processes needed to manage data effectively. For instance, they can help design workflows for data collection, validation, storage, and analysis. This ensures that data flows smoothly from one stage to another, in line with the TOM.

- **Implementing data technologies**: Data stewards help identify the right technologies and tools to manage and analyze data. For example, they might recommend a specific data management system that aligns with the organization's data strategy and fits within the TOM.

- **Ensuring data quality**: Data stewards are responsible for maintaining the quality of the organization's data. They establish data quality metrics and regularly assess the data against these benchmarks. This helps maintain the integrity of data, which is crucial for the TOM to be effective.

- **Facilitating data culture**: Data stewards promote a culture of data-driven decision-making. This cultural shift supports the TOM by ensuring that everyone in the organization understands and values the role of data in achieving strategic goals.

The TOM is the *glue* that holds together various elements of the data stewardship program, connecting strategy to operations.

This blueprint is essential not only for implementing a data stewardship program but also for ensuring seamless functionality that drives business value. By outlining how all components interact and collaborate, the TOM fosters a data-driven culture, enhances data security, and effectively connects strategy to operations to meet overall business objectives.

Let's consider the building blocks for the TOM:

- **Roles and responsibilities**: Accountable data owners and responsible data stewards who manage the quality and compliance of enterprise data subject area.

- **Data governance**:

  - Do the right things in the right ways

  - A single source of truth for the most important enterprise master data

  - End-to-end data lineage to completely track data consumption

  - A common enterprise data catalog with a discoverable, certified source of truth

  - Centralized data provisioning processes and tools that enforce common data authorization standards

- **Technology and infrastructure**:

  - Shared systems of intelligence infrastructure that bring together all data in one place for ease of discovery, life cycle management, and compliance enforcement

  - Embed data policies and standard operating procedures into the system workflows

Each of these building blocks is interconnected and mutually reinforcing, collectively forming the foundation of a robust TOM for data stewardship.

Designing the TOM

Designing a TOM for data governance involves creating a practical and efficient framework that brings together people, processes, technology, and culture to manage and utilize data effectively.

The following steps can guide the design process:

1. **Define the vision**: Establish a clear understanding of what your organization aims to achieve with data governance. This could be enhancing data quality, ensuring regulatory compliance, or driving data-driven decision-making. For example, a financial institution may aim to improve its risk management by ensuring high-quality, reliable data.

2. **Assess current state**: Evaluate the existing state of data governance, including the current culture, technologies, processes, and skills. For instance, a manufacturing firm might find that it has strong data processes but lacks a data-driven culture.

3. **Identify gaps**: Determine the gaps between the current state and the desired vision. For example, your organization may want to have a personalized recommendation service for online customers but you find that data silos exist in several departments, data quality is not up to the standard, and you have no data privacy policy in place.

4. **Design the future state**: Based on the vision and identified gaps, design a TOM that outlines how people, processes, technology, and culture will interact to support data governance. For example, a healthcare provider aiming for better patient data management might design a model that includes new data privacy technology, enhanced data processes, and a strong culture of data protection.

5. **Define roles and responsibilities**: Clearly outline who is responsible for what within the data governance framework. This could involve designating data owners, data stewards, and data users.

6. **Develop an implementation plan**: Create a step-by-step plan for transitioning from the current state to the TOM. This could involve training programs, technology upgrades, process re-engineering, and cultural change management initiatives.

7. **Measure and adjust**: Establish metrics to monitor progress and adjust the model as needed. For instance, an increase in data quality or a reduction in data breaches could indicate progress toward the TOM.

Designing a TOM for data governance is a strategic endeavor that requires careful planning and execution. However, when done effectively, it can significantly enhance the organization's ability to manage and utilize data, driving better decision-making, compliance, and competitive advantage.

Implementing the TOM

Implementing the TOM for data governance is a multi-step process that transforms the strategic vision into a practical, operational reality. Here are the key steps and potential challenges:

1. **Communicate the plan**: Convey the purpose, benefits, and expectations of the TOM to all stakeholders. Effective communication fosters buy-in and minimizes resistance. However, the challenge lies in ensuring everyone understands and supports the changes, which may require messages tailored to different stakeholder groups. Overcoming this challenge may also involve creating a comprehensive communication plan that includes consistent messaging, multiple communication channels for different business units, and opportunities for stakeholders to ask questions and provide feedback.

2. **Provide training and support**: Equip your staff with the necessary skills and knowledge to operate within the new model. This could involve data competence training or workshops on new data processes. A potential challenge is ensuring all employees, regardless of their department or level, receive the necessary training and feel confident to apply their new skills. This can be tackled by developing a training program that covers different levels of data competence and is customized to the needs of different roles. Providing ongoing support, such as a helpdesk or online resources, can also help employees feel more confident and capable in their new roles.

3. **Pilot the model**: Test the TOM in a controlled environment or within a selected department before a full-scale rollout. This allows for identifying and rectifying issues early. The challenge at this stage is selecting a representative sample for the pilot and ensuring that the findings are generalizable to the entire organization. This can be addressed by carefully selecting a pilot group that includes a range of roles, functions, and levels. It's also important to gather feedback from the pilot group and adjust the model as needed before the full-scale rollout.

4. **Roll out the model**: Implement the model across the organization, monitoring progress and addressing issues as they arise. The challenge here lies in managing the change at scale and ensuring continuity of operations during the transition. This can be managed by planning the rollout in phases, allowing for adjustments and problem-solving between each phase. Regular communication about the progress and next steps can also help manage expectations and reduce anxiety about the changes.

5. **Review and refine**: Regularly review the model's effectiveness using the predefined metrics, and make necessary adjustments. The challenge is in determining the appropriate frequency and scope of reviews and managing the potential disruption caused by refinements. This can be tackled by establishing clear review metrics and schedules from the start, and by involving stakeholders in the review process. Refinements should be communicated clearly and implemented in a way that minimizes disruption, such as during slower periods or in stages.

For instance, when a large retail corporation implemented its data governance operating model, it faced significant resistance from employees who were accustomed to legacy systems and methods. To overcome this, the company used regular communication, comprehensive training programs, and ongoing support to ease the transition, demonstrating patience and persistence throughout the process.

Evaluating and adjusting the TOM

Assessing the effectiveness of the TOM is vital for ensuring that it delivers the desired outcomes for data governance. This process involves monitoring performance indicators, gathering feedback, and making adjustments as necessary:

- **Monitor performance indicators**: Establish KPIs that align with your data governance objectives. These KPIs could include data quality metrics, the number of data incidents, compliance levels, or the extent of data usage in decision-making. For instance, a decrease in data errors could indicate effective data governance practices under the new model.

- **Gather feedback**: Collect feedback from stakeholders, including data users, data stewards, and senior management. This qualitative information can provide insights into how the model is working in practice and highlight any areas of difficulty. For instance, data stewards may provide valuable insights into the practical challenges of implementing new data processes.

- **Conduct regular reviews**: Periodically review the performance of the TOM. This review should not only look at the KPIs but also consider broader business performance and strategic objectives. For example, if the company's strategic focus has shifted toward enhancing customer data analytics, the operating model may need adjustment to support this new focus.

- **Make necessary adjustments**: Based on the outcome of performance monitoring, feedback, and reviews, adjustments should be made to the model. This could involve refining data processes, improving training programs, or enhancing data technology. For instance, if the feedback indicates that data users are struggling to use a new data management system, additional training or user support could be provided.

- **Communicate changes**: Any changes made to the operating model should be communicated to all stakeholders to ensure understanding and buy-in.

What would happen if one of the key components of the TOM underperforms?

Consider a hypothetical global retail corporation that has a well-established business strategy aimed at leveraging big data to personalize customer experiences and streamline supply chain operations. The company's desired TOM includes robust data infrastructure, clear roles and responsibilities, a data governance framework, and a culture that values data-driven decision-making.

However, let's assume that in this scenario, the company's data culture is underdeveloped. While the organization has invested heavily in state-of-the-art technology and defined processes and roles, the importance of a data-driven mindset has not been adequately communicated or embraced by the workforce. The absence of this cultural component has several impacts:

- **Lack of engagement**: Without a strong data culture, employees across various departments, including sales, marketing, and supply chain, may not understand the value of the data they handle. This can lead to a lack of engagement with the data governance processes and a failure to utilize data in daily decision-making.

- **Poor data quality**: The disengagement of employees may result in poor data quality as individuals may not see the importance of maintaining accuracy or may bypass established processes due to a lack of understanding or commitment.

- **Ineffective use of technology**: The advanced data analytics tools and platforms that the company invested in remain underutilized because employees are either unaware of their full capabilities or are resistant to adopting new technologies due to the absence of a supportive culture.

- **Inefficient processes**: The well-defined processes for data management become inefficient as employees might not follow them diligently or may not fully comprehend their purpose, leading to inconsistencies and errors.

- **Compliance risks**: An underdeveloped data culture could lead to a casual approach to data privacy and security, resulting in an increased risk of non-compliance with data protection regulations such as the GDPR, which can have serious financial and reputational consequences.

- **Missed strategic objectives**: Ultimately, the absence of a strong data culture means that the company's strategic objectives, which depend on the effective use of data, are not fully realized. The potential insights from data analytics that could drive personalized customer experience and efficient supply chain management are not leveraged, leading to missed opportunities for growth and competitiveness.

To address the challenges of an underdeveloped data culture, the company must integrate a data-centric mindset with its strategic vision and the TOM that encapsulates promoting executive endorsement of data initiatives, advancing data literacy through targeted training, recognizing and rewarding data-driven achievements, and fostering a feedback-rich environment for continual enhancement of data practices.

Evaluating and adjusting the TOM is not a one-off activity but a continuous process that helps maintain the model's relevance and effectiveness in a dynamic business environment. By being responsive and adaptive, organizations can ensure that their data governance model continues to deliver value and support their strategic objectives.

Summary

This chapter delved into the complex world of data stewardship and governance, exploring the interplay between people, processes, technology, and culture, all underpinned by a robust TOM. We emphasized the pivotal role of individuals within the organization, highlighting the need for distinct roles such as data owners and stewards, and the importance of ongoing education programs to boost data literacy.

Then, we discussed the significance of implementing a robust data governance framework, focusing on data compliance and risk management. We highlighted the crucial role of technology in establishing a robust data infrastructure, emphasizing data integration to ensure a unified view of data.

An organization's culture plays a key role in the success of data governance, with emphasis on fostering a data-driven culture and measuring the shift in attitudes toward data governance.

Finally, we walked through the steps of designing and implementing a TOM, emphasizing the need for regular evaluation and adjustments to ensure its effectiveness.

The journey toward effective data governance is a continuous one, requiring an integrative approach that considers people, processes, technology, and culture. In the following chapter, we will explore the centralized and decentralized modes of data stewardship.

Establishing a Data Governance Organization

This chapter will give you an overview of the steps needed to establish a data governance structure. It will cover the importance of establishing data governance bodies, such as a data governance team structure, and how to foster a data culture within the organization. It will also explain the importance of defining **key performance indicators** (**KPIs**) to measure the success of the data governance program. This will help you with the knowledge and tools to create a successful data governance structure and measure its success. The chapter will also provide practical advice on how to create a data governance roadmap and set up a data governance team.

We will explore the following topics to help you jumpstart the data governance journey:

- Establishing data governance bodies
- Creating a data governance roadmap
- Defining KPIs

Establishing data governance bodies

Establishing data governance bodies is a vital step in the process of implementing effective data governance within an enterprise. The **chief data officer** (**CDO**) will lead the **data steering committee** (**DSC**) to propose the data team hierarchy to the management committee for approval. This collection of talent is not random, but rather a carefully curated team designed to ensure that the company's data is properly managed, protected, and leveraged for maximum value. Let's discuss how we can build a team and define a team structure for your data governance program.

Building your team

People are the assets of your organization. They are also the competitive edge of your company. Formulating a data governance team with the right talents is the key to success. This involves assembling a group of individuals, each with unique skills and expertise, who will be responsible for strategic and operational aspects of data governance. Here are some guidelines on how to go about this:

- **Team composition**:

  - **Core members**: The team should comprise core members with experience in data governance, data policy, data privacy, and data quality. For instance, a retail company might include individuals who have previously worked on implementing data privacy regulations such as the **General Data Protection Regulation (GDPR)**.

  - **Cross-departmental members**: Representatives from various departments such as IT, business, and data teams should be included to foster a sense of ownership and to reinforce the data governance team's authority. A healthcare organization, for example, might include members from the clinical, administrative, and IT departments to ensure a comprehensive data governance strategy.

  - **External stakeholders**: The inclusion of customers, vendors, and partners can enhance the team's perspective. For example, a retail company might include key suppliers in their data governance team to ensure supply chain data is properly managed and utilized.

- **Mission definition**: The team should have well-defined short-term and long-term missions to drive business outcomes through data stewardship. A bank, for instance, may set a short-term mission to ensure regulatory compliance and a long-term mission to leverage data for customer-centric services.

- **Role definition**: Each team member's role and tasks should be clearly defined and understood. For example, a data steward in an insurance company should know their responsibility for ensuring data quality and consistency.

- **Policy understanding**: The team should comprehend the data governance policies, procedures, and KPIs that will measure the program's success. These should be documented and officially communicated.

- **Roadmap creation**: The team should develop a data governance roadmap outlining the implementation steps and timeline. This roadmap should include policy creation steps and milestones for the program's implementation. For example, a tech start-up might include milestones such as *Data Audit Completion*, *Data Governance Policy Drafting*, *Staff Training*, and *Full Program Implementation*. While the CDO and the management committee are the decision makers, data stewards can contribute by sharing their observations on the field. You can also refer to *Chapter 4, Developing a Comprehensive Data Management Strategy*, for details of data roadmap creation.

So, now you have the data governance teammates, how about the overall decision-making hierarchy, and how do all these cross-functional data roles work together as one team? Let's talk about the team structure and hierarchy.

Team structure and hierarchy

Having a proper team structure in place can ensure clarity in roles and responsibilities. Each member of the team knows their duties and whom they report to, reducing confusion and increasing efficiency. This clarity is particularly crucial in data governance, where accuracy and timeliness are paramount. Also, a structured team fosters a culture of accountability. When roles are clearly defined, each team member is accountable for their tasks. This is crucial in data governance, as accountability ensures data integrity and compliance with regulations. With a clear and transparent team hierarchy, decisions can also be made quickly at the appropriate level, reducing bottlenecks.

Figure 6.1 shows one of the common hierarchies in organizations for the authority and decision-making of data governance programs. It can vary in different organizations:

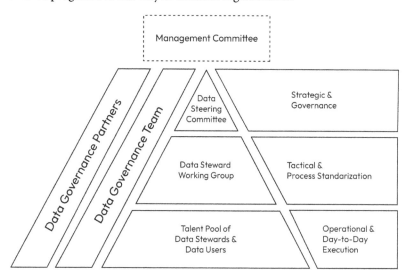

Figure 6.1 – A typical team hierarchy for a data governance program

The team hierarchy is represented in the form of a pyramid chart. The diagram shows that the talent pool of data stewards is the cornerstone of the pyramid, the data steering working group sits on top of it, followed by a data steering committee, then the management committee as the top tier. Let's look at this in more detail:

- Talent pool of data stewards and data users at an operational level:
  - Decentralized versus centralized versus federated data stewardship (see *Table 6.1* and *Figures 6.2* to *6.5*).
  - Data **subject-matter expert (SME)**.
  - Defines, produces, and uses data.
  - Maintains integrity and quality of data.
  - For example, in a decentralized model, data stewards might be spread across different departments, each responsible for their own data. In a centralized model, there may be a dedicated team of data stewards who oversee all data across the organization. A federated model might combine these two approaches, with department-specific data stewards reporting to a central authority.

- **Data steward working group (DSWG)** at a tactical level:
  - Works across **business units (BUs)** to help break down silos between divisions and promote a collaborative cross-functional environment.
  - Proposes use cases to the DSC for approval and suggests refinement to the framework.
  - Collects feedback from BUs.
  - For instance, the DSWG may propose a new data quality initiative based on feedback from marketing about inconsistent customer data.

- DSC at a data strategic level:
  - Acts as the enterprise-level decision body to ensure that firm-wide and business-specific standards are well balanced.
  - Prioritizes use cases and endorses the program roadmap submitted by the data governance team.
  - Provides overall vision, strategy, and guidance on data projects, policies, and tools.
  - For example, the DSC may prioritize a project to integrate data from a newly acquired company to ensure seamless data flow because they see it can create a new revenue stream for the company.

- Management committee at a firm-wide strategic and executive level:

  - Sponsors, approves, and champions the enterprise's strategic plan and policy.

  - Gives the final green light for data governance initiatives and ensures they align with the organization's overall strategy.

  - For instance, they might approve a new data privacy policy suggested by the DSC to ensure compliance with new regulations. This includes the approval of new headcounts, and the budget for software, hardware, and cloud services.

You can also refer to *Chapter 1* and *Chapter 2* for the illustration of data strategy, tactics, and operation.

Spanning across all layers

The data governance team and data governance partners are two unique entities that span all layers of the data governance pyramid. They play pivotal roles in connecting, facilitating, and driving the data governance effort across the entire organization. Let's take a closer look at what they do:

- Data governance team:

  - Your team!

  - A team that spans across divisions and oversees data governance at all levels.

  - Coordinating efforts between different groups, facilitating communication, and ensuring alignment with the overall data strategy.

  - For instance, they work closely with the pool of data stewards to understand their needs and challenges and relay this information to the DSWG for action planning. They also liaise with the DSC, providing them with the necessary data and insights to make informed decisions. At the management committee level, the data governance team presents updates and strategic recommendations, ensuring that the top tier is well informed about the status and progress of data governance initiatives.

- Data governance partner:

  - For example, a data custodian, external consultant, IT infrastructure, and security team.

  - Maintains the IT resources for the firm-wide data platform.

  - For example, an IT partner might provide technical solutions to help data stewards better manage and maintain data quality. Legal partners can provide advice on data privacy and compliance issues, helping to shape policies that the DSC and management committee approve.

In essence, both the data governance team and data governance partners act as a glue, bridging the different layers of the data governance pyramid. They ensure smooth interaction, effective communication, and alignment of efforts across all tiers, ultimately driving the success of the data governance program.

Mode of data stewardship

Before we discuss the detailed roles and responsibilities of data stewards in the next chapter, let's explore the three modes of stewardship in the field: centralized, decentralized, and federated.

Centralized data stewardship

A central authority/individual determines the rules of how to govern data in the organization. This individual can have many different titles, such as *chief data officer* (*CDO*), **chief data steward** (*CDS*), *data governance lead* (*DGL*), and so on. When individuals and teams execute data governance tasks, they must adhere to centrally defined processes.

Figure 6.2 illustrates an example scenario for centralized data stewardship:

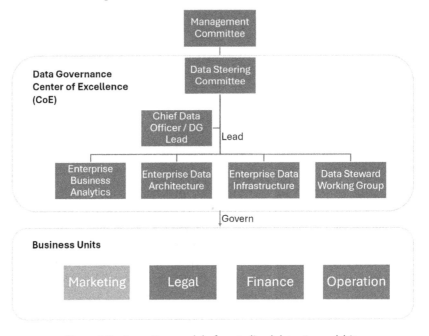

Figure 6.2 – Execution model of centralized data stewardship

In a centralized data stewardship model, a central authority, such as a CDO or DGL, sets the rules for data governance. This model provides clear governance and ensures consistency in data management across the organization. However, it may not be as responsive to department-specific needs. This model might be suitable for a smaller organization with relatively simple data needs.

For example, a start-up tech company might opt for centralized stewardship to ensure a uniform approach to data governance as it grows.

Decentralized data stewardship

The bottom-up approach is driven by the on-the-ground teammates working most closely with the data.

An instance of decentralized data stewardship is shown in *Figure 6.3*:

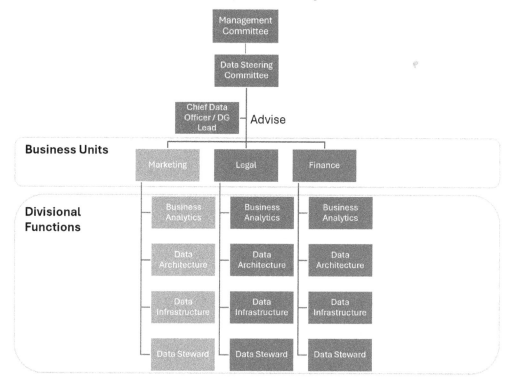

Figure 6.3 – Execution model of decentralized data stewardship

On the other hand, the decentralized data stewardship model is driven by individuals and teams who work most closely with the data. This bottom-up approach allows for greater flexibility and responsiveness to specific department needs. However, it can also lead to inconsistencies in data governance. This model could work well in larger organizations with diverse data needs across various departments.

For instance, a multinational corporation with separate BUs might choose decentralized stewardship to cater to each unit's unique data needs.

Federated data stewardship

This allows multiple groups of authority and decision-making. This also means localized data strategy and distributed organization.

A sample federated data stewardship instance is shown in *Figure 6.4*:

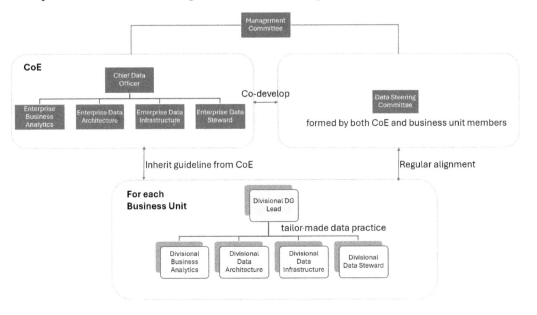

Figure 6.4 – Execution model of federated data stewardship

Lastly, the federated data stewardship model is a hybrid approach that allows for multiple decision-making authorities. This model balances the need for centralized control with the flexibility of localized data strategies. It could be an ideal choice for organizations with complex data needs that require both overarching governance and department-specific customization. For example, a healthcare organization might opt for federated stewardship to ensure compliance with industry-wide data regulations while also catering to different departments' specific data requirements.

Choosing the mode of data stewardship

So, when to use which mode of data stewardship? *Table 6.1* illustrates the pros and cons of the three modes of data stewardship:

Modes of Data Stewardship	Pros	Cons
Centralized	Faster decision-making Easier to control costs Consistent framework across all BUs The reporting structure is aligned with the existing org chart	Front-line data employees feel excluded from the process Senior managers enacting policies that do not work for data teams Operation rigidity and less flexibility to fit the unique requirements of different BUs
Decentralized	Helps focus on concrete improvements to practical, day-to-day processes All-encompassing representation from the business Each BU can define the data stewardship process that works best for them	Potentially removes the connection to business stakes understood by senior management. This may reinforce silos between groups rather than breaking them down.
Federated	Top-down decision-making regarding enterprise data with bottom-up inputs Aligns centralized data strategy with decentralized, practical implementation Assigns clear data and metadata ownership to application managers Full autonomy for BUs to develop standards, policies, and procedures	Difficult to balance enterprise-wide goals with individual unit needs Monitoring autonomous units effectively can be complex and often depends on self-reporting Managing diverse metadata across units presents significant harmonization challenges

Table 6.1 – Comparison of the three modes of data stewardship

There is no right or wrong among the three modes of data stewardship. Choosing the right data stewardship model for your organization hinges on several factors, including your organization's culture, size, data complexity, and business objectives. It is essential to evaluate these factors carefully and consider how each model might play out in your specific context.

To determine the most fitting model-be it centralized, decentralized, or federated—organizations must consider their size and structure, the complexity and scope of their data ecosystem, the regulatory environment they operate within, and their overall business objectives. For instance, a smaller organization with a more straightforward data environment may benefit from the uniformity and control of a centralized approach. In contrast, a large, geographically dispersed organization with diverse BUs might opt for a decentralized or federated model to cater to localized needs while maintaining some level of centralized control. The federated model serves as a middle ground, accommodating enterprise-wide oversight along with the agility to address specific departmental requirements. Ultimately, the chosen mode must align with the organization's data strategy and goals, ensure effective data management practices, and support the organization's capacity to derive value from its data assets. It is critical to assess these factors thoroughly and be prepared to evolve your stewardship approach as the organization grows and its data management needs change.

How about the allocation of a data steward's time across various workloads?

It depends on the stewardship mode you are operating. Here is a suggested ratio split for a typical day in the life of a data steward, focusing on three types of workloads:

- **Strategic initiatives**: This workload involves long-term planning and development of the organization's data capabilities. It includes activities such as setting data governance policies, aligning data strategies with business goals, and leading data-related projects.

- **Line-of-business (LOB) work**: This workload includes the day-to-day data operation for specific BUs and processes, including managing the quality and integrity of data. Tasks include data **quality assurance (QA)**, metadata management, handling data requests, and troubleshooting data issues.

- **Compliance and risk mitigation**: This workload involves ensuring that data practices comply with legal, regulatory, and policy requirements. It includes monitoring compliance, assessing risks, and implementing controls to mitigate potential data breaches or misuse:

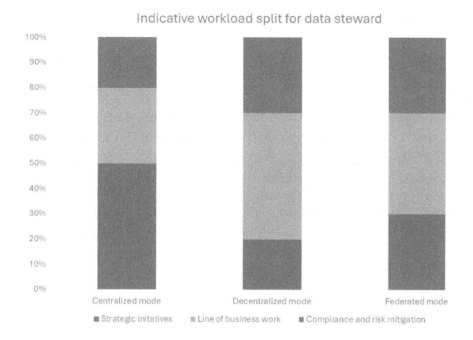

Figure 6.5 – Indicative workload split for data stewards

In *Figure 6.5*, we can see the allocation of responsibilities and workload can vary significantly depending on the chosen model of governance. Whether an organization opts for a centralized, decentralized, or federated approach, each comes with its own set of expectations and demands on a data steward's time and expertise. We will look at how the centralized model emphasizes strategic oversight and enterprise-wide consistency, how decentralization allows stewards to focus on the nuances of their specific BUs, and how a federated approach requires a careful balance of both strategic and operational responsibilities:

- **Centralized data stewardship**: In centralized models (*Figure 6.5*), data stewards often engage more in setting and enforcing frameworks and KPIs across the whole enterprise, hence the higher emphasis on strategic initiatives. Stewards dedicate a moderate amount of their day to operational tasks, ensuring that central policies are implemented consistently across the organization. Data stewards also focus on compliance at the enterprise level, ensuring uniform adherence to regulations and identifying organization-wide risks.

- **Decentralized data stewardship**: Decentralized stewards (*Figure 6.5*) are typically immersed in the specifics of their own BU, focusing on operational tasks and compliance within their domain while contributing to strategic initiatives as they align with their BU. They also concentrate on compliance within their BU, navigating the specific legal and regulatory landscape relevant to their domain.

- **Federated data stewardship**: Federated data stewards (*Figure 6.5*) need to strike a balance between operational management, strategic planning, and compliance duties, ensuring that enterprise-wide policies are adopted and adhered to within individual BUs.

In all modes, data stewards must be adept at balancing these workloads, often switching between strategic thinking and hands-on data management throughout their day. The aforementioned ratios are just indicative and can vary depending on the organization's specific needs, the projects at hand, and the maturity level of the data governance initiatives. Data stewards must remain flexible to shift focus between these areas as required by the dynamic nature of data governance.

Having explored the dynamics of centralized, decentralized, and federated data stewardship, it is crucial to understand that efficient data governance is not a one-man show. Rather, it is a collaborative effort that requires active engagement from multiple stakeholders. This notion leads us to our next topic: *Data is a team sport*.

Data is a team sport

In the era of data-driven decision-making, data governance is no longer a solitary venture but a team sport. It involves the collaboration of various departments within an organization, each contributing their unique perspectives, insights, and expertise to the process. The establishment of a diverse, cross-functional team forms the bedrock of a robust data governance body, ensuring that the data governance program remains aligned with the organization's wider strategic goals.

To get your teams in sync with data governance, here are some key points to consider:

- **Holistic view**: A cross-functional team provides a comprehensive understanding of the organization's data needs and challenges. For instance, a marketing representative can shed light on customer data needs, while a finance representative can underscore the data requirements for financial reporting. This diversity ensures a well-rounded and inclusive data governance strategy.

- **Break down data silos**: Cross-functional collaboration helps dismantle data silos, fostering a culture of data sharing across the organization. For example, data exchange between sales and customer service can offer a more exhaustive view of customer behavior, enhancing service delivery.

- **Foster buy-in**: A cross-functional team can help build consensus and support data governance initiatives across the organization. Department representatives, being part of the data governance strategy formation, are more likely to advocate for it within their respective teams.

- **Ensure alignment**: By involving representatives from different departments, cross-functional teams ensure that the data governance strategy aligns with the broader organizational strategy. This alignment is crucial for the successful implementation and sustainability of the data governance program.

However, building and managing a cross-functional team can be challenging. Differences in departmental priorities, jargon, and working styles may lead to misunderstandings or conflicts. For instance, the IT department's emphasis on data security might conflict with marketing's need for easy data access.

Here is how you can address these challenges:

- **Align a common data dictionary**: Cultivate an environment where team members can freely express their ideas and concerns and ask questions. Encourage everyone to use clear, jargon-free language to ensure mutual understanding.

- **Mitigate data privacy and security concerns**: Sharing data across teams can raise concerns about data privacy and security. These can be mitigated by implementing robust data security policies and ensuring compliance with privacy regulations.

- **Promote collaborative decision-making**: Encourage team members to make decisions collaboratively, considering the needs and concerns of all departments. This approach can help balance competing priorities and foster a sense of ownership among team members.

- **Overcome technological barriers**: Teams may use different systems or platforms, making data sharing difficult. Implementing a unified data platform or ensuring interoperability between different systems can help overcome this obstacle.

- **Provide ongoing training**: Offer regular training to help team members understand data governance principles and practices better. This can also help bridge any knowledge gaps among team members from non-technical backgrounds.

Despite the challenges, such a team can provide a comprehensive, organization-wide perspective on data governance, fostering collaboration and ensuring broad-based support for data governance initiatives.

After understanding the collaborative nature of data governance and the importance of cross-divisional cooperation, as well as the challenges associated with managing a cross-functional team, it is also crucial to establish a strategic data governance roadmap.

Creating a data governance roadmap

Constructing a data governance roadmap is pivotal in establishing a data governance structure. This roadmap outlines the program's objectives, implementation timeline, required resources, and progress monitoring plan. Here are some vital considerations when crafting a data governance roadmap:

1. **Define objectives**: Begin by delineating clear goals for the data governance program. Aligning these with the organization's overall strategy ensures a focus on achieving quantifiable results. For instance, an objective might be to enhance data quality by 20% in the first year.

2. **Identify stakeholders**: Recognize those within the organization who have an interest in the data governance program. This could range from executives and IT staff to business users. For example, the marketing team might be stakeholders, as improved data quality can enhance their targeting efforts.

3. **Form a data governance team**: This team oversees the data governance program and should comprise representatives from all stakeholder groups. Ideally, a data governance leader or CDO should spearhead this team. You should also decide which mode of data stewardship (centralized, decentralized, federated) you would like to operate for your organization and build your team accordingly.

4. **Develop policies and procedures**: Design robust policies and procedures to ensure consistent implementation of the data governance program. This involves developing data standards, setting up data security protocols, and defining roles. For instance, a policy could dictate that all customer data must be anonymized to maintain privacy.

5. **Craft a data governance roadmap**: With objectives, stakeholders, policies, and procedures in place, construct a data governance roadmap with measurable outcomes. This should detail the timeline and resources needed to achieve the data governance objectives.

6. **Monitor progress**: Regularly track and evaluate the data governance program to ensure its objectives are met. This involves tracking KPIs and assessing the program's effectiveness, such as monitoring the reduction in data errors after implementing new data quality measures. You should also review regularly the mode of data stewardship to see if any change is needed to cope with ever-changing business and regulatory requirements.

By utilizing the skills introduced in previous chapters, you can define short-term and long-term roadmaps for the organization as per the *Fulfilling the business and data strategy – where do you want to go?* section of *Chapter 4*. You can deploy some task prioritization techniques from the *Building a prioritization matrix* section of *Chapter 3* to identify which items are quick wins and which are strategic major projects.

Creating short-term and long-term roadmaps

Creating short- and long-term roadmaps for cross-team data collaboration involves setting both immediate and future goals based on the challenges identified.

Here are some ways to fulfill quick wins in a short-term roadmap:

- **Establish a common data language**: Start by creating a data dictionary that standardizes data terminologies across all teams. This will immediately help improve communication and eliminate misunderstandings. For instance, in a retail enterprise, ensure that all teams have the same understanding of terms such as **customer lifetime value (CLV)** or **average transaction value (ATV)**.

- **Define clear roles and responsibilities**: Develop a clear framework that spells out who is responsible for what in the data governance process. This could mean assigning a data steward to each team who will be responsible for maintaining and ensuring the quality of the team's data.

To enable sustainable success via a long-term roadmap, here are some guidelines:

- **Foster a culture of data sharing**: Plan regular training and awareness sessions over the next year to emphasize the importance and benefits of data sharing. Use real examples from your organization to show how cross-team data collaboration has led to better insights and decision-making.

- **Implement robust data security policies**: In the long term, focus on enhancing your organization's data security infrastructure. This could involve investing in advanced security software or hiring a data security officer. For example, in a healthcare enterprise, this would ensure patient data is secure and confidential while being available for cross-team collaboration.

- **Develop a unified data platform**: Over time, strive to integrate different data systems used by your teams. This will make data sharing easier and more efficient. As an example, for a multinational corporation, this might involve integrating data from different regional offices into one central system.

The key to successful data governance is understanding that it is a continuous, evolving process. Regularly revisit your roadmap, make adjustments as necessary, and continuously strive for improvement.

Risk management and mitigation

Risk management and mitigation are essential elements in a data governance roadmap. They involve pinpointing potential risks in the implementation of the roadmap, evaluating their potential impact, and devising strategies to preclude or lessen their effects. This practice is crucial to dodge substantial obstacles that could impede the roadmap's deployment, leading to delays, increased costs, or even the failure of the data governance initiative. Recognizing that the implementation of data governance can bring about significant changes in people, processes, technology, and culture, each of these areas could potentially pose risks, making effective risk management vital.

Table 6.2 lists some potential risks that might arise during the implementation of a data governance roadmap:

Type of Risk	Severity	Description	Management and Mitigation
Resistance to change	High	Employees may resist new processes or tools, particularly if they perceive them as adding to their workload or complicating their tasks.	The organization could implement a comprehensive **change management** (**CM**) plan. This plan might include regular communication about the benefits of the new processes, training to equip employees with the necessary skills, and support mechanisms to address concerns or difficulties during the transition.
Lack of skills or resources	Low	The organization may lack the necessary skills or resources to implement the roadmap effectively. This could lead to delays or suboptimal outcomes.	Develop strategies to prevent or minimize the impact of identified risks. This could involve providing or allocating additional resources for training, or conducting thorough system testing to prevent technical issues.
Technical issues	Med	Problems with the new data management systems, such as bugs or integration issues, could disrupt the implementation.	Recognize potential risks early in the planning stage. For example, if the roadmap includes a new data management system, there could be risks related to system compatibility, data migration, or employee training.
Regulatory compliance	High	The new processes or systems might fail to comply with relevant data regulations, exposing the organization to legal and reputational risks.	Evaluate the potential impact and likelihood of each risk. For instance, the risk of regulatory non-compliance might have a high impact due to potential fines and reputational damage but a low likelihood if the organization has robust compliance processes in place.

Table 6.2 – Potential risks for the data governance program

Having delved into the aspects of risk management and mitigation within a data governance roadmap, our next checkpoint is defining these KPIs and reporting your success to the stakeholders.

Defining KPIs

It is now time to focus on how we measure the effectiveness of our data governance efforts. This is where KPIs come into play. They provide measurable evidence of how well the governance program is achieving its stated objectives.

In *Table 6.3*, we see typical types of KPIs for data governance programs. Again, please make sure you understand the business strategy and objective first. Then, you drive the data strategy to support the business strategy. To make sure the cost of data stewardship is justified, you need to define, measure, and report your KPIs regularly:

Types of KPIs	Examples
Strategy and outcome alignment	**Strategy alignment**: % of coverage by data stewardship for the business strategy
	Roadmap progress: The progress made in implementing the data governance roadmap, including the completion of planned milestones and activities
	Policy development and approval: The time taken to develop and gain approval for data governance policies, ensuring timely establishment of governance frameworks
End-to-end data operations	**Data compliance adherence**: The level of adherence to data governance and compliance regulations throughout the data life cycle
	Data quality improvement rate: The improvement in data quality metrics, such as accuracy, completeness, consistency, and timeliness
	Data issue resolution time: The time taken to identify and resolve data-related issues or inconsistencies and SLA metrics
	Data security compliance: Measures the organization's compliance with data security standards and regulations
	Subject area compliance and monitoring: For almost all subject areas, KPIs can be used to develop a scorecard
	Technology adoption rate: The rate of adoption and utilization of data governance technologies within the organization
Data upskilling	**Awareness**: The level of awareness and understanding of data governance principles and practices among employees and stakeholders
	Training completion rate: The percentage of employees who have completed data governance training programs
	Employee engagement: The level of employee engagement and participation in data governance activities and initiatives

Table 6.3 – Different types of KPIs with examples

The KPIs should be measurable and tailored to the specific needs of the organization.

For example, if the goal of the program is to improve data quality, then the KPIs should focus on measuring the accuracy and completeness of the data. Other KPIs could include the number of data errors found, the number of data requests completed, or the amount of time it takes to process a data request.

It is also important to track the performance of the data stewardship team, such as the number of data stewards trained, the number of data stewards certified, or the number of data stewardship projects completed. By tracking these KPIs, organizations can measure and keep track of the success of their data stewardship program and identify areas for improvement.

Measuring and reporting on KPIs

By measuring and reporting on KPIs, organizations can assess the success of their data governance initiatives. This practice encompasses methodical documentation of the performance of various governance activities against set KPIs and presenting this data to stakeholders in an understandable manner to strive for continuous improvement. For instance, persistent low data quality scores could suggest a necessity for improved data cleaning procedures.

Moreover, well-structured reports provide stakeholders with a clear overview of data governance performance, aiding informed decision-making. For example, a report demonstrating high compliance with data protection regulations can reassure stakeholders of the organization's dedication to data privacy.

Tracking KPIs involves routinely collecting data on various metrics defined under your data governance initiative. For example, if *Data completeness* is a KPI, you might monitor the percentage of fully completed records in your database.

Reporting KPIs entails presenting this information in an easily understandable format. Reports should be succinct, clear, and audience-specific. For instance, senior management might prefer an overarching dashboard displaying overall performance, while data stewards might require detailed reports on specific data quality metrics. You can also refer to the *Empowering people* section of *Chapter 5* for an effective data stewardship program and more example KPIs for data stewards.

The rise of data visualization tools is a significant market trend in KPI reporting. These tools make it easier to present complex data in an intuitive, visual format, enhancing stakeholders' understanding. For instance, data quality metrics can be displayed as a heatmap where colors represent different levels of data quality across various datasets.

Take a look at this Microsoft online document `https://learn.microsoft.com/en-us/purview/concept-insights`, that provides a bird's-eye view of the current status of all data assets in a unified data governance portal. With a graphical presentation, all users are aligned on high-risk items. Regarding data visualization tools, you can also consider *Power BI*, *Tableau*, and *QlikView*.

There is an increasing use of real-time reporting these days. Thanks to advances in data processing technology, organizations can now track and report KPIs in real time, enabling quicker responses to emerging issues. For example, a sudden spike in data errors can be detected and addressed promptly to minimize its impact. Other than Microsoft Purview, Informatica, Collibra, Alation, and Talend are common tools that can help you measure and report KPIs for data governance.

Let's say your organization has set *Data accuracy* as a KPI for your data governance initiative. To track this, you might use data validation tools to detect and count errors in your database. You could then report this as a percentage of the total records checked.

Over time, if you notice that the data accuracy rate is falling, you could dig deeper to identify the source of the errors. Perhaps a new data entry tool is causing problems, or a recent organizational change has led to confusion about data entry protocols. Based on your findings, you can then take action to improve data accuracy, such as providing additional training or fixing the data entry tool.

Thus, measuring and reporting on KPIs is a crucial aspect of data governance. It provides insights into the effectiveness of the data governance program, supports decision-making, and enables continuous improvement. By leveraging modern tools and techniques, organizations can make this process even more efficient and impactful. Now, let's explore how to use KPI feedback to drive continuous improvement.

Using KPIs for continuous improvement

Leveraging KPIs for continuous improvement is a crucial aspect of data governance. It entails scrutinizing KPI data to pinpoint strengths and weaknesses in the governance framework and making necessary adjustments for enhanced performance. The data governance framework must continually adapt to meet the organization's evolving needs. KPIs provide essential feedback on the framework's effectiveness, thus serving as a critical tool for improvement. By using KPIs, the data governance framework stays relevant, leading to improved data quality, greater compliance, and more effective decision-making. For example, a KPI indicating high data errors in a department can instigate corrective actions.

The process of using KPIs for continuous improvement typically involves several steps:

1. **Analyze KPI data**: Look for trends, patterns, and anomalies in the KPI data that might indicate issues or opportunities. For instance, an insurance company might notice from its KPI data that there are consistently more errors in data entry during peak claim seasons. This could indicate an issue with the speed of data entry impacting accuracy.

2. **Identify improvement opportunities**: Based on the KPI analysis, identify areas where the data governance framework could be enhanced. This could involve refining existing processes, introducing new tools, or providing additional training. Based on the preceding example, the insurance company could identify a need for improved data validation processes during peak seasons, or a need to provide more support to data entry staff during these times.

3. **Implement changes**: Make the necessary adjustments to the data governance framework. This should be done in a controlled manner, with changes clearly communicated to all relevant stakeholders. For example, the insurance company could then introduce data validation tools to automatically check data entries for errors or inconsistencies. They could also provide additional training to data entry staff to enhance their skills and speed, and maybe even bring in temporary staff during peak seasons to manage the workload.

4. **Monitor impact**: After implementing changes, monitor the relevant KPIs to assess the impact. If the desired improvement isn't achieved, further adjustments might be needed. For example, the insurance company might observe whether there is a decrease in data errors during the next peak claim season. If the error rate remains high, additional strategies might be needed, such as further training or a review of the data entry process.

One significant accelerator is the growing use of advanced analytics and **artificial intelligence (AI)** tools for KPI analysis. These tools can process large volumes of KPI data and identify complex patterns that might be missed by manual analysis. For example, AI could detect subtle correlations between different KPIs, providing deeper insights into the performance of the data governance framework. You may refer to *Chapters 5* and *9* for more details on how we use AI for data governance.

Let's illustrate the process of using KPIs for continuous improvement with an integrated example. Suppose *Time to resolve data issues* is a KPI in your data governance program. Over a period, you observe a gradual increase in this metric, indicating a prolonged duration to rectify data issues.

Upon further analysis, you discern that this increase aligns with the rollout of a new data management system. This leads you to infer that the staff might be facing challenges adapting to the new system.

To address this, you plan and execute additional training sessions to better acquaint the staff with the new system. Post-implementation, you keep a close watch on the KPI and notice a significant reduction in the time taken to resolve data issues.

In essence, the practice of employing KPIs for ongoing enhancement is a critical aspect of data governance. It ensures the data governance framework evolves with the organization's changing needs, resulting in superior data management and well-informed decision-making.

Reviewing the fitness of your data stewardship mode

Assessing the fitness for a data stewardship mode within an organization involves a continuous evaluation process that is both introspective and forward-looking. To determine whether your organization should maintain or change its current mode of data stewardship, consider the following steps:

- **Review business objectives and data strategy**: Regularly assess whether the current stewardship mode aligns with evolving business objectives and the data strategy. If the business strategy has shifted significantly, it may necessitate a reassessment of the stewardship approach.

- **Measure effectiveness against KPIs**: Establish clear KPIs related to data quality, compliance, and business outcomes. If the current mode is underperforming against these KPIs, it may be time to consider an alternative approach.

- **Solicit feedback from data users**: Continually gather feedback from those who interact with the data most—data users, data stewards, and business leaders. If there are persistent challenges or dissatisfaction with the current mode, explore other options.

- **Monitor organizational changes**: Stay attuned to changes in organizational structure, such as mergers, acquisitions, or reorganizations. Such changes may necessitate a different stewardship model to better integrate data management practices.

- **Evaluate changes in a regulatory environment**: Keep abreast of changes in the regulatory environment. New data protection laws or industry standards may require a more centralized approach to ensure compliance.

- **Analyze data management maturity**: As your data management practices mature, the organization might be ready to transition from a centralized to a federated model, allowing greater autonomy while retaining oversight.

- **Assess scalability and flexibility**: If the organization is rapidly growing or diversifying, evaluate whether the current stewardship mode can scale effectively. A federated model might offer the needed flexibility and scalability.

- **Examine technological advancements**: New technologies can impact how data is managed. If emerging tools or platforms can better support a different stewardship mode, it may be worth transitioning.

- **Consider costs and efficiencies**: Evaluate the cost-effectiveness and operational efficiencies of the current stewardship mode. If it's overly resource-intensive or creates bottlenecks, a different approach may be more efficient.

- **Engage in scenario planning**: Perform scenario planning for potential changes in the data ecosystem. This can help anticipate when a different stewardship mode may be required.

Choosing the best fit for a data stewardship mode is not a one-time decision but an ongoing process that should be revisited regularly. It requires a balance between current capabilities and future aspirations, ensuring that the organization remains agile and responsive to changes in its data environment and business landscape.

Summary

This chapter has provided an overview of the steps needed to establish a data governance organization. It has discussed the importance of establishing data governance bodies, such as a data governance team, and how to foster a data culture within the organization. It has also explained the importance of defining KPIs to measure the success of the data governance program. Finally, we have practical advice on how to create a data governance roadmap and set up a data governance team.

In the next chapter, we will shine a spotlight on the roles and responsibilities of data stewards, including best practices for managing data quality and classification.

7

Data Steward Roles and Responsibilities

This chapter will provide you with an overview of the roles and responsibilities of a data steward. We will discuss the importance of establishing data quality and lineage principles and practices, setting up data access control and security, and monitoring and ensuring compliance with regulations. This information will help you understand the roles and responsibilities of a data steward and the importance of data governance to your organization. We will also provide you with the knowledge and skills you need to become a successful data steward.

We'll reinforce the foundation of data governance by exploring the following topics:

- Understanding high-level roles and responsibilities
- Establishing data quality and lineage principles and practices
- Setting up data classification, access control, and security
- Monitoring and ensuring data privacy and compliance

Understanding high-level roles and responsibilities

Imagine stepping into the shoes of Alex, a seasoned data steward, to get a glimpse of the daily whirlwind of activities that define the role. Alex's day begins with a steaming cup of coffee and a review of the latest data quality reports. These reports, which are generated overnight, highlight any anomalies or discrepancies in the organization's critical data elements. With an eye for detail, Alex analyzes the metrics, identifies a few potential issues, and reaches out to the relevant **subject matter experts** (**SMEs**) for their insights. Together, they determine whether these discrepancies are true errors needing correction or acceptable variances due to recent business events.

As the morning progresses, Alex turns their attention to a new project requiring the establishment of data lineage for a critical financial reporting process. Collaborating with IT specialists and report analysts, Alex meticulously documents the flow of data from its initial entry points in the organization to its final use in executive-level reports. This exercise not only ensures compliance with regulations such as SOX but also aids in understanding the impact of proposed changes to data structures down the line.

After a brief lunch break, Alex conducts a data classification review for a set of newly introduced data elements. Working closely with the information security team, they assess the sensitivity of this data and define appropriate access controls, ensuring that only authorized personnel can view or modify it. This careful categorization is crucial for maintaining data security and upholding the organization's data privacy standards.

In the afternoon, Alex leads a training session for a group of new employees, educating them about the organization's data governance policies and the importance of adhering to established data access protocols. Following the training, Alex meets with the data governance committee to discuss the progress of ongoing initiatives, leveraging the insights provided by report analysts to advocate for necessary adjustments to data policies.

The day concludes with Alex reviewing the data compliance dashboard, which monitors the organization's adherence to various data privacy regulations. A new regulatory update requires adjustments to data processing activities, prompting Alex to plan a meeting with the legal team for the following day to discuss the implications and necessary actions.

That is a day in the life of a data steward.

Through diligent oversight, proactive problem-solving, and cross-functional collaboration, Alex plays a pivotal role in maintaining the integrity, security, and value of the organization's data. It is a role that is both demanding and rewarding, as each day brings new challenges and opportunities to enhance data governance and empower data-driven decision-making.

Now, we will focus on different activities data stewards undertake to accomplish their objectives.

Day-to-day activities for data stewards

In the ever-evolving digital landscape, the role of data stewardship has become increasingly pivotal in managing and safeguarding an organization's data assets. As businesses strive to unlock the inherent value of data, understanding the roles and responsibilities of a data steward is critical. A data steward serves as a guardian of data, ensuring its quality, security, compliance, and usability.

A data steward is also a role within an organization that's responsible for the fitness and freshness of data, both the business content and metadata. While data governance sets the policies around data, data stewardship is about the execution and alignment with those policies. In the realm of data management, data stewards serve as the conduits between data governance policy-making bodies (such as the data steering committee) and the data management activity that implements data policies.

Data stewards take direction from the data steering committee and are responsible for reconciling conflicting definitions, defining value domains, and reporting on quality metrics. From an organizational perspective, data stewards generally sit on the business side but they should have the ability to speak the language of IT to ensure smooth and effective communication among the team.

You may also refer to *Figure 4.7* in *Chapter 4* for the engagement model among the data governance team, business units, and IT team.

Data stewards can be organized in several ways: by business unit or top-level data domain, such as by product, function, system, or project. You can refer to *Figures 6.2, 6.3,* and *6.4* in *Chapter 6* for different types of data stewardship. The key to success in any data stewardship organization is granting authority to the stewards to oversee data and bring in a sense of belonging from business stakeholders.

More examples of the day-to-day duties of data stewards are as follows. We will also discuss them in detail in upcoming sections:

- **Establishing data quality and lineage principles and practices**: A data steward is responsible for ensuring that data is accurate, complete, and up to date. This includes developing data quality metrics, establishing data lineage, and monitoring data quality.

- **Maintaining inventory of critical data elements (CDEs)**: A data steward performs integrity checks during onboarding and ongoing maintenance of CDEs.

- **Setting up data access control and security**: A data steward is responsible for setting up access control and security measures to protect data from unauthorized access. This includes developing policies and procedures, setting up user access controls, and monitoring access logs.

- **Monitoring and ensuring compliance with regulations**: A data steward is responsible for monitoring and ensuring compliance with applicable laws and regulations. This includes developing policies and procedures, monitoring data usage, and responding to regulatory inquiries.

- **Providing data-driven insights**: A data steward is responsible for providing data-driven insights to support decision-making. This includes supporting data analysis and visualization via dashboards to provide a bird's-eyes view to the data steering committee.

- The miscellaneous day-to-day activities of data stewards include the following:

  - Reviewing the data profiling result

  - Communicating the new or changed data requirements to end users, the data steward working group, and the data steering committee

  - Creating clear definitions of data and more

  - Defining a range of acceptable values, such as max or min value for selected numeric fields

  - Enumerating value definitions for the enumerated data type

It is common to see various roles related to data in a professional team or workgroup, among which the positions of data custodian and data steward are notable. Although these roles are related, they encompass different responsibilities and expertise. A data custodian, for instance, plays a more technical role, aligning more closely with IT operations. The main responsibility of a data custodian is to ensure that systems and applications are working properly to enforce data policies and conduct data quality checks. Comparatively, the role of a data steward is more operational, focusing on the overall management and governance of an organization's data.

SMEs, for instance, bring deep domain knowledge that is critical for defining accurate data models, establishing relevant data quality checks, and interpreting data correctly for the business's benefit. Report analysts, on the other hand, work closely with data stewards to ensure that reports are accurate, reliable, and reflect the true state of the business. Their analytical skills are indispensable in translating raw data into actionable insights.

Figure 7.1 illustrates various roles in the data team and their responsibilities:

Figure 7.1 – Various roles in the data team

Next, we'll use the RACI matrix to align the job scopes of different roles in the data governance team.

RACI matrix for data governance

A RACI matrix is a project management tool that's used to define and document the roles and responsibilities of individuals or teams involved in a project. RACI stands for **Responsible, Accountable, Consulted, and Informed**; these are the four key roles identified in the matrix. The RACI matrix helps to avoid confusion, ensures clear communication, and prevents duplication of efforts within a project. It helps stakeholders understand who is involved in each task, who has the final decision-making authority, and who needs to be kept informed about the progress:

- **Responsible (R)**: This role is responsible for completing the task or activity
- **Accountable (A)**: This role is ultimately accountable for the completion of the task and for making decisions

- **Consulted (C)**: This role provides input and expertise during the task but does not have any final decision-making authority

- **Informed (I)**: This role needs to be kept informed about the progress and outcomes of the task but is not directly involved in its completion

In the context of data governance, the RACI matrix can be used to clearly define roles and responsibilities, ensuring that everyone knows their specific duties and who they should report to or consult with. For instance, data stewards could be responsible for maintaining data quality, the data owner is held accountable for the signoff of data quality, and so on. This clear delineation of tasks and responsibilities can greatly enhance the effectiveness and efficiency of a data governance program.

Table 7.1 shows a sample RACI matrix for the data governance program:

Activity	Process	CDO	DSC	DA	DO	DS	DC	IS
Data strategy	Define data vision and roadmap	A	R	C	C	C		
	Define the current and target state of data architecture	A	C	R		C		
Data policy	Define data life cycle management policy	A	R		C	I	I	
	Define an information security policy	C	C	I	I	I	I	R, A
Metadata management	Maintain business data glossary	A	R	C	R	R	I	
	Maintain data catalog and data lineage	A	R	R	C	C		
Data quality	Define data quality rules and metrics	A	R		R	C,I	I	
	Remediation and monitor	C	C	C	A	R	R	
Data operation	Operationalize **standard operating procedure (SOP)**				A	R	R	R
	Monitor and report to the management committee				A	R	R	R

Table 7.1 – RACI matrix for the data team

Here are the abbreviations for the roles in the data governance team shown in *Table 7.1*:

- **CDO**: Chief data officer
- **DSC**: Data steering committee
- **DA**: Data architect
- **DO**: Data owner
- **DS**: Data steward
- **DC**: Data custodian
- **IS**: Information security specialist

Having delved into the roles and responsibilities within a data governance team using the RACI matrix, let's turn our attention to the foundational elements of data stewardship – data quality and data lineage.

Establishing data quality and lineage principles and practices

Establishing data quality and lineage principles and practices is an important role of a data steward. This involves developing data quality metrics to measure the accuracy, completeness, and timeliness of data, as well as establishing data lineage to track the flow of data from its source to its destination. The data steward must also monitor data quality to ensure that it meets the established standards.

Data quality

Data quality is the prerequisite of data-driven decision-making. It is both the quick win and long-term strategic goal you should attain. In this section, we will talk about the basic elements of data quality, the operation of data quality programs, and the reporting mechanism.

The common elements of data quality are as follows:

- **Accuracy**: Information reflecting what it is designed to measure. A retail company could experience issues with data accuracy when its inventory management system fails to correctly record the quantity or type of products sold. This could lead to discrepancies between the actual and reported stock levels, impacting the company's ability to fulfill customer orders and maintain customer satisfaction.
- **Timeliness**: The release of current and updated data within specific time constraints. In the field of financial trading, any delay in the release of market data could have significant implications. If the data on stock prices is not updated in real time, traders could make decisions based on outdated information, resulting in financial losses.

- **Completeness**: No unexpected missing data in both row and column dimensions. A healthcare organization might face data completeness issues when patient records are not filled out or updated. This could result in doctors not having all the necessary information to make accurate diagnoses or treatment plans, potentially compromising patient care.

- **Credibility**: A trustworthy data source with a measurable data quality benchmark. A business might use data from an external source to make strategic decisions. If this source is not reliable or the data is not validated, the business could make decisions based on inaccurate or misleading information, leading to strategic missteps.

- **Consistency**: A stable mechanism that collects and stores the data without contraction. In a multinational corporation, different regional branches might use different systems or standards to collect and store data. This could lead to inconsistencies in the data, making it difficult to compare performance across regions or to aggregate data at the corporate level.

Later in this chapter, in *Figure 7.3*, you will see a sample data quality scorecard based on these five elements.

To ensure a comprehensive approach to data quality, SMEs are often engaged to validate and confirm the business relevance of data quality metrics. Their expertise ensures that the data quality efforts align with business objectives and provide true value. Likewise, report analysts play a key role in interpreting the outcomes of data quality assessments, often serving as the bridge between data stewards and end users who rely on reports and dashboards for decision-making.

The DQM cycle

DQM is an integral part of data governance that focuses on the condition and health of data. DQM processes are designed to maintain and improve the accuracy, consistency, completeness, relevance, and reliability of data.

The **data quality management cycle(DQM cycle)** suggests breaking down tasks into smaller, manageable chunks to perform quality checks and profiling. This process begins with planning and selecting the dataset, the metrics to be used, and the desired outcome. We then move on to profiling and identifying any outliers, investigating the root causes and potential solutions, presenting the findings to the business for review and approval, and, finally, implementing the necessary remediation and maintaining the process.

Figure 7.2 illustrates the flow of data quality management to ensure you have trustworthy datasets for decision-making:

Figure 7.2 – The DQM cycle

In short, data profiling is about understanding your data, data cleansing is about fixing it, and data monitoring is about maintaining it.

Let's consider the stages in the DQM cycle:

- **Data profiling**: Data profiling is the process of examining data to understand its structure, content, and quality. Through data profiling, potential data quality issues can be identified and prioritized for further analysis. To facilitate this process, data profiling tools can be employed to automatically scan and analyze data to detect issues such as outliers, missing values, duplicate records, and inconsistencies. The aim is to identify potential problems and understand the nature of the data before any cleaning or transformation takes place.

- There are tools available in the market that aid in data profiling:

  - **Informatica Data Explorer**: This tool offers comprehensive data profiling capabilities, helping organizations to understand data patterns, relationships, and anomalies.

  - **Talend Data Profiler**: This open source tool allows organizations to assess the quality of data by providing detailed statistics and insightful information on data.

  - **Azure data catalog**: This tool examines the data in your catalog and collects statistics and information about that data. This feature helps you determine the suitability of the data to solve your business problem and identify data inconsistency, duplicates, and anomalies.

- **Data inspection and cleansing**: Data cleansing is the process of making sure data is accurate and consistent. Automated tools can be used to fix errors such as typos, discrepancies, and formatting problems. In cases where automated tools cannot fix errors, manual data cleansing may be necessary. This might involve standardizing data formats, removing duplicate records, or filling in missing values. We will explain more in the *Data quality monitoring and reporting* section and *Chapter 8* regarding data incident management.

- Some tools can help in data inspection and cleansing:

  - **IBM InfoSphere QualityStage**: This tool allows for data inspection, cleansing, and monitoring. It uses a rules-based method to review and cleanse data, ensuring consistency and accuracy.

  - **Trifacta**: This tool offers data wrangling capabilities, which include data inspection and cleansing. It also provides features for data preparation, such as structuring, cleansing, enriching, validating, and publishing.

- **Data monitoring**: Data monitoring is the process of continually evaluating and assessing data after it has been cleaned to ensure its accuracy and consistency. Data monitoring can involve setting up automated rules or alerts to flag potential issues, such as sudden changes in data values, trends, or patterns that deviate from the norm. Tools such as data monitoring software can be used to detect changes in data, detect missing values, identify outliers, and detect anomalies. For instance, in a company's sales data, an unusually large order might significantly increase the average sales figure. If this outlier is not identified and treated appropriately, it could lead to inaccurate forecasting or budgeting. You may want to consider Collibra or Microsoft Purview for the data estate insight feature, which allows users to view and manage key health metrics across their hybrid data estate.

The data quality lead and data steward should review and prioritize data quality issues registered in the backlog. We should also identify if there is a one-off issue, such as a network outage causing data to not be updated. We can try to uncover fundamental issues that require long-term solutions. For instance, say the data provider frequently gives incorrect data. In this case, you may want to change to another data provider. During each stage of the data life cycle (details will be provided in *Chapter 8*), you should review what data quality check you want to put in place. To maximize the **return on investment** (**ROI**), you may want to focus on the CDE first. For the definition and key considerations about CDE, you may refer to *Chapter 5*.

Types of data quality checks

In any robust data governance strategy, meticulous data quality checks are of utmost importance. These checks are integral to ensuring the reliability, accuracy, and usability of data. There are primarily two types of data quality checks that organizations typically conduct – technical inspection and business inspection. Each serves a different purpose and focuses on different aspects of the data. Technical inspection is about confirming the data's format or type, while business inspection involves validating the data against business rules or logic. Both are critical to maintaining high-quality data that can facilitate accurate decision-making and efficient business operations. Let's delve into each one to understand their significance and how they work:

- **Technical inspection**: This refers to the process of verifying whether the data aligns with the expected or predefined format, type, or structure. This evaluation ensures that the data is in a usable and consistent format that adheres to specified technical standards. In essence, a technical inspection is an initial step in data quality management that ensures raw data is formatted correctly and is technically sound before it is integrated into further analysis, processes, or systems. You are recommended to review if tools such as his Markit EDM or Fencore can be deployed to embed the technical inspection into the data management flow. For instance, it would involve checking if a price field is numeric, or if a country code adheres to the ISO three-character format. This step ensures that raw data is in a usable format before it is integrated into downstream processes and systems.

- **Business inspection**: Business inspection in the context of data quality refers to the process of validating data against established business rules or logic. This form of inspection goes beyond merely checking the structure or format of the data. It involves confirming that the data makes sense in the context of business operations and decision-making. The primary purpose of business inspection is to ensure that the data aligns with business expectations and realities. It helps to identify any inconsistencies, inaccuracies, or anomalies that might impact business decisions or operations. This form of inspection is crucial for maintaining data integrity, enhancing operational efficiency, and supporting informed decision-making.

- Here are some examples of business inspection checks:

  - **Horizontal check**: While handling stock data, at the same given time instance, you compare the stock price from multiple data providers for the same stock. Then, you can flag it as a potential issue when it exceeds the 1% difference. For instance, on the same trade day, Bloomberg tells you Microsoft's stock close price is 370 while Refinitiv suggests it is 390. This will be flagged as a potential data issue as the difference is more than 1%.

  - **Vertical check**: For the same data provider (for example, a POS system), you compare today's sales record with yesterday's. You want to have it flagged if there is more than a 5% difference since business stakeholders define it as abnormal to have such a big delta for any two given consecutive days.

  - **Range or outlier checks**: You want to be alerted if a certain data field is below or over a certain range so that you can review and action as soon as possible.

Everyone has different expectations and definitions of data quality programs. Thus, you should work with the chief data officer and the data steering committee to align with business stakeholders on the expected outcome. Now let's turn our focus to how to monitor quality of the data.

Data quality monitoring and reporting

As part of the data quality monitoring and reporting process, report analysts are also crucial in interpreting the data quality scorecards, similar to the one depicted in *Figure 7.3*. They assist in identifying trends, pinpointing areas of concern, and communicating these findings to the data governance team for appropriate action. Their analytical prowess ensures that data quality issues are not just recorded but also understood and addressed effectively.

Figure 7.3 is a sample data quality spider web scorecard for your team and stakeholders to get aligned on the current health of your organization's data. When users complain about data quality, you should verify if it is reflected in this scorecard and whether the data quality logic is documented and implemented. As always, priority should be given to CDEs:

Figure 7.3 – Sample data quality daily scorecard

What else? You should define what exactly needs to be done after a data quality incident is flagged. Who should review the data quality issue? Do we need to notify the data owner? Should we update the **master data** (that is, the golden copy) or the raw data? We will discuss data incident management in the next chapter.

Data quality best practices

Organizations should create a data quality program that encompasses policies, procedures, and guidelines for data management. This program should include regular training and education for staff to ensure they comprehend the significance of data quality and how to maintain it. By implementing these data quality best practices, organizations can ensure the accuracy and integrity of their data:

- Conduct regular data assessment and constant monitoring.

- Establish data quality metrics and a measurable scale.

- Educate the entire organization on the basics and value of data quality and train stakeholders on their roles in maintaining it.

- Use Data quality as the OKR/KPI of the performance review of the business and IT team. **OKR**, which stands for **Objectives and Key Results**, is a goal-setting framework that helps organizations set, track, and achieve their goals. Objectives define what the organization aims to achieve, and key results are measurable ways to track the progress toward these objectives.

Data governance and data quality is a team sport! To ensure that data quality is upheld, organizations need to foster collaboration between business, IT, and data governance teams. You may refer to *Figure 4.7* for the engagement model in *Chapter 4, Developing a Comprehensive Data Management Strategy*.

Organizations should create a data quality program that encompasses policies, procedures, and guidelines for data management. You may refer to the frameworks from EDM Council (`https://edmcouncil.org`) and DAMA (`https://www.dama.org/cpages/home`). This program should include regular training and education for staff to ensure they comprehend the significance of data quality and how to maintain it. By implementing these data quality best practices, organizations can ensure the accuracy and integrity of their data.

Data lineage

Data lineage is a critical aspect of data management that helps us understand the origin, transformation, and movement of the data throughout its life cycle.

Data lineage is metadata; we need both business and technical perspectives to help the organization understand how data transforms from one state into another.

One example is the management report for senior executives. For most, if not all, of the fields on the financial and sales record report, we have end-to-end lineage to explain how we calculate the figures from the raw data. *Figure 7.4* shows how we visualize the data movement and transformation process along the data life cycle for management reporting.

The process of documenting and maintaining data lineage often requires the involvement of SMEs. They possess the necessary knowledge to identify and validate the key data elements and transformations that should be captured. Their input ensures that the data lineage diagrams, such as the one shown in *Figure 7.4*, are not only technically accurate but also meaningful from a business standpoint:

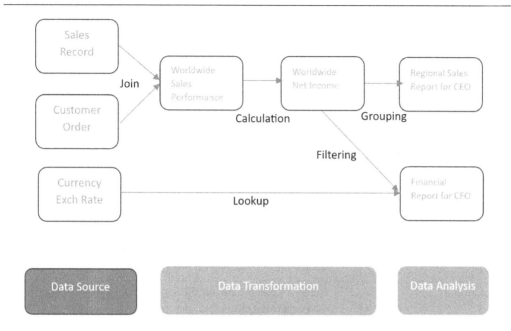

Figure 7.4 – Sample data lineage diagram for end-to-end lineage

The importance of data lineage

Data lineage provides traceability, allowing stakeholders to understand how data is transformed, aggregated, and used in different processes, as well as auditing and logs to help in compliance and regulatory requirements.

It also improves data quality by identifying potential issues or inconsistencies in the data flow, understanding the downstream effects of changes to data sources or transformations, which help us in impact analysis, and supporting data governance initiatives by identifying data ownership, and stewardship. For the technical team, it also provides a better grounding for the impact analysis when they consider updating the definition of a data field.

Challenges and recommendation

Data lineage, whether automated or manual update, and whether forward or reverse, presents some challenges, such as complex data transformations, data lineage across multiple systems, and a lack of metadata, which can lead to confusion in data definition and understanding.

So, how can you effectively document data lineage?

First of all, do not boil the ocean. If you ask the business stakeholders, they will just say they want all data lineage documented for all data fields!

Even if you can finish all with amazing software, business users may end up just taking a look at the 10 to 20% of the data fields for the lineage.

Your organization has limited resources; you should focus on the critical business process, CDE, and the critical report. These will determine what data source and data transformation you need to document the lineage.

Whether you document the data lineage manually or automatically, you should include key attributes alongside your metadata management system, as illustrated in *Table 7.2*:

Attribute	Description
Data source	The original data source or system
Data destination	The destination or target system
Source and destination schema	Describes the schema of the source and destination system (for example, tables, fields, and relationships)
Data mapping	The relationship between the source and the destination structure (for example, source columns mapped to destination fields)
Data transformation logic	Describe the specific data transformation processes applied to the source data (for example, cleaning, filtering, aggregation, joining, and so on)
Reference documentation	Reference any relevant documentation, such as design specifications, data dictionaries, or business process diagrams
Last update and review date, information of owner and reviewer	How and when the data lineage documentation is reviewed or updated

Table 7.2 – Key attributes of a data lineage record

Having explored the intricacies of data lineage, its importance, the challenges faced during its implementation, and the recommended best practices, it is clear how vital this aspect is in overall data governance. Now, let's pivot our attention to another equally critical aspect: data classification, access control, and security. These are fundamental to protecting and managing our data effectively.

Setting up data classification, access control, and security

Establishing data classification, access control, and security is the cornerstone of data stewardship. Data classification is the process of categorizing data based on its sensitivity and importance. This helps organizations determine who should have access to what data and how to protect it. **Access control** is the process of granting and denying access to data based on user roles and permissions. Security measures are used to protect data from unauthorized access, such as encryption, authentication, and data masking. A data steward is responsible for setting up and maintaining data classification, access control, and security measures to ensure data is properly protected.

Data classification

Data classification is the process of categorizing data into various types, based on factors such as its sensitivity, criticality, and regulatory requirements. It's a crucial step in data stewardship and governance for several reasons:

- **Enhanced data protection**: By understanding what types of data you possess and how sensitive they are, you can apply appropriate levels of protection. For instance, highly sensitive data, such as **personally identifiable information** (**PII**), may require encryption at rest and in transit, while less sensitive data may not.

- **Regulatory compliance**: Many regulations require businesses to handle different types of data in specific ways. By classifying data, you can ensure compliance with these regulations and avoid penalties.

- **Improved data management**: Classification helps organizations understand what data they have and where it resides, making it easier to manage, retrieve, and archive data.

- **Cost savings**: By classifying data, organizations can optimize their storage strategies. Instead of storing all data in high-cost, high-performance storage, they can store less critical or infrequently accessed data in cheaper, lower-performance storage.

- **Risk management**: Data classification helps in identifying potential risks and taking appropriate measures to mitigate them. It aids in understanding the potential impact of data loss, which means it can guide disaster recovery and business continuity planning.

You may consult your information security team for the existing classification scheme of your organization. *Table 7.3* shows a typical example for enterprises:

Classification	Description	Example
Public	Information that may be broadly distributed without causing damage to the organization, its employees, and stakeholders. The information may be disclosed or passed to people outside the organization.	Marketing materials authorized for public release, such as advertisements, brochures, and internet web pages
Internal	Information whose unauthorized disclosure, particularly outside the organization, would be inappropriate and inconvenient. Disclosure to anyone outside of the organization or contractual parties covered by NDAs requires management authorization.	Most corporate information falls into this category Internal training materials, policy and operating procedures, and marketing information (before authorized release)
Confidential	Sensitive or valuable information. This must not be disclosed outside of the organization without the explicit permission of a director-level senior manager with full audit details and risk acceptance sign-off.	Information about the company's confidential projects, passwords, credit and debit card numbers, account data, and PII (for example, employee HR record and social security number)

Table 7.3 – Data classification scheme

Data access control

Data access control is a method of ensuring that only authorized individuals have access to certain data. This is achieved by implementing systems that can identify, authenticate, and authorize individuals or groups who have rights to specific datasets.

In the context of data stewardship and governance, access control plays a significant role for several reasons:

- **Protection of sensitive information**: With access control, sensitive data such as personal information, intellectual property, or financial records can be protected from unauthorized access, thereby reducing the risk of data breaches.

- **Regulatory compliance**: Many regulations, including GDPR and HIPAA, mandate specific access control measures to protect personal data. Implementing robust access control helps organizations comply with these regulations and avoid potential legal penalties.

- **Principle of least privilege**: This principle states that a user should have the least amount of privileges necessary to perform their job function. Access control systems enforce this principle, reducing the risk of accidental or deliberate misuse of data.

- **Auditability**: Access control systems typically keep logs of who accessed what data and when. These logs can be crucial for audits, investigations, and demonstrating regulatory compliance.

- **Data integrity:** By limiting who can access and modify data, access control systems help maintain the accuracy and consistency of data over its life cycle.

- **Enhanced productivity:** By ensuring employees have access to the data they need when they need it, access control systems can enhance productivity and efficiency.

A key concept in data access control and data security is **role-based access control** (**RBAC**).

RBAC is an access control model that grants access to system resources based on the roles of individual users within an organization, as shown in *Figure 7.5*:

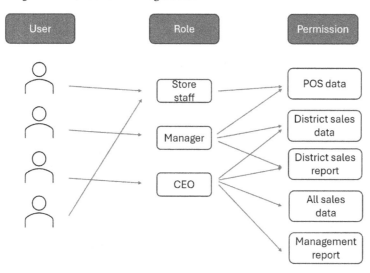

Figure 7.5 – RBAC example

RBAC is a method of restricting access to computer systems, networks, or applications based on the roles of individual users within an organization. This type of access control system is designed to limit user access to only those resources that are necessary for them to perform their job duties. RBAC can be used to define user roles, assign users to roles, and control access to resources based on the roles assigned to each user. By assigning users to roles, RBAC can ensure that users only have access to the resources that are necessary for them to do their job.

In the example illustrated by *Figure 7.5*, instead of granting individual users access to datasets and reports, you should create a user group called *Manager*, then assign relevant users to this group and grant this group to access sales datasets and reports. When there is a new joiner or someone leaves the company, you just need to review the group membership instead of revoking data access from multiple systems.

You can also reference the typical access control approval flow chart shown in *Figure 7.6*:

Figure 7.6 – Data access control approval flow

Data security and protection

Data security and protection is a critical component of any organization's overall data and security strategy. Usually, you would involve the **chief information security officer** (**CISO**) to advise the security operation and roadmap. While the terms **data security** and **data protection** are often used interchangeably, they do have distinct meanings in the realm of data management.

Data protection is a broader term that includes data security. Data protection refers to the practices and legal measures that ensure data is only used for its intended purpose. It involves making sure that data is not misused or exploited and that the privacy rights of the individuals are respected.

On the other hand, data security refers to the defensive measures put into place to prevent unauthorized access to databases, computers, or saved files. It encompasses the safeguards that protect data from deliberate attacks, such as hacking, phishing, and other forms of cyber threats. It involves techniques such as encryption, which protect data across all applications and platforms.

With a **standard operating procedure** (**SOP**), your data will be protected in a consistent and compliant way. SOPs for data security are a set of step-by-step instructions compiled by an organization to help workers carry out complex routine operations. These procedures aim to achieve efficiency, quality output, and uniformity of performance while reducing miscommunication and failure to comply with industry regulations. They generally include specific practices related to data access, data sharing, data storage, and incident response.

For example, an SOP might stipulate that all employees must use a particular, approved method for sharing sensitive data with external partners. Another SOP might outline the steps to take in the event of a data breach, including who needs to be notified, what immediate actions should be taken to mitigate the breach, and how to document the incident for future review and learning.

When it comes to the technologies and tools for data security, organizations have a wide array to choose from, depending on their specific needs. Here are a few categories of tools that are commonly used:

- **Data encryption tools**: Let's zoom into the various types of encryption for your data security deployment:

  - **Encryption at rest**: Encryption at rest is the process of encrypting data when it is stored. This type of encryption is used to protect data that is stored on physical media, such as hard drives, tapes, and USB drives. Encryption at rest ensures that the data is secure even if the physical media is stolen or lost. You can have client-side and service encryption as per your use cases.

  - **Encryption in transit**: Encryption in transit is the process of encrypting data when it is transmitted over a network. This type of encryption is used to protect data that is being sent over the internet or other networks. Encryption in transit ensures that the data is secure even if the network is compromised.

  - **Encryption in use or memory**: Encryption in memory is the process of encrypting data when it is stored in memory. This type of encryption is used to protect data that is stored in RAM. Encryption in memory ensures that the data is secure, even if the system is compromised.

  - The tool can convert data into code to prevent unauthorized access. Examples include Azure Disk Encryption, file encryption tools such as AxCrypt, and end-to-end encrypted messaging services such as Signal.

- **Network security tools**: These help protect the integrity of your network and data. They include firewalls, **intrusion detection systems (IDSs)**, and **intrusion prevention systems (IPSs)**. Examples are the firewall solutions from Cisco and Fortinet.

- **Identity and access management (IAM) tools**: These tools manage who has access to what data. They include **single sign-on (SSO)** systems, **multi-factor authentication (MFA)** tools, and privilege access management systems. CyberArk provides the IAM solution that protects against cyberattacks, which use insider privileges. Azure Active Directory also offers SSO and MFA capabilities.

- **Data loss prevention (DLP) tools**: These tools monitor and control endpoint activities, filter data streams on corporate networks, and monitor data in the cloud to protect data at rest, in motion, and in use. For example, Symantec DLP can discover, monitor, and protect sensitive data.

- **Security information and event management (SIEM) tools**: These tools provide real-time analysis of security alerts generated by applications and network hardware. They are used for log management and information management related to security incidents. Azure Sentinel is a cloud-native SIEM solution with built-in AI and automation to help you detect and respond to threats quickly.

Remember that these tools alone are not enough. Regular training and awareness campaigns are crucial to ensure that all employees understand the importance of data security and know how to follow the SOPs. A secure data environment is only as strong as its weakest link, so everyone in the organization needs to be part of the solution.

Having thoroughly examined the standard operating procedures and tools essential for robust data security, we are aware that protecting data is a multi-faceted task. However, the responsibility of managing data extends beyond just security. In our interconnected digital world, data privacy and compliance have become equally significant considerations. We will cover this next.

Monitoring and ensuring data privacy and compliance

Data privacy and compliance are integral parts of data stewardship. A data steward is responsible for monitoring and ensuring compliance with applicable laws and regulations related to data privacy and security. This includes developing policies and procedures for data privacy, setting up user access controls, monitoring access logs, and responding to regulatory inquiries. This includes identifying and addressing potential risks to data privacy, as well as ensuring that data is collected, stored, and used in a secure and compliant manner.

The data steward must ensure that data is protected from unauthorized access and that data is used as per applicable laws and regulations. The data steward must also be aware of any changes in the legal landscape and be prepared to adjust their data privacy and security policies accordingly.

The first step in monitoring and ensuring data privacy and compliance is to develop and implement a data privacy and compliance policy as per the business needs and regulatory requirements. This policy should clearly outline the organization's expectations and requirements for handling data, as well as the consequences for not adhering to the policy.

An example data privacy and compliance policy for company X would contain these core elements:

- **Scope**: This policy applies to all employees, contractors, and third parties who process data on behalf of company X.
- **Principles**:
  - **Data minimization**: We will collect and process only the data that is necessary for specified, explicit, and legitimate purposes
  - **Lawful processing**: We will always process data lawfully, fairly, and in a transparent manner
  - **Data accuracy**: We will make every reasonable effort to ensure that data is accurate, complete, and kept up to date
  - **Data security**: We will apply appropriate security measures to protect data against unauthorized access, alteration, disclosure, or destruction

- **Responsibilities**: All employees are responsible for adhering to this policy. Department heads are responsible for enforcing this policy within their teams. **The data protection officer (DPO)** is responsible for overseeing the overall compliance with this policy and related regulations.

- **Incident reporting**: Any suspected data breaches must be reported to the DPO immediately.

- **Consequences of non-compliance**: Non-compliance with this policy may result in disciplinary action, up to and including termination of employment.

- **Policy review**: This policy will be reviewed annually or as required by changes in laws and regulations.

Once the policy is in place, organizations should monitor data usage to ensure that it complies with the policy. This can be done through regular audits, reviews, and assessments of data usage. For example, you can introduce the annual certification exercise to all the data assets to have a full body check on your organization's data. You should also consider implementing tools and technologies to help monitor data usage and detect any potential violations of the policy with an operation dashboard.

Organizations should also have a process in place for responding to any violations of the policy. This is known as data incident management, which includes notifying the appropriate parties, conducting an investigation, and taking corrective action. We will talk about the data incident management in the next chapter.

Finally, organizations should regularly review and update their data privacy and compliance policy to ensure that it is up to date with any changes in laws and regulations, as well as any changes in the organization's data usage.

Here are some of the suggestions to safeguard the continuous health of your organization's data assets:

- **Annual certification**: Annual data certification is a process that's used to ensure that data within an organization is accurate, complete, and up to date. It is an important part of data governance and stewardship and helps to ensure that data is reliable and trustworthy to support your decision-making. The process typically involves reviewing data sources, data elements, and data relationships to ensure that the data is accurate and up to date. The process also involves identifying any discrepancies or errors and the resolution of those issues. Once the data has been certified, it can be used with confidence by the organization.

- **Security penetration test**: A **security penetration test**, also known as a **pen test**, is a simulated attack on a computer system, network, or web application to identify security vulnerabilities that an attacker could exploit. It is a method of evaluating the security of a system or network by simulating an attack from malicious outsiders, or malicious insiders. The purpose of a penetration test is to identify and exploit vulnerabilities in a system, application, or network to assess the security posture of the target. The test typically includes gathering information about the target, identifying possible entry points, attempting to break in, and reporting back the findings. Your organization should schedule a regular pen test to have a third-party expert view on the overall security health.

- **Learn the latest data privacy landscape in the industry:**

  - **General Data Protection Regulation (GDPR):** The GDPR is a regulation in EU law on data protection and privacy for all individuals within the **European Union (EU)** and the **European Economic Area (EEA).** It also addresses the transfer of personal data outside the EU and EEA areas. The GDPR's primary aim is to enhance individuals' control and rights over their data and to simplify the regulatory environment for international business.

  - **Hong Kong Personal Data (Privacy) Ordinance (PDPO):** The PDPO is a comprehensive data protection law in Hong Kong that was passed in 1995 and took effect in December 1996. In 2021, the PDPO underwent major amendments. These amendments aim to combat doxing acts that are intrusive to personal data privacy, through the criminalization of doxing acts, and conferring on the privacy commissioner for personal data statutory powers to issue cessation notices demanding the cessation or restriction of disclosure of doxing content.

  - **Health Insurance Portability and Accountability Act (HIPAA):** The HIPAA is a federal law in the United States that sets national standards for the protection of certain health information. It applies to health plans, healthcare clearinghouses, and healthcare providers that conduct certain healthcare transactions electronically. The HIPAA requires organizations to protect the privacy and security of individuals' health information and to provide individuals with certain rights regarding their health information.

As we highlighted earlier, data is a team sport. When establishing data classification, access control, and security protocols, collaboration with SMEs ensures that the sensitivity and importance of data are assessed accurately. Similarly, report analysts can provide insights into which reports contain sensitive data, necessitating stringent access controls. Their collaboration with data stewards is essential to the protection and correct usage of the organization's data assets. You should also work with the CISO to make sure your data operation adheres to the firm-wide security standard.

Summary

Overall, this chapter provided a comprehensive overview of the roles and responsibilities of data stewards, as well as related topics such as data quality management, data lineage, data classification, access control, data security, and data privacy and compliance.

Data stewards bridge the gap between data governance policy-making bodies and the implementation of data policies. Some of their key responsibilities include reconciling conflicting definitions, defining value domains, reporting on quality metrics, establishing data access control and security, monitoring and ensuring compliance with regulations, providing data-driven insights, and more.

In the next chapter, we will dive deeper into the stages in the data life cycle, the importance of data incident management, and the framework of data ownership. Join us as we continue to unlock the value of data in enterprise environments.

Effective Data Stewardship

This chapter will provide you with an overview of effective data stewardship. It will cover the principles of data stewardship, such as defining core principles, designing the data domain, and establishing data ownership. It will also discuss how to handle data incidents and what good data stewardship looks like, such as transparent communication accountability and continuous upskill training. By the end of this chapter, you will have more understanding to become a proficient data steward.

Let's deep dive into these topics for effective data stewardship:

- Establishing data stewardship principles and standardizing data **incident management**

- Defining and implementing data ownership

- Defining a target state –What does good data stewardship look like?

Establishing data stewardship principles and standardizing data incident management

Data stewardship principles serve as the foundation for the effective management, control, and protection of an organization's critical data assets. These principles provide a direction that guides the development of policies, procedures, and practices to ensure data is used and maintained in a manner that aligns with the organization's objectives. Importantly, the data steward plays a pivotal role in this setting. As custodians of data, they are responsible for its quality, integrity, and security. They foster collaboration among data producers and consumers, ensuring everyone adheres to these principles. Thus, establishing robust data stewardship principles is not just a nice-to-have but a critical component in the successful realization of a company's data-driven agenda. The importance of these principles and the role of data stewards become even more significant as we move toward a digital future where data is the new oil.

Let's look into real-life examples in the area of the data life cycle, principles and policies, and data **incident management (IM)**.

The data life cycle

Data can be in text, number, graphic, sound, or video format. Data assets include all structured and unstructured data. The data life cycle refers to the series of stages that a data asset goes through, from its initial creation or capture, through processing, storage, utilization, and eventually to its disposal. The importance of this alignment cannot be overstated. Each stage of the data life cycle plays a crucial role in harnessing the full potential of the data. If one stage is misaligned, it could compromise the integrity and value of the data. Therefore, it is vital for data stewards to ensure that all stages of the data life cycle are in sync, from the moment data enters an organization to its eventual disposal.

Business units (**BUs**) and data owners shoulder the responsibility to delineate the requirements of origins, transformation, standardization, and destinations for the diverse types of data used. The data governance team is responsible for defining and operationalizing the data governance framework, plus promoting the data culture. The IT team is responsible for maintaining the infrastructure.

Typical stages of the data life cycle are illustrated in *Figure 8.1*:

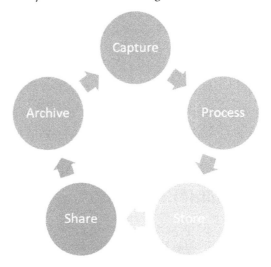

Figure 8.1 – Data life cycle

The data goes through various stages in its lifetime in an organization:

1. **Capture**: This is the first stage in the data life cycle, involving the collection or creation of data. It can be anything from collecting customer information through forms on a website, capturing sales transactions in a retail store, or recording environmental data through sensors. The data steward ensures that the methods of data capture align with the organization's principles and policies for data quality and privacy.

2. **Process**: Once data is captured, it often needs to be processed or transformed to make it useful. This could involve cleaning data to remove errors, aggregating data from different sources, or analyzing data to extract insights. For example, a data steward in a financial institution might oversee the processing of transaction data to detect fraudulent activity.

3. **Store**: After processing, data is stored for future use. This could involve saving data in databases, data warehouses, or cloud storage systems. The data steward ensures that the storage methods used are secure and reliable and align with the organization's data retention policies. For instance, a hospital data steward would ensure patient records are securely stored and only accessible to authorized personnel.

4. **Share**: Sharing refers to the distribution of data within or outside the organization. This could be sharing sales data with a company's marketing department, sharing patient data with healthcare providers, or sharing financial data with regulators. The data steward plays a crucial role in ensuring data is shared responsibly, protecting sensitive information, and maintaining compliance with data privacy laws.

5. **Archive**: The final stage in the data life cycle is archiving. This involves moving data that is no longer actively used to long-term storage. Archiving helps to maintain the availability of historical data while freeing up resources for current data needs. For example, a data steward at a research institution might oversee the archiving of older research data, ensuring it remains accessible for future studies.

You should consider and implement a governance process for each of the stages in the target operating model as automated as possible. An effective data steward will ensure that the data life cycle is managed in a way that maximizes data value while minimizing risks. Let's see how data stewards can fit in during the data life cycle with measurable **key performance indicators** (**KPIs**) in *Table 8.1*:

Stage	Data steward's duties	Example KPI
Capture	The data steward is responsible for ensuring that the data captured is accurate, relevant, and adheres to the organization's data collection policies. They also ensure that data is collected in a manner that respects privacy laws and regulations.	Percentage of data collected that meets the organization's quality standards
Process	The data steward oversees the processing of data, ensuring it is done in a way that maintains data integrity and quality. They ensure that data is cleaned, validated, and transformed according to the organization's standards.	Percentage of data processed without errors
Store	The data steward ensures that data storage practices are secure, efficient, and aligned with the organization's data retention policies. They work to protect data from unauthorized access, loss, or corruption.	Number of data breaches or loss incidents

Stage	Data steward's duties	Example KPI
Share	The data steward is responsible for managing the distribution of data within and outside the organization. They ensure data is shared responsibly, protecting sensitive information and maintaining compliance with data privacy laws.	Number of data-sharing violations or incidents
Archive	The data steward oversees the archiving process, ensuring data is stored in a way that maintains its accessibility and usefulness while complying with the organization's data retention policies.	Percentage of archived data that can be retrieved within a set time frame

Table 8.1 – Data steward's involvement in the data life cycle

As we delve into the next topic of our discussion on establishing data stewardship principles, we will explore the critical role of principles and policies in shaping an organization's data management practices. Let's unpack their importance and the role of the data steward in defining and implementing these principles and policies.

Principles and policies

Data stewardship principles and policies serve as the backbone of data governance, providing the framework within which data stewards operate. They define the *what*, *why*, and *how* of data stewardship, guiding every decision and action concerning data in the organization. They reflect the organization's commitment to data quality, security, integrity, and privacy. Well-defined principles and policies can also help mitigate risks associated with data management, such as data breaches, loss of data integrity, and non-compliance with regulations. Effective data stewardship principles and policies enable organizations to unlock the true value of their data. They ensure data is not just collected but is processed, stored, shared, and archived in ways that maximize its usefulness and value.

Table 8.2 talks about some core principles for data stewardship:

Principle	Description	Implications
Value	Data should be treated as a valuable organizational resource that requires appropriate management.	Data must be carefully managed to ensure that the user knows its location, can rely upon its accuracy, and can access it when needed.
Openness	Ensuring easy access to accurate data is crucial for enhancing the quality and effectiveness of decision-making, analysis, and comprehension across the organization.	Non-sensitive corporate data is accessible to all users by default. Clear accountability and straightforward technical processes are in place to request access to data deemed sensitive.
Security	Limiting access to confidential information on a need-to-know basis and data classification are the prerequisites of open sharing of information.	The infrastructure on which data is stored, analyzed, or accessed must conform fully to firm-wide data security controls. Appropriate logging, monitoring, and alerting, auditing of data access, and control distribution.
Standardization	A common business glossary is essential for effective communication across BUs and data exchange. The infrastructure used for data storage and analysis should be standardized and reused whenever feasible to reduce the need for system integration.	Data should be defined consistently, with definitions that are understandable and available to all users. The core data governance team is ultimately responsible for classification and categorization standards group-wide.

Table 8.2 – Four core principles of data stewardship

So, what is the difference between principles and policies?

Data stewardship principles are strategic and set the broad direction.

On the other hand, policies translate these principles into actionable guidelines, providing a clear blueprint on how data should be captured, processed, stored, shared, and archived. The role of a data steward in this context is to champion these principles and policies, ensuring they are ingrained in the day-to-day operations of the organization. Let's take a look at some examples:

Principle	Policy
Value	**Data lineage**: Every **critical data element** (CDE) should be traceable from origin to usage, with a strictly controlled data structure to manage the impact of any changes on business and systems effectively.
	Data quality: Every enterprise data source must meet approved standards with measurable quality, including accuracy, completeness, timeliness, credibility, and consistency, defined by the group's data risk appetite. Relevant control measures such as data validation, correction, and cleansing ensure data fitness across its life cycle. Quality metrics for all CDEs should be developed with business users and expanded upon.
	Mastering data: Adopt a master data management approach for critical operational data across the group to ensure consistency. Initially, focus on establishing a governance model and onboarding impactful datasets.
Openness	**Data accessibility and transparency**: Data should be open by default, protected, and audited where required. Organizations should keep a data catalog of all assets, accessible to users, to dissolve data silos, foster innovative data use, and unlock data asset value.
	Reuse data: BUs should maximize data source reuse across the group, such as checking for existing datasets or dashboards before creating new ones and making data readable to other systems with appropriate access control.
Security	**Data security, controls, ownership, and classification**: Every business data piece should have a security classification and a data owner to guide user access and data security measures, including **Personally Identifiable Information** (PII) data encryption. All actions must adhere to group security policies, legal regulations, and privacy laws, and, where feasible, data should be logged in an auditable, traceable way.
	Data IM: A data IM workflow with the RACI matrix defined for data issues should be embedded in the target operating model.
Standardization	**Data definition**: Adopt international, national, or industry standards for common data definitions whenever possible; otherwise, develop organizational ones. All CDEs should have a unified business definition approved by the **Data Steering Committee** (DSC), written in user-friendly language, and accessible to all users.
	Reference data: Data that is required to classify other data (for example, currency code, country code, account status) must be compliant with enterprise reference data principles that will be defined by business users and approved by the DSC.

Table 8.3 – Example data policies

Transitioning from the establishment of data stewardship principles and policies, our next focus is data IM. This crucial aspect of data stewardship involves anticipating, preparing for, and effectively handling data-related incidents. Let's dive deeper into this critical responsibility of a data steward, exploring how they can build robust systems for managing data incidents and ensure a swift, effective response when issues arise.

Data incident management

Data incident management (IM) refers to a comprehensive set of processes and protocols designed to identify, assess, and respond to data-related incidents swiftly and effectively. These incidents can range from data breaches and leaks to issues related to data quality, integrity, or accessibility. In our increasingly data-driven world, effective IM is not just important but absolutely critical. It safeguards the organization's data assets, ensures compliance with data protection regulations, and helps to maintain trust with stakeholders.

The data steward plays an irreplaceable role in this process. As the custodian of data, they are responsible for putting in place robust mechanisms to monitor and detect potential incidents. They also lead the response when an incident occurs, coordinating with different stakeholders to mitigate the impact and to ensure that the incident is thoroughly investigated and resolved. By ensuring effective IM, data stewards can significantly enhance the resilience of an organization's data management system, protect its valuable data assets, and uphold its reputation. Whenever there is a data incident, a ticket should be created manually or automatically with the owner and a priority and escalation path defined.

Data incidents can manifest in a variety of ways, depending on the nature of the data, the systems in place, and the vulnerabilities present. Some common examples of data incidents include the following:

- **Data breaches**: This is when unauthorized individuals gain access to confidential data. This could be due to hacking, employee negligence, or system vulnerabilities. The consequences can be severe, especially if the data includes sensitive information such as customer details or proprietary business information.

- **Data leakage**: This refers to situations where data is unintentionally exposed. For example, an email containing sensitive information might be sent to the wrong recipient, or a document with confidential data might be inadvertently made public.

- **Data corruption**: This happens when an error in the system or a software bug alters data, making it inaccurate or unusable. This can seriously impact business operations and decision-making processes that rely on corrupted data.

- **Data loss**: This occurs when data is accidentally or intentionally deleted, or when storage devices fail. The loss of data, especially if not backed up, can be disastrous for an organization.

- **Data availability issues**: This can happen when network or system failures, natural disasters, or cyber-attacks prevent users from accessing critical data when they need it.

- **Non-compliance incidents**: These are situations where the organization fails to adhere to data protection laws and regulations, potentially leading to legal penalties and reputational damage.

- **Data quality**: This results from a business or technical data validation rule, and an alert should be raised to data stewards.

Data IM cycle

Data IM is a proactive, cyclical process designed to ensure the swift resolution of issues and the continuous improvement of data systems. Let's look at each stage of the cycle in detail in *Figure 8.2*:

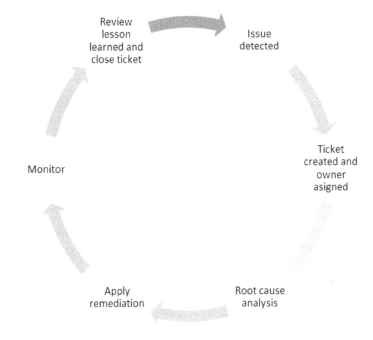

Figure 8.2 – Data IM cycle

Effective management of data incidents is not a solitary task but a symphony of actions performed in concert by data stewards, data owners, IT personnel, security teams, and senior management. Let's look at the different stages involved:

1. **Issue detected**: This is the initial stage where a data incident is identified. The detection of a data incident can occur through various channels. It might be an automated alert from a data monitoring tool, a report from a customer, or an observation by a staff member. IT personnel, who manage the technical infrastructure, play a key role here, as do data stewards, who monitor data quality and usage. At this stage, communication between IT and data stewards is crucial to quickly assess the potential scope and impact of the incident.

2. **Ticket created and owner assigned**: Once an incident is detected, a ticket is created in the IM system. This is often the responsibility of the IT helpdesk or the data stewardship team. The ticket must include all relevant details of the incident and is then assigned to a data steward or an IT specialist, depending on the nature of the incident. The data owner may also be involved at this stage, particularly if the incident pertains to data they are accountable for.

3. **Root cause analysis (RCA)**: The data steward or IT specialist assigned to the ticket undertakes an RCA. They may need to collaborate closely with data owners and **subject matter experts (SMEs)** who understand the business context of the data, as well as security teams if there is a suspicion of a breach. At this stage, it is all about gathering information and understanding how and why the incident occurred. Understanding the root cause is key to finding an effective solution and preventing similar incidents in the future.

4. **Apply remediation**: With the root cause identified, the next step is to implement a solution to resolve the issue. Remediation actions are taken to resolve the incident. IT personnel may work on technical fixes, such as patching software vulnerabilities or restoring data from backups. Data stewards coordinate with data owners and SMEs to ensure that data integrity is maintained and that any data-related processes are amended if necessary. They may also work with the legal and compliance teams if there are regulatory implications arising from the incident. The aim is to restore normal operations as quickly and smoothly as possible.

5. **Monitor**: After remediation, the situation is closely monitored to ensure the solution is working and that the issue has been fully resolved. Monitoring also helps to detect any new or recurring issues promptly. Continuous monitoring is often under the radar of the IT team, with data stewards keeping an eye on data quality and usage aspects.

6. **Review lesson learned and close ticket**: After successful remediation and monitoring, a review is conducted to learn from the incident. This review should involve data stewards, data owners, IT, security teams, and potentially senior management if the incident is significant. Lessons learned are documented, and policies or processes are updated accordingly. The ticket is then closed, with the data steward typically responsible for ensuring that all follow-up actions have been completed.

Throughout all these stages, the role of senior management is to provide support and ensure that adequate resources are allocated for data IM. They may also be involved in communication with external stakeholders, such as customers or regulators, and in making strategic decisions if the incident has significant business implications.

Effective data IM relies on clear communication channels and predefined processes that outline each role's responsibilities. By establishing and practicing these protocols, organizations can ensure a rapid and coordinated response to data incidents, thereby minimizing any potential damage and maintaining trust in their data governance capabilities.

First things first

Prioritizing data incidents effectively is crucial to managing them efficiently and minimizing their impact. Not all incidents are created equal. Addressing them in the right order can make a significant difference. Key considerations when prioritizing incidents are severity, urgency, and business impact, as illustrated in *Figure 8.3*:

Figure 8.3 – Key considerations when prioritizing data incidents

Let's take a closer look at these:

- **Severity**: This refers to the extent of the damage caused by the incident. Higher severity incidents might result in significant data loss or corruption or expose highly sensitive data. These incidents often require immediate attention to mitigate their effects.

- **Urgency**: Urgency relates to the time sensitivity of resolving the incident. Some incidents might cause a minor issue now, but if left unresolved could escalate into a major problem. Understanding the urgency helps to allocate resources effectively and prevent small issues from becoming big problems.

- **Business impact**: This considers how the incident affects the organization's operations. An incident that disrupts a critical business process or compromises key data has a high business impact. Such incidents need to be prioritized to ensure **business continuity** (**BC**).

Last but not least, make sure you have an escalation path for data incidents so that users know what to do in emergency situations.

The escalation path in data IM is a predefined plan or procedure that outlines the steps to escalate an incident to higher levels of management or specialized teams when necessary. It designates who should be involved at each stage, and when and how to escalate the issue if it cannot be resolved at the current level.

The escalation path is critical for several reasons. Firstly, it ensures that serious incidents receive the appropriate level of attention and resources needed for their resolution. Secondly, it provides clarity and structure, reducing confusion and delays in the response process. Lastly, it ensures accountability and keeps all relevant parties informed about the incident and the actions being taken.

For example, when there is a leakage of sensitive data, you want to have a clear guideline on what to do and communicate among the teams, just as with the examples shown in *Figure 8.4*:

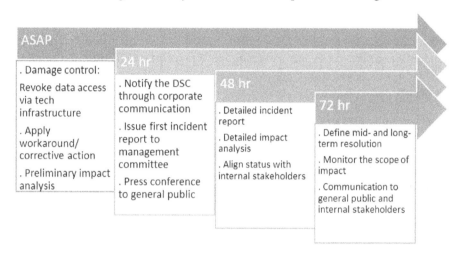

Figure 8.4 – Example escalation path of a data incident

The data steward plays a crucial role in the escalation process. As the primary owner of the data incident, they are often the first to decide if an incident needs to be escalated. They need to be able to assess the situation accurately and make informed decisions about when to involve higher management or specialized teams. This requires a deep understanding of the data, the incident, and potential risks and impacts.

Once the decision to escalate is made, the data steward is also responsible for communicating the issue effectively. They need to provide all relevant information about the incident, actions taken so far, and potential implications. This enables the higher-level management or specialized teams to take over and manage the incident effectively.

Overall, the escalation path is a crucial part of the data IM process, and the data steward is at the heart of it. Their ability to navigate this process effectively can significantly influence the organization's ability to respond to and recover from data incidents.

Having delved into the intricacies of data IM and the principles of data stewardship, we will now shift our focus to another crucial aspect of effective data management: data ownership.

Defining and implementing data ownership

Data ownership is a fundamental element of data governance that refers to the assignment of responsibility for data quality, integrity, and security to specific individuals or teams within an organization. This concept goes beyond the mere possession of data, extending to encompass responsibility for its appropriate use, its protection, and maintenance of its accuracy and reliability. The importance of data ownership cannot be overstated. It fosters accountability, ensures compliance with data standards and policies, and facilitates efficient decision-making.

In the context of data governance, data ownership is pivotal. It is the backbone that supports data policies, standards, and procedures, ensuring they are effectively implemented and adhered to. It empowers individuals or teams, known as data owners, with the authority to make decisions about the data they oversee, including who can access it, how it can be used, and how it should be protected.

Data stewards often work closely with data owners in managing and enhancing data quality. While the data owner is ultimately accountable for the data, the data steward provides the necessary support to ensure that the data is fit for its intended uses in operations, decision-making, and planning. Together, the data owner and the data steward form an essential partnership in the effective governance and management of data within an enterprise.

Defining and designing a data domain

What is a data domain?

A **data domain** is a set of data elements or attributes that have a common purpose or are related to each other in some way. It is the basis for data governance and stewardship, as it helps to define the scope of the data and the rules and policies that should be applied to it. Data domains can be used to define the structure of a data model, access rights to the data, and processes and procedures that should be followed when managing the data. Data domains can also be used to ensure data quality and consistency across different systems and organizations. Examples of a data domain include customer data, trade processing data, and financial data.

How do data domain and data ownership work together for the greater good of data governance?

Each data domain is typically overseen by a specific individual or team—the data owner. The relationship between data ownership and data domains is symbiotic. By establishing clear data domains, an organization can more effectively assign data ownership. Conversely, having clearly defined data owners helps maintain the integrity of each data domain, as there is a designated person or team accountable for that data.

There are at least three ways to design a data domain scheme for your organization:

- **By BU or organization chart**: This approach involves defining data domains based on divisions or **organizational units** (**OUs**) within the organization. This approach allows for the data to be divided into distinct domains that can then be managed and monitored by the appropriate teams. This approach also allows for the data to be organized in a way that is easy to understand and maintain. This approach is popular because it is easy for the team to follow the existing organization chart.

- **By system**: This approach involves defining data domains based on systems or applications within the organization. This is driven by the system and application landscape in the organization.

- **By data product**: This approach involves defining data domains based on data products within the organization. It allows for the data to be tailored to the specific needs of the organization, ensuring that the data is being used to its fullest potential.

Assigning an owner to a data domain

After the scheme of the data domain is confirmed, we should assign one and only one data owner to each data domain. I do not believe in co-ownership as it will just introduce confusion and political tension. You may consider primary and secondary data owner models if you are afraid the primary data owner may take extended leave. Still, for each data domain, you should have one and only one data owner at a time.

Assigning an owner to a data domain is an important step in data governance and stewardship. This is because the owner is responsible for ensuring that the data is properly managed and maintained. The owner should be knowledgeable about the data domain and be able to provide guidance and direction to the team responsible for managing the data. The owner should also be able to identify potential risks and develop strategies to mitigate them. Additionally, the owner should be able to communicate the importance of data governance and stewardship to the organization and ensure that the data is used in an ethical and responsible manner.

So, how do we identify and assign a data owner(s)?

To make data ownership successful, we need to find the right people and get them to take on the role, then ensure they are adding value.

Personally, a top-down approach is the way to go.

To identify and assign data owners to data domains, we need to engage leaders to get their support first. The leaders will then help identify owners. This should be done through face-to-face 1-1 meetings before submitting to the DSC for endorsement. Putting yourself into others' shoes, why do you want to take on the data owner role? It is important to explain the benefits of taking on the role, such as career and network benefits. Additionally, it is important to provide training that is specific and focused so that data owners understand what is expected of them and how they can benefit from the role. Finally, it is important to maintain success by providing ongoing benefits to data owners, such as addressing high-priority data issues and integrating new data sources.

Figure 8.5 shows a sample data domain and dataset (in highlighted blocks) with a data owner assigned in two departments:

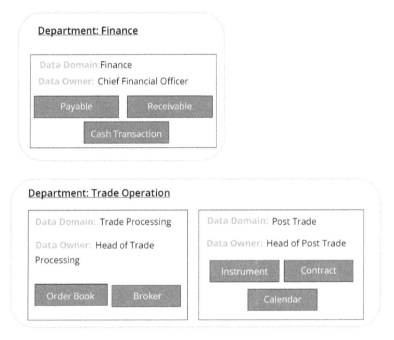

Figure 8.5 – Sample design of a data domain

Data governance is not a one-off project; it is a **business-as-usual** (**BAU**) activity.

To keep the momentum of a robust data governance framework, you should embed data ownership into the *target operating model* and approval process via an automated workflow platform. You may refer to *Chapter 4, Developing a Comprehensive Data Management Strategy*, and *Chapter 5, People, Process, Technology*.

With a comprehensive understanding of data domain and data ownership, we are now ready to move to the next stage of our discussion about defining the target state of your data stewardship journey.

Day 2 for data ownership and domain

Day 2, or the period following the establishment of a data domain structure, is a critical phase in data governance where the theoretical framework meets practical application. It is a time when the organization starts to see the real-world implications of the data domain approach it has chosen and begins to refine and embed these practices into everyday operations.

In the context of business models and allocating data domains, there are several approaches an organization can explore *(Table 8.4)*.

Approach	Focus	Day 2 operation
Product-led	This approach categorizes data domains based on specific products or services offered by the organization. Each product becomes a domain with its own data that reflects its unique life cycle, from creation to customer delivery. This approach aligns well with organizations that have distinct product lines, as it allows for focused management and optimization of data related to each product.	In the product-led approach, data stewards monitor and manage data quality, usage, and policies specific to their product data. The data domain is evaluated for its efficiency in delivering product insights, supporting product development, and contributing to cross-functional strategies.
Data-led	This approach organizes data domains around the types of data the organization manages, such as customer data, financial data, or operational data. It is centered on the nature and purpose of the data itself, rather than the organizational structure or product lines.	Data stewards focus on ensuring the consistency, accuracy, and security of data within their domain. They work closely with data owners and IT teams to address any data quality issues and to support the specific needs of different BUs that rely on their domain's data.
Functional group	In this approach, data domains are aligned with functional groups such as sales, marketing, or HR. Each function's data is treated as a separate domain, reflecting the specific data requirements and workflows of that area.	Functional data domains require stewards to have a deep understanding of the department's processes and needs. They must ensure that the data supports the function's objectives and is integrated with the wider organizational data strategy.

Approach	Focus	Day 2 operation
Process-centric	Data domains are structured around key business processes, such as **customer relationship management** (**CRM**) or supply chain operations. Data associated with these processes is grouped into domains to streamline management and optimization.	Stewards in a process-centric model focus on the end-to-end flow of data, ensuring it facilitates process efficiency and effectiveness. They work to remove silos and encourage cross-functional collaboration.
Hybrid	This approach combines elements of the preceding models to best fit the organization's complexity and goals. Data domains might be organized by product lines in one area and by functional groups in another.	The hybrid approach calls for flexible data stewardship, where stewards may wear multiple hats, managing data quality and governance across diverse domains. They must navigate the interplay between different domain structures and ensure cohesive governance practices.

Table 8.4 – Approaches of allocating data domains

Regardless of the approach, Day 2 for data domains is about operationalizing the data domain framework. It involves the following:

- **Monitoring and measuring**: Data stewards track key metrics related to data quality, usage, and compliance within their domains

- **Continuous improvement**: Stewards and owners regularly review domain performance and seek opportunities for optimization

- **Communication and collaboration**: Regular interactions take place between stakeholders within and across domains to ensure alignment

- **Governance and policy enforcement**: Ensuring that data policies are adhered to and governance standards are maintained across all domains

- **Training and support**: Providing the necessary training and resources to all personnel involved in data management within the domains

Refer to *Chapter 11, Theory versus Real Life*, for more details on how a **data mesh** can help the implementation of a data domain.

Defining a target state – What does good data stewardship look like?

Defining a target state is essentially creating a clear vision of what an optimized data governance and stewardship program looks like. It involves setting specific goals and KPIs that reflect the organization's data management aspirations. This vision should encapsulate the desired data quality, compliance, security, and accessibility, among other critical factors.

The target state plays a pivotal role in shaping the data stewardship program. It serves as a guidepost, providing direction and clarity to the various data stewardship initiatives. It sets the bar for what the organization aims to achieve, enabling data stewards to align their efforts with these goals and measure their progress.

Understanding the level of data complexity

Before we define the target state of data stewardship, let's align on the various levels of data complexity in the data journey. As organizations evolve, so does the complexity of their data. It is crucial for data stewards and owners to recognize that data complexity is not a static metric—it grows with the scale of data assets, the diversity of data types, and the intricacy of data interrelationships.

Let's look at the levels of data complexity:

1. **Basic complexity**:

   - In the initial stages, data complexity is relatively low. Data sources are few, formats are uniform, and data is used for straightforward operational purposes.

   - Data management tasks involve simple collection, storage, and retrieval processes.

   - The organization's data maturity is in its infancy, with rudimentary governance structures in place.

2. **Moderate complexity**:

   - As the organization grows, the number of data sources increases, and the organization begins to integrate data from various systems.

   - Data is now used not just for operational needs but also for analytical insights, leading to more sophisticated data management requirements.

   - Data governance practices become more formalized, with clearer roles and policies.

3. **High complexity**:

- At this level, an organization deals with a large volume of data from a multitude of sources, including structured, semi-structured, and unstructured data.

- Advanced analytics, such as predictive modeling and **machine learning** (**ML**), are in use, increasing the demand for high-quality, well-governed data.

- Data governance is mature, with established processes for data quality, compliance, and stewardship.

4. **Extreme complexity**:

- In the most advanced stage, the organization's data landscape includes real-time data processing, **Internet of Things** (**IoT**) inputs, and massive data lakes.

- Data governance is a strategic priority, with a focus on enterprise-wide consistency, advanced data privacy concerns, and cross-border data flow regulations.

- The organization's data maturity is high, with a strong culture of data-driven decision-making and continuous innovation in data management practices.

Each level of complexity requires a tailored approach to data stewardship and governance. As complexity increases, so does the need for sophisticated tools, advanced skills, and more robust governance frameworks. Understanding where your organization falls on this spectrum is critical to determining appropriate strategies for data management and the necessary investments in technology and training. You may refer to *Chapters 3* and *4* for a gap analysis of data maturity for your organization.

Defining a target state

There are challenges when defining a target state. It requires a deep understanding of the organization's data landscape, its business objectives, and potential obstacles to good data governance. It also necessitates engagement and buy-in from various stakeholders, including data owners, data stewards, and senior management.

Addressing these challenges often involves a thorough assessment of the current data management practices and identifying gaps and areas for improvement. You may refer to *Figure 4.5* of *Chapter 4* for a visualization of gap analysis by comparing the current state to the target state. It also requires fostering a data-driven culture within the organization, where data is viewed as a valuable asset that needs to be managed properly. Clear communication and collaboration between all stakeholders is essential, ensuring that everyone understands the vision and is committed to achieving it. With a well-defined target state, organizations can navigate their data stewardship journey more effectively and unlock the full value of their data.

Next, let's explore the target state of data governance by three different dimensions:

- **Defensive versus offensive**: The target state of data governance should be one that takes into account both a defensive and offensive view. This means that data governance should be able to protect data from misuse while also enabling the organization to use data to its fullest potential.

- **Defensive data governance** focuses on protecting data from misuse and abuse. It involves setting up controls, standards, and policies to ensure data privacy, security, and compliance. An example of a defensive strategy would be a healthcare organization adhering to **Health Insurance Portability and Accountability Act (HIPAA)** regulations to protect patient data. On the other hand, **offensive data governance** refers to using data as a strategic asset to drive business value. It involves leveraging data for decision-making, innovation, and competitive advantage. For instance, a retail business might use customer data to tailor marketing strategies, thus driving sales. In reality, an effective data governance program should balance both approaches. A financial services firm, for example, must protect sensitive customer information (defensive) but also use that data to offer personalized services (offensive).

- **Run the business (RTB) versus change the business (CTB)**: Data governance should also be implemented from both an RTB and CTB perspective. The data governance operating model should be able to maintain the current state of data operations while also enabling the organization to adapt and innovate with data. RTB focuses on maintaining current operations and improving the efficiency and effectiveness of existing processes. For example, a manufacturing firm may use data governance to ensure the accuracy and timeliness of its production data. CTB, in contrast, is about using data to drive innovation and transformation. An e-commerce company, for example, might use data governance to support the launch of a new AI-driven recommendation engine. Both perspectives are critical for a successful data governance program. Data stewards play a key role here, ensuring data quality and accessibility for RTB while also supporting strategic data initiatives for CTB.

- **Top-down versus bottom-up**: Data governance should be driven from the top of the organization, with the senior leadership team setting the vision and goals for data governance while also enabling the organization to tap into the knowledge and expertise of individual data stewards and data owners. This ensures that data governance is not only driven from the top but also from the bottom, ensuring that the organization is able to benefit from the expertise of its data stewards and data owners.

- **Top-down data governance** involves senior leadership setting the vision, goals, and policies. For instance, a pharmaceutical company's leadership might set a goal of achieving data-driven research and development.

- **Bottom-up data governance** taps into the knowledge and expertise of data stewards and data owners. These are the individuals who understand the data's nuances and can provide insights into its quality, usage, and challenges. For example, in a logistics company, data stewards might identify recurring data quality issues that affect supply chain efficiency.

A comprehensive data governance program should leverage both approaches. Leadership sets the strategic direction (top-down), and data stewards and data owners provide operational insights (bottom-up). This ensures that the data governance program is aligned with the organization's strategic goals while being grounded in the realities of day-to-day data management.

Now, let's zoom in on a crucial but often overlooked role—the data owner.

What does good look like for data owners?

Data owners are pivotal in the data governance framework, as they hold accountability for data quality, integrity, and security within their domain. Here's what good looks like for data owners:

- **Clarity of role and responsibility**: Effective data owners have a clear understanding of their roles and the responsibilities that come with them. They know what data they are accountable for and what outcomes are expected from their stewardship. This includes an awareness of compliance requirements and the operational use of the data.

- **Active engagement**: Good data owners are actively engaged with their data. They don't simply oversee data management; they are involved in strategic discussions about the use and value of data. They regularly participate in data governance meetings, contribute to policy development, and are accessible to data stewards and other stakeholders for consultation and decision-making.

- **Collaborative approach**: Strong data owners recognize the need for collaboration. They work closely with data stewards to establish and maintain data quality and work across teams to ensure data is used to support organizational objectives. They understand the interconnected nature of data and seek input from various business functions to ensure data meets the needs of all users.

- **Data quality advocacy**: An effective data owner is committed to maintaining high data quality standards. They understand the impact of data quality on business decisions and operations and advocate for resources, tools, and processes that support data accuracy, completeness, and reliability.

- **Strategic vision**: Good data owners have a strategic vision for the data they manage. They align this vision with the organization's broader goals and identify opportunities where their data can contribute to innovation and competitive advantage. They think beyond day-to-day operations and consider the long-term implications of data usage and governance.

- **Risk management**: Effective data owners are proactive in identifying and mitigating risks associated with their data. They understand potential security threats, privacy concerns, and compliance issues and work closely with IT and security teams to safeguard data assets.

- **Continuous improvement**: Good data owners are not complacent. They seek to continually improve data governance practices. They are open to feedback, willing to learn from incidents, and adapt policies and processes accordingly. They encourage a culture of continuous improvement within their teams.

- **Clear communication**: Strong data owners communicate effectively about their data. They ensure that data definitions, policies, and governance practices are well documented and understood by stakeholders. They are transparent about the state of the data and any issues or limitations that might affect its use.

- **Empowerment and accountability**: Effective data owners empower their teams to manage and use data correctly. They delegate authority where appropriate but also hold themselves and their teams accountable for the data's condition and adherence to data governance policies.

- **Performance measurement**: Good data owners regularly measure and report on the performance of their data domains. They use KPIs to track data quality, usage, and governance activities, ensuring that they meet the set objectives and contribute value to the organization.

As we conclude our discussion on setting the target state for a data stewardship program, it is important to visualize what a mature data governance framework looks like. In the ideal scenario, an organization has well-defined policies and procedures that ensure the quality, security, and privacy of its data. Operating within this framework, there exists a dedicated data governance team, appointed by the DSC. This team is entrusted with the responsibility of setting, implementing, and enforcing data governance standards.

To measure the progress of the data governance program and to gauge its success, a detailed data governance roadmap is indispensable. This roadmap should clearly outline the steps to be taken and include measurable KPIs that align with data governance objectives. Moreover, an effective data governance framework includes robust mechanisms to monitor and audit data governance activities, ensuring compliance and continual improvement.

All these elements contribute to nurturing a new data culture within the organization. This culture, centered on responsible and strategic data management, can become a significant competitive advantage, driving innovation, efficiency, and growth. This is the vision that every data steward should strive for as they embark on their data stewardship journey.

Summary

Data stewardship principles are the backbone of a robust data governance framework. The design of an organization's data policy should balance between safeguarding data assets and empowering the organization to leverage data optimally.

Data IM is one of the essential facets that ensures swift and effective responses to data breaches or other incidents. A well-defined process outlining roles, responsibilities, investigative steps, mitigation strategies, and stakeholder communication is crucial. Further, the implementation of data ownership is vital for efficient and effective data management. It assigns clear responsibilities, enhancing accountability and ensuring that data is used to its full potential.

However, it is important to remember that these guidelines are not universally applicable in their raw form. Every organization has unique needs, so the data policy, IM, and data ownership principles should be customized accordingly. Moreover, these principles are not static. They should be reviewed and updated periodically to ensure their relevance and efficacy in a dynamic business environment.

With these principles in place, organizations can work toward achieving their target state of data governance—a state that optimizes data value, fosters a data-driven culture, and provides a competitive edge.

In the next chapter, we will demystify the world of GPT in the context of data stewardship.

Supercharge Data Governance and Stewardship with GPT

Now that you have a basic understanding of data stewardship, how about GPT?

OpenAI is a research organization that aims to create and promote **artificial intelligence (AI)** that can benefit humanity without causing harm or being misused. As of this writing, Sam Altman is still the OpenAI CEO after some dramatic changes in their board of directors (`https://time.com/6338789/sam-altman-openai-return-timeline/`).

GPT stands for **generative pre-trained transformer**. GPT is a series of language models developed by OpenAI that use deep learning to generate natural language texts on various topics and tasks. GPT models are trained on large amounts of text data from the web, such as Wikipedia, news articles, blogs, social media posts, and more. GPT models can learn from the patterns and structures of natural language and produce coherent and relevant texts based on a given input or prompt.

So, how does GPT fit into data governance?

In this chapter, we will explore how AI and GPT can accelerate your data governance and stewardship program:

- Pairing data and AI
- Leveraging AI and GPT for data governance
- Understanding the challenges and limitations
- Embracing a responsible AI framework
- Future of AI for data governance

Pairing data and AI

Using AI, particularly GPT, can transform enterprise data management, enhancing decision-making, insights, and efficiency. The integration of data governance, stewardship, and AI fosters improved enterprise operations.

Data is the fuel that powers AI, and AI is the engine that drives actionable insights from data. By bringing together data and AI, you can achieve the following:

- Uncover and leverage emerging trends by analyzing large volumes and varieties of data from multiple sources: Data stewards can use AI to manage vast and diverse data, helping data analysts to uncover and seize industry and market opportunities.

- Automate customer segmentation: AI can analyze consumer behavior patterns within data, allowing data stewards to automate segmentation and deliver tailored customer experiences.

- Optimize digital marketing: Data stewards maintain good quality customer data for AI-powered personalized marketing while ensuring ethical use, data privacy, and compliance, thus optimizing digital marketing campaigns effectively and responsibly.

- Enhance data quality and protection: AI can automate data cleansing, identifying and rectifying errors, outliers, duplicates, and missing values. This ensures data stewards maintain high data integrity. Furthermore, AI can enhance data protection by automating access controls, ensuring that sensitive data are handled only by authorized personnel in a manner that safeguards privacy and meets regulatory obligations.

- Extract quick insights: AI can analyze raw data rapidly, employing techniques such as natural language processing, computer vision, and sentiment analysis. This empowers data stewards to deliver timely insights, such as the real-time monitoring of data breach incidents.

- Support decision-making: AI can provide data-driven recommendations, predictions, and feedback, enabling quicker and more effective decisions.

- Unlock new data sources: AI can access unstructured or semi-structured data, such as text, images, and social media posts, which constitute over 80% of data. This allows data stewards to tap into previously inaccessible data for analytics.

To leverage the full potential of data and AI for your business and data governance, you need to do the following:

- Prioritize data, analytics, and AI to drive your business outcomes and align them with your strategic goals. A data steward with a clear understanding of the organization's data landscape and strategic goals can ensure that data and AI initiatives are aligned with these goals. For instance, if a telecommunication company aims to reduce customer churn, the data steward can facilitate the use of AI algorithms to analyze customer data and predict churn trends. You may refer to *Chapter 3, Getting Started with the Data Stewardship Program*, for use case prioritization and business value alignment.

- Build your data strategy around a data lakehouse or data mesh architecture, which unifies data, analytics, and AI on a single platform. A data steward ensures that the data is accurate, reliable, and accessible to analytics and AI. For example, in a healthcare firm, the data steward might ensure that patient data from various sources are correctly integrated into a centralized data infrastructure, making it ready for AI-driven analysis and domain-driven self-service. You may refer to *Chapter 11, Theory versus Real Life*, for the details on data meshes.

- View data management and governance as an organization-wide initiative that involves all your stakeholders across individual business units and departments. The data steward acts as the liaison between different business units and departments, fostering collaboration for data governance. They ensure that all stakeholders understand their roles and responsibilities towards data management. In a retail enterprise, this might mean coordinating between marketing, sales, and IT departments to ensure uniformity in customer data handling.

- Secure your data and AI by implementing policies, standards, controls, and audits to ensure the privacy, security, ethics, and compliance of your data assets and activities. The data steward is responsible for implementing and monitoring the adherence to data-related policies, standards, and controls. This includes ensuring data privacy, security, and ethical use. For example, in a financial institution, they would ensure that customer financial data are securely stored and used in compliance with regulations such as GDPR.

- Adapt and improve your data and AI solutions over time to keep up with the changing data landscape and expectations of your customers, partners, regulators, and competitors. As the data landscape evolves, the data steward ensures that the organization's data and AI capabilities also evolve. They continuously assess and improve the data quality and AI models to meet changing expectations. For instance, a logistics company might adapt data and AI strategies to better predict delivery times as e-commerce trends evolve.

Data and AI are not mutually exclusive but complementary. By combining them in a synergistic way, you can achieve greater business performance and efficiency while ensuring effective data governance for your organization. Now, let's examine how integrating AI, especially GPT, revolutionizes data governance.

Leveraging AI and GPT for data governance

By leveraging the capabilities of AI and GPT, organizations can automate data management processes, derive insightful analytics, and enhance decision-making capabilities. The potential benefits of these technologies are extensive, ranging from improved data quality to enhanced regulatory compliance and risk management. Amid this transformative shift, the role of a data steward becomes increasingly important. As the custodians of data, stewards have the opportunity to demonstrate their value by facilitating the integration of AI and GPT into governance strategies, ensuring data integrity, and driving efficient data usage to deliver strategic insights and drive business outcomes.

Let's see how we can achieve greater efficiency, accuracy, and innovation in the data governance space by using the latest AI technologies.

Enhancing data quality and trust

As the foundation of any data governance strategy, maintaining data quality and trust is the cornerstone. AI and GPT can be instrumental in enhancing these aspects, paving the way for reliable insights and informed decision-making:

- Enhancing your data documentation and metadata management with automated text generation and summarization, as per the compliance requirements:

- You can consider using GPT models to generate natural language descriptions, definitions, labels, tags, and annotations for your data assets, such as tables, columns, fields, values, schemas, and more. You can also use GPT models to summarize the key information, insights, and statistics from your datasets, such as the number of records, the distribution of values, the correlations among variables, and more. *Figure 9.1* illustrates how you set the background and ask questions to a GPT model.

Generate a summary of the below conversation in the following format:
Customer problem:
Outcome of the conversation:
Action items for follow-up:
Customer budget:
Departure city:
Destination city:

Conversation:
User: Hi there, I'm off between August 25 and September 11. I saved up 4000 for a nice trip. If I flew out from San Francisco, what are your suggestions for where I can go?
Agent: For that budget you could travel to cities in the US, Mexico, Brazil, Italy or Japan. Any preferences?
User: Excellent, I've always wanted to see Tokyo. What kind of hotel can I expect?
Agent: Great, let me check what I have. First, can I just confirm with you that this is a trip for one adult?
User: Yes it is
Agent: Great, thank you, In that case I can offer you 15 days at HOTEL Sugoi, a 3 star hotel close to a Palace. You would be staying there between August 25th and September 7th. They offer free wifi and have an excellent guest rating of 8.49/10. The entire package costs 2024.25USD. Should I book this for you?
User: That sounds really good actually. Please book me at Sugoi.
Agent: I can do that for you! Can I help you with anything else today?
User: No, thanks! Please just send me the itinerary to my email soon.

Figure 9.1 – Sample GPT prompt

- In *Figure 9.2*, you can see the output generated by a GPT model, as per the requirements in *Figure 9.1*.

Summary:
Customer problem: The customer wants to take a trip within a budget of 4000 USD between August 25 and September 11 from San Francisco to a destination suggested by the agent.
Outcome of the conversation: The agent suggested Japan and offered a 15 day stay at a 3-star hotel called HOTEL Sugoi which costs 2024.25 USD. The customer agreed to the offer and asked the agent to book it for them.
Action items for follow-up: The agent needs to send the itinerary to the customer's email.
Customer budget: 4000 USD
Departure city: San Francisco
Destination city: Tokyo

Figure 9.2 – Sample GPT completion

- Improving your data quality and integrity with data validation and anomaly detection using natural language understanding and generation: You can also use AI technologies, such as natural language processing (NLP) and natural language generation (NLG), to validate the accuracy, completeness, consistency, timeliness, and relevance of your data. AI can be used to detect anomalies or outliers in your data, such as missing values, incorrect values, duplicate values, inconsistent values, unexpected ranges, and more. You can use GPT models to generate natural language explanations or recommendations for resolving data quality issues or anomalies. Imagine you have an AI copilot for your data governance program. For example, *Figure 9.3* shows the sample data:

> Please highlight the outliers in the data below and give explanation:
> - Apple
> - Banana
> - Coconut
> - Data Steward

Figure 9.3 – Sample GPT prompt for outlier detection

- Observe how a GPT model can figure out the outlier and an explanation for this result (*Figure 9.4*):

> In the given list, 'Data Steward' is the outlier. While 'Apple', 'Banana', and 'Coconut' are all categories of fruit, 'Data Steward' is a professional role, specifically in the field of data management. It does not belong to the same category as the other items in the list. Therefore, 'Data Steward' stands out as an outlier in this context.

Figure 9.4 – Sample GPT completion of outlier detection

Automation and enrichment

By leveraging AI and GPT, repetitive and manual data governance tasks can be automated, enriching data completeness and freeing up data stewards to focus on strategic initiatives:

- Automate data compliance and policies using natural language understanding and generation:

  - You can leverage AI technologies, such as NLP and NLG, to automate the creation, implementation, monitoring, and enforcement of your data compliance and policies. You can use NLP to extract the relevant rules, regulations, standards, and best practices from various sources of text, such as laws, contracts, agreements, guidelines, frameworks, and more. You can use NLG to generate natural language texts that express your data compliance and policies in a clear, concise, and consistent manner. You can also use NLG to generate natural language reports or alerts that inform you of the status or performance of your data compliance and policies. Let's look at the long text form in *Figure 9.5* that we need to summarize:

Provide a summary of the text below that captures its main idea.

At Microsoft, we have been on a quest to advance AI beyond existing techniques, by taking a more holistic, human-centric approach to learning and understanding. As Chief Technology Officer of Azure AI Services, I have been working with a team of amazing scientists and engineers to turn this quest into a reality. In my role, I enjoy a unique perspective in viewing the relationship among three attributes of human cognition: monolingual text (X), audio or visual sensory signals, (Y) and multilingual (Z). At the intersection of all three, there's magic—what we call XYZ-code as illustrated in Figure 1—a joint representation to create more powerful AI that can speak, hear, see, and understand humans better. We believe XYZ-code will enable us to fulfill our long-term vision: cross-domain transfer learning, spanning modalities and languages. The goal is to have pre-trained models that can jointly learn representations to support a broad range of downstream AI tasks, much in the way humans do today. Over the past five years, we have achieved human performance on benchmarks in conversational speech recognition, machine translation, conversational question answering, machine reading comprehension, and image captioning. These five breakthroughs provided us with strong signals toward our more ambitious aspiration to produce a leap in AI capabilities, achieving multi-sensory and multilingual learning that is closer in line with how humans learn and understand. I believe the joint XYZ-code is a foundational component of this aspiration, if grounded with external knowledge sources in the downstream AI tasks.

Figure 9.5 – Sample GPT prompt

- Now take a look at *Figure 9.6*, which is the summarized version of the example in *Figure 9.5*, as per GPT:

> Microsoft has been working to advance AI by taking a more human-centric approach to learning and understanding. The team has developed a joint representation called XYZ-code which combines monolingual text, audio or visual sensory signals, and multilingual signals. This approach has enabled them to achieve human-level performance on a range of AI tasks, and they hope to use XYZ-code to achieve a leap in AI capabilities, closer to how humans learn and understand.

Figure 9.6 – Sample GPT completion

- Automate data enrichment and master data elements with AI: You can use various AI technologies, such as **machine learning (ML)**, **computer vision (CV)**, **speech recognition (SR)**, **sentiment analysis (SA)**, and many more, to enrich your data with additional information or features that can enhance its value or usability. For example, you can use ML to classify or cluster your data into meaningful categories or groups. You can use computer vision to extract information from images or videos in your data. You can also use speech recognition to transcribe audio or voice in your data. Sentiment analysis can help gauge public opinion about your products or services among a massive amount of social media posts. It can identify positive, negative, and neutral sentiments, helping you understand customer satisfaction and feedback on a deeper level. Then, you can also use AI to create master data elements that represent the most accurate or authoritative sources of information for your data. Here is a real-life success story of AI automation related to customer success in a supermarket chain: `https://customers.microsoft.com/en-US/story/1459768210983092445-jumbo-supermarkten-retailers-azure-en-netherlands`.

Driving innovation and insight

With AI and GPT, data governance transcends traditional boundaries. It becomes a wellspring of innovation, providing granular insights that can steer strategic business decisions and stimulate growth:

- Enriching your data analysis and visualization with natural language query and report generation:

  - You can use GPT models to enable **natural language query** (**NLQ**) and **natural language report** (**NLR**) for your data analysis and visualization. NLQ allows you to ask questions about your data in natural language and get answers in natural language or visual formats. NLR allows you to generate natural language summaries or narratives that highlight the key findings or insights from your data analysis or visualization. Let's look at an example of an NLQ prompt for GPT in *Figure 9.7*.

    > Over the last five years, our company has tracked the sales performance of our five products: Product A, Product B, Product C, Product D, and Product E. Our analysis shows that Product A has consistently been the top-selling product, with an average of 10,000 units sold per year, generating $2 million in annual revenue and a profit margin of 15%. However, the profit margin for Product A has decreased over the past two years, indicating a need for re-evaluation of our pricing strategy. Product B and Product C have also shown steady sales and profitability, with an average of 7,500 units sold per year, generating $1.5 million in annual revenue, and a consistent profit margin of 20%. Product D has seen a slight decline in sales over the past two years, with an average of 5,000 units sold per year, generating $1 million in annual revenue, and a profit margin of 10%. Our analysis suggests that we may need to adjust our marketing or product development strategies to improve its performance. Product E has shown the lowest sales and profitability among the five products, with an average of 2,000 units sold per year, generating $400,000 in annual revenue, and a profit margin of 5%. Further investigation and potential changes to our product offering or marketing approach are necessary to improve the performance of Product E. Overall, our sales performance analysis suggests that we should focus on maintaining the profitability of our top-selling products while exploring ways to improve the performance of our less successful products.
    >
    > Compare the performance of each product and determine which one is the most profitable.

    Generate   ↩   ○   **Tokens:** 329 ⓘ

Figure 9.7 – Sample GPT prompt for NLQ

Figure 9.8 illustrates the chain of thoughts by GPT to answer the query shown in *Figure 9.7*:

Based on the data provided, the most profitable product is Product B, which has a consistent profit margin of 20% and generates $1.5 million in annual revenue. Product A, which consistently sells the most units, has a profit margin of 15%, generating $2 million in annual revenue. Product D has a profit margin of 10%, generating $1 million in annual revenue. Product E has a profit margin of 5%, generating $400,000 in annual revenue. Product C has not been assigned a profit margin in the data provided. However, its consistent sales performance suggests that it is likely profitable. Therefore, Product B is the most profitable product based on the data provided.

Figure 9.8 – Sample GPT completion

- Accelerating your data innovation and value creation with data synthesis and augmentation using natural language generation:

  - Another possibility of using GPT models is to synthesize or augment your data with new or additional information or features that can increase their diversity or quality.

  - For example, you can use GPT models to generate synthetic data that mimic the characteristics or patterns of your real data but without revealing any sensitive or confidential information. You can also use GPT models to augment your existing data with new variables or values that can improve its completeness or richness. In *Figure 9.9*, we have informed GPT of sample product names to seek ideas for a new product.

Generate product name ideas for a yet to be launched wearable health device that will allow users to monitor their health and wellness in real-time using AI and share their health metrics with their friends and family. The generated product name ideas should reflect the product's key features, have an international appeal, and evoke positive emotions.

Seed words: fast, healthy, compact

Example product names:
1. WellnessVibe
2. HealthFlux
3. VitalTracker

Figure 9.9 – Sample GPT prompt

- *Figure 9.10* demonstrates that GPT can learn and mimic the examples to give more options for this scenario:

Product names:
1. HealthPal
2. FitVista
3. VitalEase
4. SwiftHealth
5. ThriveLink
6. HealthSnap
7. FastWell
8. HealthSense
9. QuickCare
10. HealthTune

Figure 9.10 – Sample GPT completion

You may also refer to this online resource for more details: `https://www.mercity.ai/blog-post/using-chatgpt-to-build-synthetic-datasets#how-to-generate-synthetic-data-with-chatgpt`.

Here are more-depth tutorials and examples that you can refer to to craft effective GPT prompts:

`https://github.com/f/awesome-chatgpt-prompts`

`https://github.com/dair-ai/Prompt-Engineering-Guide`

While the integration of AI and GPT in data governance offers immense potential, it does not come without its share of challenges and limitations. In the following section, we will delve into these obstacles and explore how they can be addressed to harness the power of these groundbreaking technologies fully.

Understanding the challenges and limitations

While AI and GPT possess the transformative power to automate and streamline data governance processes, they are not the silver bullet that can instantly resolve all data-related issues. While promising, incorporating AI into data governance presents its own set of challenges and limitations. The primary obstacle lies in the sheer volume and complexity of enterprise data. There are some considerations when you deploy the AI solutions for data governance:

- Fueling the right AI with the right data for data governance in a real-time manner: AI and GPT models require large amounts of high-quality data to learn from and generate outputs. However, the data are often scattered, siloed, incomplete, inconsistent, or outdated in many organizations. Data governance itself is a complex and dynamic process that involves multiple stakeholders, roles, processes, communications, metrics, and tools. There is a question mark to ensure that the right AI models are fed with the right data at the right time to support data governance tasks.

- For instance, consider a global financial organization that has data distributed across various departments, each housing its separate databases. When the organization attempts to implement AI for data governance, it may face the challenge of scattered and inconsistent data. The AI model might receive inaccurate information from an outdated database, leading to wrong predictions or inefficient data management.

- To address this, the organization needs to adopt a robust data governance framework that ensures data quality, integrity, and accuracy. This is where a data steward comes into play. Data stewards can help ensure the AI model is fed with the right, high-quality data. They can facilitate this by implementing stringent data quality checks, data validation, and standardization processes to prevent inconsistencies and errors. The steward can also implement a system to update the data in real time or at regular intervals to avoid the use of outdated information. Moreover, the data steward can work closely with the AI team to understand the specific data requirements of the AI model and ensure these requirements are met. They can also serve as the bridge between different stakeholders, ensuring clear communication and alignment in terms of data needs and usage.

• Ensuring the accuracy, reliability, and ethics of the generated texts and data: AI is not infallible. AI can make mistakes, errors, or biases in their outputs. It can also generate texts or data that are misleading, inappropriate, or harmful to individuals, organizations, or society. Therefore, it is challenging to ensure that the texts and data generated are accurate, reliable, and ethical and that they comply with the relevant rules, regulations, standards, and best practices.

- Picture a news agency that employs AI for automated journalism, using it to generate news reports from raw data. If the AI model is not well-trained, it could produce misleading or biased reports, which might lead to misinformation.

- To tackle such scenarios, the organization needs to embrace a responsible AI framework (details in next section) that reinforces the transparency, accountability, and ethics of the AI models used. Adopting a robust AI governance framework that includes regular audits, checks, and balances is essential. A data steward can play an instrumental role in this scenario. As the custodian of data, the steward can ensure that the AI model is trained on high-quality, unbiased, and representative data. They can implement data quality checks and validation processes to ensure the accuracy and reliability of the data fed into the AI model. In terms of the AI outputs, the data steward could implement a system of checks and balances. This might involve setting up a review process for AI-generated content, using human oversight to catch any inaccuracies or biases that the AI might have missed.

- Balancing the trade-offs between human oversight and machine autonomy: AI and GPT models can automate many data governance tasks that are tedious, repetitive, or complex for humans. However, they cannot replace human judgment, creativity, or intuition. Thus, it is challenging to balance the trade-offs between human oversight and machine autonomy in data governance. Too much human oversight can limit the potential of AI and GPT models to improve efficiency, accuracy, consistency, transparency, compliance, innovation, and value for data. On the other hand, too much machine autonomy can increase the risks of errors, biases, or harm from AI and GPT models.

    - Consider a large retail chain that uses AI to automate its inventory management. The AI model predicts future inventory needs based on past sales data, helping the business maintain an optimal stock level and minimize losses due to overstocking or understocking. However, if the model is entirely autonomous, it might fail to consider certain external factors, such as extreme weather conditions, upcoming holidays, local events, or current trends, potentially leading to inaccurate predictions. On the other hand, if the company relies too heavily on human oversight, it could limit the efficiency gains from the AI model. The manual checking of every AI-generated prediction could slow down the inventory management process, reducing the effectiveness of the AI system.

    - To strike a balance, the organization needs a combination of human oversight and machine autonomy. The AI model can handle the bulk of the data analysis, and human experts review and validate the model's predictions, especially in critical or non-standard situations. A data steward plays a vital role in achieving this balance. They can work with the organization to define the level of human oversight required for different tasks. For routine tasks with low risk, the AI model can operate with a high level of autonomy. For complex, high-risk tasks, the steward can ensure more stringent human oversight.

- Adapting the GPT models to your specific data domains and contexts: GPT models are general-purpose models that can generate natural language texts on various topics and tasks. However, they may not be able to capture the nuances, jargon, or terminologies of your specific data domains or contexts. Therefore, it is challenging to adapt the GPT models to your specific data domains or contexts without losing their generality or quality. You may need to fine-tune or customize the GPT models with your own datasets or vocabularies to make them more suitable for your data governance needs.

    - Consider a pharmaceutical company that decides to utilize GPT models for data governance to manage and process a wealth of data from diverse sources such as clinical trials, R&D, and patient records. However, these domains have unique terminologies and context-specific nuances that a general-purpose GPT model might not fully comprehend. For instance, the term "vector" in clinical trials has a different meaning than in mathematics or computing. The GPT model might struggle with such domain-specific language, leading to misunderstandings or inaccuracies. To overcome this challenge, the organization might need to fine-tune the GPT model by using its own datasets. This involves training the model on domain-specific data so that it learns the unique language and nuances of that domain. However, this requires a vast amount of high-quality, labeled data, and the process can be time-consuming and resource-intensive.

- A data steward can play a crucial role in this process. They can work with the AI team to identify the specific data needs of the GPT model and ensure these are met. They can oversee the data collection and labeling process, ensuring that the data used for fine-tuning is of high quality and is representative of the domain.

These challenges and limitations are not insurmountable but require careful consideration and planning when using AI and GPT for data governance. You may need to adopt best practices, such as data quality assurance, data lineage tracking, data access control, data audit and monitoring, human-in-the-loop review, model explainability and interpretability, model fairness and accountability, model security and privacy protection, model fine-tuning or customization, and more, to overcome these challenges and limitations.

As we navigate the challenges and limitations of AI and GPT in data governance, it becomes clear that a structured approach is necessary. This leads us to the next critical piece of the puzzle: embracing a responsible AI framework.

Embracing a responsible AI framework

A **responsible AI framework** is crucial for ensuring that AI systems are not only effective but also ethical, fair, and transparent. It is about making sure that as we harness the power of AI, we do so in a way that respects human values and societal norms. The Microsoft responsible AI framework (`https://www.microsoft.com/en-us/ai/responsible-ai`) is a set of guidelines and best practices for building and using AI systems in a way that respects human values and ethics. It is based on six principles: fairness, reliability and safety, privacy and security, inclusiveness, transparency, and accountability, as shown in *Figure 9.11*:

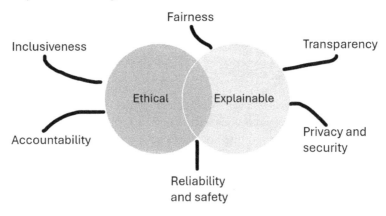

Figure 9.11 – Responsible AI framework

The framework can help ensure the effective use of AI for data governance by considering the following:

- **Fairness**: Ensuring that the AI systems do not create or reinforce unfair biases or outcomes for different groups of people or data subjects. For instance, a hiring AI tool could unintentionally discriminate against certain demographics if it is trained on biased data. A data steward can prevent this by ensuring the AI model is trained on diverse and representative data and by regularly auditing the model's decisions for signs of bias.

- **Reliability and safety**: Ensuring that the AI systems perform consistently and reliably and that they can handle errors, failures, or adversarial attacks without causing harm or damage. Imagine a self-driving car AI system; if it's not reliable, it could lead to accidents. A data steward can ensure reliability by implementing stringent data quality checks, validating the AI's actions, and ensuring the model is trained to handle different scenarios safely.

- **Privacy and security**: Ensuring that the AI systems protect the data and the identities of the data subjects and that they comply with the relevant data protection laws and regulations. For example, a healthcare AI system must protect patient data in compliance with regulations like HIPAA. A data steward plays a critical role in this by implementing robust data protection measures, monitoring data access, and ensuring compliance with data protection laws.

- **Inclusiveness**: Ensuring that the AI systems are accessible and usable by diverse groups of people or data subjects and that they reflect their needs, preferences, values, and cultures. For instance, a voice recognition AI might struggle to understand accents if it is not trained on diverse voice data. A data steward can ensure inclusivity by making sure the data used for training are representative of the diverse user base, ensuring the AI system works effectively for all users.

- **Transparency**: Transparency in AI refers to the openness about the purpose, functionality, and operation of AI systems. An explainable AI system can clearly communicate how it arrived at a specific conclusion or decision. This is crucial, as it allows data subjects and stakeholders to understand and trust the system's outcomes. Take, for example, a credit-scoring AI system. It's not enough for it to provide a credit score; it should also explain how it arrived at that score. This explanation could include the various factors considered, such as credit history, income level, and existing debts and their respective weightage. It could also explain any biases in the system and how they're being addressed. A data steward plays a critical role here. They work closely with the AI team to ensure that the explanations provided by the AI system are clear and comprehensive. They ensure that the AI's decision-making processes are understandable to non-technical users. This involves creating a balance between technical accuracy and simplicity in explanations, which is a key responsibility of a data steward in enhancing AI transparency.

- **Accountability**: Ensuring that the AI systems are subject to appropriate oversight, governance, audit, and feedback mechanisms and that they can be challenged or corrected if they violate any of the other principles. For instance, if a predictive policing AI system wrongfully targets a certain demographic, there should be mechanisms to hold it accountable. A data steward can ensure accountability by setting up governance mechanisms that allow for the auditing, challenging, and correction of AI systems when they violate fairness, reliability, privacy, inclusiveness, or transparency principles.

By following these principles, Microsoft's responsible AI framework can help build trust, confidence, and value for the data subjects and other stakeholders who interact with the AI systems for data governance. It can also help mitigate the risks and challenges of using AI for data governance, such as malicious or unethical use, data quality issues, human-machine trade-offs, or domain adaptation issues.

Best practices for responsible AI in data governance

Let's review some of the best practices that can help operationalize responsible AI for data governance:

- Involve people with diverse skill sets and perspectives in the AI lifecycle, such as product owners, model developers, model validators, and model deployment engineers. The team can help define the business objectives, data requirements, model specifications, validation criteria, deployment strategies, and monitoring mechanisms for the AI and GPT models.

- A real-life example could be a large retail chain implementing AI to forecast inventory needs. Product owners provide insights on what objectives the AI model should aim for, such as reducing overstocking costs. Model developers build the AI model using these objectives and data requirements provided by data stewards. Model validators ensure the model is accurate and reliable before it's deployed by engineers. Each role brings unique perspectives and skills that contribute to the successful implementation of the AI model.

- Use the appropriate methods and parameters for the GPT models, such as choosing the right engine, setting the right temperature, frequency penalty, presence penalty, stop sequence, logprobs, and best of parameters. These parameters can help control the quality, diversity, coherence, relevance, and length of the generated texts. You may refer to the online resource here for details: `https://learn.microsoft.com/en-us/azure/ai-services/openai/reference`.

- A real-world example is a news organization using GPT models to generate news reports. The team could adjust the temperature parameter to control the randomness of the generated text. A lower temperature could result in more focused and consistent texts, while a higher temperature could lead to more diverse and creative texts. Adjusting the frequency penalty could help avoid the overuse of certain phrases or words. By fine-tuning these parameters, the organization can ensure the quality and relevance of the AI-generated news reports. Let's take the following example in *Figure 9.12*, which shows the background and question:

> Write a product launch email for new AI-powered
> headphones that are priced at $79.99 and available at
> GoBuyStore. The target audience is tech-savvy music
> lovers and the tone is friendly and exciting.

Figure 9.12 – Sample GPT prompt

Figure 9.13 illustrates the AI-generated content with a parameter temperature set to 1:

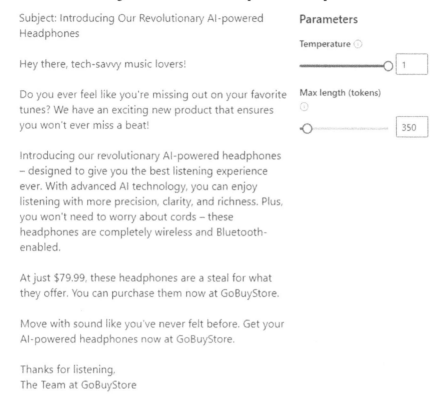

Figure 9.13 – Sample GPT completion; temperature = 1

- Increasing the temperature will result in more unexpected or creative responses. *Figure 9.14* is the outcome when using 0 temperature. Lowering the temperature means that the model will produce more repetitive and deterministic responses:

Dear Tech-Savvy Music Lovers,

We are thrilled to announce the launch of our revolutionary AI-powered headphones!

These headphones are designed to provide you with the ultimate listening experience. Our AI-powered technology automatically adjusts the sound to match your preferences and environment, so you can enjoy your music the way it was meant to be heard.

Plus, they are incredibly affordable at just $79.99. You can find them exclusively at GoBuyStore.

We know you'll love the sound quality and convenience of our AI-powered headphones. So don't wait – get yours today and experience the future of music listening!

Sincerely,

The GoBuyStore Team

Parameters

Temperature ⓘ

0

Max length (tokens) ⓘ

350

Figure 9.14 – Sample GPT completion; temperature = 0

Ensure data quality, compliance, and security at scale by using advanced data technologies such as AI and ML. They can help automate data cleansing, standardization, enrichment, validation, classification, anonymization, encryption, and more. For instance, a healthcare organization handling sensitive patient data could use AI and ML technologies to ensure data quality and security. They could use AI to automate data cleansing and standardization, ensuring the data fed into their AI models is accurate and reliable. Machine learning algorithms could be used for data classification and anonymization, ensuring sensitive patient data are adequately protected. These technologies can help the organization manage and govern its data effectively, even as the volume of data grows.

Operationalizing a responsible AI Framework

To operationalize the principles of a responsible AI framework within data governance structures, organizations can adopt the following actionable steps:

1. **Policy development and training**:

   - Create robust policies that encapsulate the core tenets of responsible AI—fairness, reliability, privacy, inclusiveness, transparency, and accountability. These policies will serve as a blueprint for AI system deployment and operation.

- Educate and raise awareness among data stewards and relevant personnel through consistent training. This will ensure that all stakeholders are knowledgeable about the ethical aspects of AI and the organization's dedication to upholding responsible AI standards.

2. **Oversight and transparency**:

- Establish mechanisms for continuous oversight, including regular audits and evaluations, to ensure that AI systems comply with the responsible AI framework and maintain adherence to ethical guidelines.

- Promote transparency by thoroughly documenting AI methodologies and outcomes. This practice should enable stakeholders to understand AI systems' functionality, data utilization, and decision-making processes.

3. **Feedback and collaborative governance**:

- Implement feedback channels that allow stakeholders to voice concerns and propose enhancements related to AI applications, fostering a culture of accountability and ongoing refinement.

- Facilitate cross-functional collaboration by bringing together data stewards, data scientists, legal experts, and ethicists. This diverse team will tackle complex ethical issues and provide comprehensive guidance on responsible AI deployment.

4. **AI impact assessment**:

- Last but not least, you are recommended to regularly conduct a responsible AI impact assessment so that you have a better understanding of the impact that AI systems may have on people, organizations, and society. Here is a list of recommended resources that you can use to carry out responsible AI impact research:

  - Responsible AI impact assessment template: `https://blogs.microsoft.com/wp-content/uploads/prod/sites/5/2022/06/Microsoft-RAI-Impact-Assessment-Template.pdf`

  - Responsible AI impact assessment guide: `https://blogs.microsoft.com/wp-content/uploads/prod/sites/5/2022/06/Microsoft-RAI-Impact-Assessment-Guide.pdf`

Remember, your AI is only as good as your data.

Now, let's take a sneak peek at the future.

Future of AI for data governance

In the digital age, AI is set to revolutionize data governance. As data-driven decision-making grows, AI's role in managing, protecting, and leveraging data becomes crucial. AI can automate tasks and predict trends, bringing unprecedented efficiency to data governance.

As we look to the future, the impact of AI on data governance is only set to grow.

Here are the trends:

- The use of AI and machine learning will revolutionize data quality measurement, data discovery, classification, and lineage. This not only enhances data governance but also allows data stewards to focus on strategic tasks.
- With the increasing volume and variety of data, AI can boost efficiency, accuracy, and scalability, making data governance more manageable.
- AI's ability to detect anomalies and inconsistencies will significantly improve data quality.
- Sophisticated AI models can predict future trends from historical data, empowering organizations to make proactive decisions.
- Integrating OCR, speech-to-text, and IoT technologies will simplify data governance tasks, allowing data stewards to command AI via instant or voice messages.

In terms of regulation, initiatives such as the global partnership on AI aim to promote responsible and human-centric AI, potentially leading to a more principled use of AI. This initiative will introduce recommendations, standards, and best practices for AI governance:

- More countries are updating their laws to address the privacy, security, ethical, and social implications of AI.
- Stakeholders, including practitioners, privacy advocates, and government regulators, are working together to understand AI's potential, risks, and challenges.

However, the use of AI in data governance also comes with risks. AI models are only as good as the data they are trained on, so any biases or errors in the training data can lead to unfair or inaccurate outcomes. The use of AI can also raise privacy and security concerns, as AI models often require access to large amounts of sensitive data. The complexity and opacity of some AI models can also make it difficult for organizations to understand and explain how these models make decisions, leading to a lack of transparency and accountability.

To stay ahead of the curve, data stewards need to upskill themselves in several areas:

- Understand AI and machine learning basics: how it works and the benefits, limitations, and applications of data governance
- Learn about AI ethics and regulations for responsible, lawful AI use

- Develop data science skills for collaboration with data scientists on AI model creation and tuning, including data preprocessing, feature engineering, and model training

- Improve communication and leadership skills to articulate AI benefits and risks, advocate responsible AI practices, and lead AI strategy

These skills will help navigate AI's opportunities and risks in data governance, unlocking the value of data.

Summary

AI and GPT models can supercharge your data governance and stewardship program by enhancing your meta-data documentation and data quality with automated text generation and natural language understanding.

By leveraging the capabilities of AI and GPT for your data governance tasks, you can achieve greater efficiency, compliance, and value for your data. However, there are challenges and limitations to using AI and GPT models for data governance, such as ensuring the accuracy of the generated texts and adapting the GPT models to your specific data domains. Ensuring responsible AI practices through fairness, reliability, safety, privacy, security, inclusiveness, transparency, and accountability is a crucial aspect of harnessing AI's full potential. Data stewards play a pivotal role in this journey by implementing these principles at every step of the journey.

The future of data governance is being shaped by the advances in AI, offering exciting opportunities for automation, prediction, and efficient data management. The rise in global AI regulation and best practices is set to guide organizations in their AI adoption, addressing privacy, security, and ethical concerns. Welcome to the new era of data governance and AI! In the meantime, data stewards must continually upskill and adapt to manage these AI technologies effectively.

As we transition into the next chapter, we shift our focus toward the best practices in data stewardship.

Part 3: What Makes Data Stewardship a Sustainable Success?

In *Chapters 10* through *12*, you will be equipped with the best practices in data stewardship, navigate the practical challenges that differentiate theory from real-world application, and learn from compelling case studies. These sections are critical for understanding how to create a culture of accountability, align team mindsets for success, and apply continuous improvement to data governance efforts. Real-life examples provide a rich context for the strategies discussed, showcasing their effectiveness in diverse organizational environments.

This part has the following chapters:

- *Chapter 10, Data Stewardship Best Practices*
- *Chapter 11, Theory versus Real Life*
- *Chapter 12, Case Studies*

10

Data Stewardship Best Practices

This chapter will provide you with the best practices for data stewardship. It will explain how to align the mindset and upskill the team to ensure successful data stewardship. Also, it will provide guidance on creating a culture of accountability and ownership. This information will be useful to you as it will help you understand the importance of data stewardship and how to ensure a sustainable implementation.

By following these best practices, you will be able to create an effective data stewardship program that meets your organizational needs.

Let's cast a spotlight on the following topics for the best practices of data stewardship:

- Rolling out a people-first operational model
- Executing day-to-day data processes
- Fast-tracking your data journey with technology
- Valuing and protecting data as an asset

Rolling out a people-first operational model

Data stewardship is fundamentally a *people-first* operation, necessitating an operational model that prioritizes human engagement and involvement. This model recognizes that while data and technology are integral components of an organization, it is the people who interpret, manage, and utilize this data that truly drive the enterprise's success. As we delve into the era of data-driven decision-making, the role of data stewards has become critical to ensuring that data usage aligns with organizational strategies and legal and ethical requirements. A data steward acts as a bridge between technical and non-technical stakeholders, facilitating communication and understanding. For instance, in a healthcare setting, data stewards ensure that sensitive patient information is appropriately managed and used, safeguarding the trust of the individuals while enabling data-driven medical advancements.

A people-first approach prioritizes the people element over processes and technology. It is about recognizing that people – the data stewards, users, and beneficiaries of data – are the core drivers of value. The rationale behind this emphasis is simple: data, in and of itself, is inert. It is the application of data by skilled individuals that transforms it into an invaluable asset.

Market trends increasingly indicate a shift toward this people-centric model. Organizations are realizing that technology alone cannot solve all data-related challenges. There is a growing acknowledgment that the people component – with its creativity, adaptability, and insight – is irreplaceable. Companies that have recognized this are already experiencing benefits, such as improved compliance with data regulations, enhanced decision-making capabilities, and a more robust data culture.

A successful rollout of data stewardship hinges on a people-first approach, which emphasizes the value and capabilities of the individuals within the organization. Understanding and adopting a mindset that combines starting small with keeping the bigger picture in mind is pivotal for a smooth and effective rollout of data stewardship.

To foster this mindset, consider the following strategies:

- **Define the broader vision**: Begin by clearly articulating the overarching vision for data stewardship within your organization. This vision should encapsulate the long-term goals and the anticipated impact on business strategy, operational efficiency, and competitive edge. It sets the stage for all stakeholders to understand the ultimate objectives of the program.

- **Start with achievable objectives**: Within this broader vision, identify smaller, achievable objectives that can be tackled in the short term. These should be steps that are manageable and can demonstrate value quickly. By securing early wins, you build momentum and create a sense of progress, which is essential for gaining and maintaining stakeholder support.

- **Engage and empower your people**: Recognize that the success of data stewardship is driven by the people involved. Engage with employees at all levels to understand their needs, challenges, and perspectives. Empower them with the right tools, training, and authority to make decisions that align with the data stewardship vision. Encourage a culture of ownership where each person feels responsible for the data's accuracy, privacy, and strategic use.

- **Iterate and expand**: Use the feedback and results from these initial objectives to refine and enhance your approach. As you achieve quick wins and build credibility, gradually expand the scope of your data stewardship program. This iterative process allows you to continuously align your efforts with the bigger picture, adapting to new insights and shifting business needs.

- **Celebrate successes and learn from setbacks**: Regularly recognize and celebrate the successes of your team, no matter how small. This reinforces the value of their contributions and fosters a positive culture around data stewardship. Similarly, view any setbacks as learning opportunities to improve and strengthen your program.

Adopting a people-first strategy can also become your organization's competitive edge. Consider the example of a leading financial services company that was grappling with data quality issues. They implemented a people-first approach by establishing a data stewardship program that prioritized training, empowering, and incentivizing their employees. This initiative led to a significant improvement in data quality, with the added benefit of heightened employee engagement. The company not only solved its immediate data challenges but also cultivated a workforce that was more invested in the company's data-driven success. You may refer to `https://one.oecd.org/document/DSTI/CDEP(2022)6/FINAL/en/pdf` for more findings around the potentials and challenges of data stewardship.

Aligning data mindset and continuous learning

Aligning the mindset of your organization's employees with the principles of data governance and stewardship is important to ensure that everyone in the organization understands the importance of data and how it can be used to drive business value.

Without the alignment of data mindset, different teams may have different expectations and understanding of data stewardship and data value, which can lead to confusion, inefficiencies, and even risk. Aligning the data mindset involves creating a shared understanding of the importance of data and how it can be used to drive business value. This can be achieved by providing regular training sessions, workshops, and seminars on data governance and stewardship. For example, you could provide training on how to classify data elements, how to tag them appropriately for proper contextual usage, and how to identify how data is used.

It is also important to ensure that everyone in the organization understands their role in managing data and is held accountable for the quality of the data they manage. This can be achieved by establishing clear roles and responsibilities for data management, providing regular feedback on data quality, and incentivizing employees to take ownership of their data.

How do data stewards fit in the picture?

Data stewards serve as educators and advocates, promoting a culture where data is valued as a critical business asset. To solidify the data mindset, data stewards should engage with various teams to communicate the vision and importance of data management. They can facilitate workshops and training sessions to educate employees on best practices, data classification, and the impact of data quality on the organization's success. By doing so, they help create a shared language and understanding of data value across departments.

Here are some **key performance indicators (KPIs)** that you can use to track the maturity of the data-driven culture for your organization:

- **Decision impact analysis score**: This KPI evaluates the outcomes of decisions made based on data analysis. By measuring the success rate or impact of these decisions, organizations can assess how effectively data is being utilized to drive business strategies. This score can be derived from a combination of factors, including the achievement of decision objectives, performance against targets, and the overall **return on investment** (**ROI**) from data-informed decisions. For example, for each decision, evaluate the following:

  I.   **Objective achievement**: Determine whether and to what extent the decision met its intended objectives, using an appropriate scale (binary, ordinal, or percentage-based).

  II.   **Target performance**: Assess how the decision's outcome aligns with predefined targets or benchmarks, quantifying the result as a percentage of the target met.

  III. **ROI of decisions**: Calculate the ROI by comparing the benefits gained from the decision to the costs incurred for data analysis, and represent this as a percentage.

  To use this KPI, compare the score over time to track the effectiveness of data-driven decisions. If the score increases, it indicates that data analysis is contributing positively to decision-making. If the score decreases, it suggests that the process of data analysis or the application of its results in decision-making needs to be improved. This KPI can also be used to identify and learn from the most and least successful data-informed decisions.

- **Training participation rate**: Measure the percentage of employees who have completed data governance and stewardship training to ensure wide-reaching knowledge dissemination. You can follow these steps to compute this KPI.

  I.   Identify the total number of employees who are required to complete the data governance and stewardship training.

  II.   Track the number of employees who have actually completed the training. You can even include the knowledge check quiz in the training.

  III. Divide the completions by the required participants and multiply by 100 to determine the participation rate percentage.

  To use this KPI, monitor the training participation rate regularly to assess the effectiveness of your training program. A high rate indicates that most employees are completing the training, which suggests that the program is accessible and engaging. A low rate, on the other hand, may indicate that employees are not finding the training useful or are facing challenges in completing it. In this case, you may need to revise the training content, delivery method, or schedule. This KPI can also be used to identify departments or groups with low participation rates, which can be targeted with specific interventions to improve their training completion rates.

- **Policy adherence rate**: Calculate the rate at which employees adhere to data policies and procedures, which reflects the level of alignment with the data governance framework.

To compute this KPI, you can follow these steps:

I.   Identify the total number of instances where data policies and procedures should be applied. This could be based on the number of data-related tasks performed, the number of datasets handled, or any other suitable metric.

II.   Track the number of instances where the data policies and procedures were correctly followed.

III. Divide the adherent instances by the total opportunities and multiply by 100 for the adherence rate percentage.

To use this KPI, monitor the policy adherence rate regularly to assess the effectiveness of your data policies and procedures. A high rate indicates that employees understand and are following the data governance framework, while a low rate suggests that there may be issues with policy communication, comprehension, or enforcement. This KPI can also help identify areas or groups with low adherence rates, indicating where targeted training or reinforcement of policies may be needed. Furthermore, tracking this KPI over time can provide insights into the impact of any changes made to data policies and procedures.

- **Data insights utilization and penetration rate**: This not only measures the frequency and effectiveness of data usage in decision-making processes but also tracks the penetration of these data insights across different levels and functions of the organization.

Here is how you can compute this KPI:

I.   Identify various decision-making instances across the organization, from strategic planning to operational processes and tactical decisions.

II.   Determine the frequency and effectiveness of data insights used, applying a binary or rating scale.

III. Compute the utilization rate by comparing effective use instances with total decision-making instances, expressed as a percentage.

IV.   Similarly, calculate the penetration rate by dividing the number of organizational levels or functions using data insights by the total number of levels or functions. Multiply by 100 to get a percentage.

V.   Average the utilization and penetration rates to derive the data insights utilization and penetration rate.

To use this KPI, monitor it regularly to assess how deeply and effectively data-driven decision-making has been ingrained in the organization. A higher rate indicates a strong data culture and effective data governance, while a lower rate may highlight areas where further training, better data accessibility, or improved data governance practices are needed. This KPI also helps in identifying departments or levels where data usage is low and needs to be improved.

By aligning the data mindset across different teams in the organization, you can ensure that everyone is working toward a common goal of creating an effective data stewardship program that meets your organizational needs. This will help you create a sustainable implementation with measurable business value.

Now, let's turn our focus to another crucial aspect – creating a culture of accountability and ownership. This is the bedrock on which an effective data stewardship program is built.

Creating a culture of accountability and ownership

Creating a culture of accountability and ownership around data is important to ensure that everyone in the organization understands their role in managing data and is held accountable for the quality of the data they manage. This can be achieved by establishing clear roles and responsibilities for data management, providing regular feedback on data quality, and incentivizing employees to take ownership of their data. For example, you could establish a data stewardship program that empowers employees to take ownership of their data by providing them with the tools and resources they need to manage it effectively.

In enterprises with complex hierarchies and reporting structures, there are several challenges that can arise when implementing data governance and stewardship programs. Here are some of the most common challenges and how to address them:

- **Limited resources**: One of the biggest challenges in implementing data governance and stewardship programs in complex organizations is the lack of resources, including budget and manpower, to maintain an ongoing program. To address this challenge, it is important to allocate resources for data governance and stewardship programs each year or quarter. You can also harness automation in your business processes to lighten the load on employees and get maximal value out of the data you collect.

- **Siloed data**: In complex organizations, data often ends up being compartmentalized or segregated, making it challenging to obtain a holistic and accurate view of business operations. To overcome this issue, it is crucial to dismantle these data silos to promote data accessibility, sharing, and collaboration across various teams within the organization. This process requires the implementation of a strategic data governance program that facilitates communication, coordination, and the linking of data for cross-silo insights.

- **Discrepancies in business terminology, master data, and hierarchies**: Data that lacks clear business definitions and rules is prone to misinterpretation and confusion. Utilizing data, such as merging or amalgamating datasets from various sources, demands a deeper understanding of the data beyond its physical formats. Integrating data assets from multiple repositories for enhanced data analytics and insights necessitates uniformity. This involves aligning with consistent master data, reference data, data lineage, and hierarchies. The construction and preservation of these structures demand the policies and coordination brought forth by effective data governance.

- **Data privacy and security**: The management of the growing volume, utilization, and complexity of new data presents significant data privacy and security challenges. With the increase in digital collection and storage of personal or sensitive data, the risks of data violations and cyber threats escalate. To tackle these issues and practice conscientious data stewardship, organizations must invest in solutions that safeguard their data against unauthorized access and breaches.

Data is a people problem at its core and we need a people solution. Putting yourself into other's shoes is the key to practical data stewardship.

After a deep dive into fostering a culture of accountability and ownership, we now turn our attention to the practicalities of day-to-day operations that ensure the sustained success of data stewardship within an organization.

Executing day-to-day data processes

In the ever-evolving landscape of data management, executing day-to-day data processes is akin to navigating a complex and dynamic ecosystem. At the heart of this ecosystem is change management, a critical component that ensures data processes are adaptable and responsive to the shifting demands of business and technology. Embracing change management is not only about implementing new systems or protocols but also about cultivating a mindset that is ready to accommodate and leverage change for better data outcomes. Simultaneously, handling data process modifications with agility and precision is paramount. It involves a keen understanding of the nuances of existing procedures and the foresight to anticipate the impact of changes.

Here are some of the best practices for change management in the data process:

- **Impact analysis**: Before making any changes, perform a thorough impact analysis to understand the repercussions across various facets of the data ecosystem.

- **Incremental implementation**: Roll out changes in manageable phases rather than all at once. This allows for smoother transitions and the ability to address issues as they arise without overwhelming the system.

- **Version control**: Use version control for data processes to track changes over time. This allows for the rollback of modifications if needed and helps in auditing processes.

- **Testing**: Rigorous testing of process modifications should be carried out in controlled environments before deployment to minimize disruptions to operational systems.

- **Change authorization**: Implement a formal process for change authorization to ensure that only approved and vetted modifications are put into effect.

- **Business continuity planning**: Have contingency plans in place to ensure that critical data processes can continue or be quickly restored in the event of any disruption caused by modifications.

Last but not least, stakeholder engagement and clear communication are the cornerstones of change management.

Who does what, by when, and approved by whom?

Data lifecycle management (**DLM**) is a policy-based approach of best practices to oversee the flow of an information system's data through its lifecycle, from creation to deletion. It includes stages such as storage, backup, archiving, and disposal, and is employed by organizations that manage sensitive, private data subject to regulatory compliance.

The **Who does what, by when, and approved by whom?** principle is a key aspect of DLM.

Yes, I invented this wordy phrase after several rounds of trimming.

This principle outlines the roles and responsibilities of different stakeholders in the DLM process. It specifies who is responsible for performing specific tasks, when those tasks should be performed, and who must approve them.

For example, in the data collection phase of DLM, organizations must establish rules to collect data in standardized formats, create policies for different types of data (e.g., employee, partner, and accounting), and develop policies for personal data according to data privacy regulations. The principle would specify who is responsible for creating these policies, when they should be created, and who must approve them. Similarly, in the data storage and maintenance phase of DLM, organizations must process, merge, aggregate, classify, and select data to ensure its accuracy and completeness.

By following the principle in DLM, organizations can ensure that everyone involved in the DLM process understands their roles and responsibilities. This can help ensure that data is managed effectively throughout its lifecycle.

Having established a robust framework for DLM, identifying roles, timelines, and approval hierarchies, we now transition to the equally critical realm of data mapping and metadata management.

Data mapping and metadata management

This section will focus on the importance of data mapping and metadata management in data stewardship. Let us first understand these concepts and common pitfalls faced by organizations.

Data mapping is the process of creating a visual representation of how data flows through an organization. It involves identifying the sources of data, how it is transformed, and where it is stored. Data mapping is the cornerstone of data lineage. It is essential to understand how data is used and ensure that it is accurate and complete. However, data mapping can be challenging in complex organizations with multiple data sources and systems. We will address some of these challenges shortly. Its importance lies in its ability to create a clear picture of how data moves through an organization, from its source to its ultimate storage destination. It also aids in the identification of data bottlenecks, inefficiencies, and redundancies, thereby allowing for more effective data management and optimization.

Metadata management on the other hand involves managing descriptions or descriptive data about other data. Metadata provides context for data elements, such as their meaning, origin, usage, and format. The management of metadata is essential for ensuring that data is accurate, complete, and accessible. Metadata is a crucial aspect of data as it provides context, making data understandable and usable. Effective metadata management ensures that data is not only accurate and complete but also accessible and understandable. It facilitates data discovery, as well as making the data easier to analyze and interpret. Furthermore, metadata management supports data governance by helping to enforce data policies, standards, and procedures. It aids in maintaining data quality and consistency, fostering trust in the data and enabling its effective use across the organization.

Let's take a look into some common challenges associated with data mapping and metadata management:

- **Lack of standardization**: Inconsistent or incomplete metadata can make it difficult to understand how data is used and where it comes from

- **Data quality issues**: Poor quality data can lead to inaccurate or incomplete metadata, which can make it difficult to use the data effectively

- **Complexity**: In complex organizations with multiple data sources and systems, it can be challenging to create a comprehensive view of how data flows through the organization

Some best practices organizations often to overcome these issues are discussed as follows:

- **Standardize metadata**: Standardizing metadata is essential for ensuring that it is consistent and complete across different systems. This can be achieved by establishing clear standards for metadata, including naming conventions, data types, and data formats. Metadata standards should be designed to meet the specific needs of your organization and should be reviewed and updated regularly to ensure that they remain relevant.

- **Ensure data quality**: Ensuring data quality (including metadata) is critical to effective data stewardship. Data quality measures how well a dataset meets criteria for accuracy, completeness, validity, consistency, uniqueness, timeliness, and fitness for purpose. To ensure data quality, organizations should establish clear rules for data collection, storage, and usage. With the right tooling and technology, metadata maintenance and quality can be automated. They should also implement regular audits to ensure that data quality standards are being met.

- **Simplify data mapping**: Whenever possible, you should also try reengineering and simplifying the business process first. Then, you can create a visual representation of how data flows through an organization and make it accessible to all relevant users.

- **Automate metadata management**: The automation of metadata management can assist in maintaining uniformity and completeness of metadata across various systems. This can be accomplished by utilizing tools and technologies that amplify the organization's understanding of the location and usage of its vital data. Ideally, these instruments should possess the capability to enforce protective measures such as encryption, data masking, and redaction of sensitive documents. They should also automate reporting to simplify audit processes and ensure compliance with regulatory requirements.

- **Data security and privacy**: Ensuring data security and privacy is a crucial part of proficient data stewardship. It's imperative for organizations to establish rules and processes to shield digital data from unauthorized interference, contamination, or theft across its entire lifespan. This encompasses the protection of physical hardware and storage apparatus, as well as the management of access controls. Furthermore, organizations need to utilize tools and technologies that augment their understanding of the location and usage of their critical data.

Let's look at a few examples of how data mapping and metadata management are being applied in practice:

- **Data governance**: Data governance programs often rely on metadata management to ensure that data is accurate, complete, and accessible

- **Data integration**: Data integration projects often involve creating a visual representation of how data flows through an organization to identify areas where improvements can be made

- **Data quality management**: Data quality management programs often rely on metadata management to ensure that data quality issues are identified and remediated quickly

Data risk assessment and mitigation

In the scope of executing day-to-day data processes, the significance of data risk assessment and mitigation is undeniable. It is the proactive armor against potential data breaches, losses, or compliance failures. The aim is to not only identify and assess the risks associated with data management but also to develop and implement strategies that mitigate these risks before they can impact the enterprise. This proactive approach is essential for maintaining the integrity, availability, and confidentiality of data assets.

A best practice in data risk assessment also involves a comprehensive and systematic approach that includes the identification of potential risks, assessment of their likelihood and potential impact, implementation of controls to mitigate identified risks, and ongoing monitoring and review of both the risks and the effectiveness of the controls in place.

To facilitate this process, there are several tools, frameworks, and processes available:

- **Tools**: Data risk management software can help automate and streamline the risk assessment process. Examples include RSA Archer, LogicGate, and RiskLens. These tools can help identify, assess, and track risks, and can also aid in planning and implementing mitigation strategies.

- **Frameworks**: Standardized risk management frameworks such as ISO 31000 (`https://www.iso.org/iso-31000-risk-management.html`) or NIST's Risk Management Framework (`https://csrc.nist.gov/Projects/risk-management/about-rmf`) can provide guidelines for establishing a comprehensive risk management program. These frameworks outline best practices for risk identification, assessment, mitigation, and monitoring.

- **Processes**: Implementing a systematic risk management process can help ensure that all potential risks are identified and assessed and that appropriate controls are put in place. This process should be ongoing and should involve regular reviews and updates to ensure that the risk management plan remains effective and relevant.

For instance, a financial institution might employ data risk assessment by conducting regular audits of its data processes to check for any vulnerabilities that could lead to financial fraud or data theft. By assessing the levels of access to sensitive financial data, the institution can implement stringent access controls and encryption methods to protect against unauthorized access, thereby mitigating the risk of data breaches.

Data stewards ensure that the data risk assessments are conducted regularly and in line with the latest regulatory and technological landscapes. They collaborate with various departments to understand the specific data risks that might affect each area and help in crafting bespoke mitigation strategies. Data stewards raise data risk awareness within the organization, training personnel to recognize and respond to data risks proactively.

In practice, a data steward might oversee the development of a risk register that catalogs identified risks and tracks the status of implemented controls. They might also facilitate risk assessment workshops or simulations to prepare and educate the workforce on potential data risk scenarios. By maintaining an active role in the continuous improvement of data risk management practices, data stewards ensure that the organization's data assets are protected and that the organization can swiftly respond to and recover from any incidents that do occur.

You can refer to this online resource to understand more about data risk management: `https://www2.deloitte.com/content/dam/Deloitte/us/Documents/risk/us-risk-value-based-data-risk-management.pdf`.

The future trend of data risk assessment and mitigation is moving toward an increasingly predictive and integrated approach, powered by advanced technologies and broader risk intelligence. Here are some key developments that are shaping the future of this field:

- **Predictive analytics**: The use of machine learning and AI to predict potential data breaches and vulnerabilities before they occur. This involves analyzing patterns and anomalies that could indicate a risk, allowing organizations to proactively address issues.

- **Automated risk assessments**: Automation tools and software are being developed to streamline the risk assessment process, reducing the time and resources required while increasing consistency and accuracy.

- **Real-time monitoring**: With the growth of IoT and connected devices, real-time monitoring of data and systems is becoming more feasible and necessary, allowing for immediate detection and response to threats.

- **Increased use of blockchain**: Blockchain technology will be leveraged more for its ability to provide secure and immutable records, aiding in data integrity and the reduction of certain types of risks.

After examining the foundational aspects of data risk assessment and mitigation, let's shift our focus toward the accelerating force of technology in our data journey.

Optimizing your data journey with strategic technological integration

In the quest to fast-track your data journey, the intersection of data integration and the seamless interoperability of systems play a crucial role. As the enterprise landscape becomes increasingly complex with a mix of legacy and modern systems, the ability to effectively integrate and facilitate communication between disparate data sources is paramount. **Interoperability**, in the context of data stewardship, refers to the ability of different systems and applications to communicate, exchange, and make use of information. It is a key component in the data journey as it ensures that data flows seamlessly across different platforms, enhancing the value of the data by making it accessible and usable in various contexts.

This section will shed light on the best practices that ensure a cohesive data ecosystem, where the old and the new not only coexist but also complement and enhance each other's capabilities. We will explore strategic approaches to integration that not only bridge the gap between different systems but also prepare the groundwork for future technological advancements, ensuring your data assets remain agile, relevant, and above all, actionable.

Some of the best practices for data integration and interoperability include the following:

- **Use middleware solutions**: Implement middleware to act as a translator between systems, allowing them to communicate without the need for extensive custom coding. For instance, Apache Kafka (`https://kafka.apache.org`) is a popular middleware solution that provides low end-to-end latency with durability.

- **Leverage APIs**: Utilize **application programming interfaces** (**APIs**) to enable different applications to interact with each other, streamlining the process of data sharing and integration. For example, the Google Maps API allows developers to embed Google Maps on web pages using JavaScript.

- **Embrace a microservices architecture**: Adopt a microservices architecture to create a suite of independently deployable, small, modular services that run unique processes and communicate through well-defined APIs. Netflix, for example, uses a microservices architecture to enable its vast and diverse range of services.

- **Conduct thorough assessments**: Regularly evaluate legacy systems to understand their functionality, limitations, and the data they hold. This informs decisions on integration, upgrade, or replacement. For example, a financial institution may assess its old mainframe system to understand how it processes transactions, which can inform decisions on whether to integrate, upgrade, or replace it.

- **Gradual phasing**: When introducing new systems, do it gradually. Run legacy systems in parallel with new systems during a transition period to ensure business continuity. A good example would be a hospital upgrading its patient record system. It would run the old and new systems concurrently until staff are fully trained and any bugs in the new system have been resolved.

- **Continuous modernization**: Implement a continuous modernization strategy, which allows for incremental updates to legacy systems. This limits disruption and spreads out the cost and effort involved in updates over time. For instance, a retail business might gradually update its inventory management system, modernizing one function at a time to limit disruption to operations.

Now, let's pivot our attention to the tools and technologies specifically designed to enhance the efficacy and impact of data stewards in their critical role.

Data stewardship tools and technologies

In the rapidly evolving digital landscape, the arsenal of tools and technologies at the disposal of data stewards is more powerful and essential than ever. To uphold the integrity and maximize the value of an organization's data assets, data stewards must leverage a suite of sophisticated resources.

We will now explore the pivotal technologies that fortify data stewardship practices, including data lineage tools that track the origin and evolution of data, **master data management** (MDM) systems that ensure uniformity, accuracy, and accountability, and data catalog tools that enable the organization and discovery of data across the enterprise. These instruments are not just facilitators of order and compliance; they are the enablers of insights and strategic decision-making that can propel a company to new heights of data maturity and business excellence:

- **Data lineage**: Data lineage is the process of tracking the flow of data from its source to its destination. Data lineage tools, such as Microsoft Purview or Collibra, help organizations understand how data is transformed as it moves through different systems and processes. This information can be used to ensure that data is accurate and trustworthy.

- Here are some best practices:

  - **Prioritize key areas**: Begin with a focused approach by mapping the data lineage for critical management reports and essential business processes, rather than attempting to document the entire organization's data flow all at once

- **Utilize automation**: Take advantage of modern technologies that automatically scan and document data lineage, providing up-to-date insights and freeing data stewards from manual tracking efforts

- **Regular certification**: Implement a routine, such as an annual review, to certify the accuracy and completeness of the data lineage records, ensuring ongoing reliability and compliance

- **Maintain documentation**: Keep thorough and accessible documentation of the data lineage to support transparency and facilitate troubleshooting and impact analysis

- **Master data management**: MDM is the process of creating a single, consistent view of an organization's critical data. It involves identifying the most important data elements, standardizing them, and ensuring that they are accurate after the consolidation from multiple data sources. MDM is essential for ensuring that data is trustworthy and consistent across different systems. We also refer to it as the **single source of truth (SSOT)**. For example, you should only have one master customer dataset for the whole company and all downstream systems should connect to this SSOT for customer information. While you can use an in-house IT team to build the MDM from scratch, you need to review the ROI and time-to-market. Here are some best practices:

  - **Establish an SSOT**: Ensure that there's a unified master dataset for critical entities such as customers, products, or employees, which all systems across the company can reference

  - **Standardize data elements**: Work toward standardizing data definitions, formats, and values to maintain consistency and accuracy after consolidating data from various sources

  - **Leverage third-party solutions**: Consider the use of established third-party MDM software to accelerate deployment and benefit from advanced features without the need for extensive custom development

  - **Focus on business rules**: Concentrate efforts on defining clear, comprehensive business rules within the MDM system to govern data harmonization, quality, and maintenance

We will now move our focus to the data catalog and metadata, which are the other two common building blocks for your data stewardship program. Let's review their practices for future-proof deployment of the data journey.

Data catalog and metadata

When you walk into a restaurant, you ask for the menu so that you know what you can order. You get the names of the dishes, their ingredients, and the prices.

The **data catalog** is the menu of your organization's data assets, while the **metadata** is the information shown on the menu.

You may refer to `https://learn.microsoft.com/en-us/purview/how-to-search-catalog` for examples of a data catalog and metadata.

Metadata management is the process of collecting, storing, and managing metadata. Metadata is information about data that describes its structure, content, quality, and other characteristics. Metadata management tools help organizations create and maintain metadata repositories that can be used to support data governance, data quality, and other data management activities.

A data catalog is a metadata management tool that provides a comprehensive inventory of all data assets in an organization. A data catalog helps users discover, understand, and trust the data they need to make informed decisions. It can also help organizations manage their data assets by providing a centralized location for storing metadata.

Here are some best practices for data catalog and metadata management:

- **Comprehensive inventory**: Ensure that the data catalog provides a complete and accurate representation of the organization's data assets, including datasets from all departments and business units.

- **Standardized metadata**: Develop and enforce standards for metadata creation and maintenance to ensure consistency and quality across the entire data catalog.

- **Accessibility and usability**: Design the data catalog to be user-friendly, ensuring that users can easily navigate and understand the metadata to find the data they need.

- **Integration with data governance**: Align the data catalog and metadata management practices with the overall data governance framework, ensuring that metadata supports data quality, privacy, and compliance standards. For example, when new regulations come into effect, a data steward could use the data catalog to quickly identify which datasets contain sensitive information, such as personal data, and work to ensure that proper controls are in place to meet compliance requirements.

- **Regular updates and maintenance**: Keep the metadata and data catalog current by establishing processes for regular updates, validation, and certification of the cataloged information.

- **Leverage profiling and discovery tools**: Utilize data profiling tools to proactively identify and address data quality issues, such as missing values, and data discovery tools to enhance the efficiency of locating and understanding data. All this information can be used to improve the efficiency of data analysis and decision-making. Through data profiling, a data steward might uncover that certain critical financial reports contain a high percentage of null values. They would then initiate a data quality improvement project to rectify this issue, ensuring that subsequent decision-making is based on complete and reliable data.

Blockchain and AI

Blockchain technology presents a transformative approach to secure and transparent data management. At its core, **blockchain** is a distributed ledger that records transactions across multiple computers in a way that ensures each transaction can be neither altered nor deleted once recorded. This immutable characteristic is highly relevant to data management, particularly in areas such as data provenance, where it is critical to have an unalterable historical record of data creation, modification, and movement.

Blockchain's ability to provide a secure and unchangeable record makes it an ideal technology for enhancing data security and integrity. By using cryptographic hashing and consensus mechanisms, data stewards can create a secure environment where data breaches are significantly less likely and data tampering can be easily detected. As a data steward, you should understand the benefits of blockchain to data stewardship but you do not need to go deep down to the coding level.

One of the possibilities is that we can use blockchain to manage access controls and to log data access and changes, thereby creating a verifiable and secure audit trail that enhances data credibility.

Other than blockchain, we can also use machine learning algorithms to automate the process of data quality management by learning from data patterns and anomalies. These algorithms can cleanse, standardize, and enrich data without human intervention, reducing errors and improving efficiency. They can also continuously learn and adapt to new data patterns, ensuring data quality over time. We can also deploy predictive analytics, which uses statistical algorithms and machine learning techniques to identify the likelihood of future outcomes based on historical data. For data stewards, this can mean predicting how data quality, usage, and relevance might change over time, allowing for more proactive DLM.

The synergy between blockchain and AI can lead to a robust data stewardship framework by ensuring that data not only remains secure but is also of high quality and ready for advanced analytics. Before we end this chapter, let's take a look at how we should value and protect data as a corporate asset.

Valuing and protecting data as an asset

Valuing and protecting data as an asset is a cornerstone in the context of data stewardship. In the digital era, information is not just a by-product of operations, but rather, a vital asset that can drive growth, innovation, and competitive advantage. However, just like any other asset, data needs to be accurately valued and effectively protected to yield its maximum potential. A data steward is key in valuing and safeguarding data as an asset. They validate data quality, manage metadata, enforce data security, and set data governance rules. Consider an e-commerce firm that uses customer data for personalized marketing. If this data is flawed, the campaign could fail, causing lost sales. But with the data steward ensuring data accuracy, it becomes a valuable asset that enhances revenue growth. Similarly, in the health sector, inaccurate patient data can lead to serious medical errors, but with effective stewardship, it can enhance care quality and patient safety. Now, we will explore the best practices in different areas of data valuation and protection:

- **Strategic planning**:

    - *Think with the big picture in mind but start small*: Data governance involves people, processes, and technology. Start with hiring the right people, who can then develop effective processes and incorporate suitable technology, ensuring a successful implementation of data governance.

    - *Pilot for selected user before the full-scale rollout*: This can encourage a progressive transformation and gather user feedback to fine-tune the operating model to be a cultural fit for your organization.

- **Realizing business value via data**:

    - *Define your business goal before onboarding the data*: Always start with your business objective and then work backward to decide what data you need. Try to reuse the existing dataset and dashboard as much as possible.

    - *Build a business case*: Securing leadership support is crucial for data governance success. Build a compelling business case highlighting benefits such as increased revenue, improved customer experience, and enhanced efficiency. This will clarify the effort required and potential rewards.

    - *Define a use case prioritization model*: The prioritization model helps focus on high-impact, low-effort use cases, enabling quick wins to build stakeholder trust before expanding to the next phase. Please refer to *Chapter 3* for details.

- **Day-to-day activities**:

    - *Metrics and more metrics*: Metrics are important to track progress and measure success. Identify KPIs that will help you measure progress toward your goals. These KPIs should be **specific, measurable, achievable, relevant, and time-bound (SMART)**.

    - *Ensure your data and data catalog are accessible to the relevant users*: With **role-based access control (RBAC)**, you can make sure the right group of users has access to the right data and enhance transparency.

    - *Communicate early and often*: Communication is key when it comes to data governance. Make sure everyone involved understands what is expected of them and how they can contribute to success. Communicate early and often to ensure everyone is on the same page.

- **Fostering the data culture**:

    - *Be collaborative*: Data stewards should facilitate user queries about data usage. This can be achieved through educational seminars, maintaining open communication channels, sharing best practices, and providing insights into data applications for everyday decision-making.

- *Account for the fact that data governance is a marathon, not a sprint*: Data governance is a continuous process demanding constant refinement. As a data steward, be ready to adapt and improve processes, such as identifying and rectifying customer record errors, based on your organization's needs.

Realizing short- and long-term business value via data

In the journey of realizing business value from data, it is imperative to understand and communicate the balance between quick wins and delayed benefits. Quick wins serve as immediate proof points that build confidence and support for the data stewardship program, while delayed benefits represent the long-term ROI that ensures ongoing investment and commitment.

Here are some strategies to effectively demonstrate this balance:

- **Identify and showcase quick wins**: Quick wins are tangible successes that can be achieved relatively quickly and with minimal effort. They provide immediate value and serve to demonstrate the efficacy of data stewardship initiatives. Examples might include cleaning a critical dataset that leads to improved customer targeting or resolving a data quality issue that reduces the error rate in reporting.

- **Articulate delayed benefits**: While quick wins are important, it is also critical to articulate the delayed benefits that accrue over time. These are often strategic and may include improved compliance posture, enhanced decision-making capabilities, or increased operational efficiencies. Delayed benefits can be projected through ROI models that estimate the financial impact of data stewardship over a longer horizon.

- **Develop a balanced scorecard**: Create a scorecard that captures both quick wins and delayed benefits. This scorecard should include KPIs linked to business outcomes, demonstrating the immediate impact of quick wins alongside the projected growth or savings from delayed benefits.

- **Communicate value effectively**: Regularly communicate the successes of quick wins and the progress toward achieving delayed benefits to stakeholders. Use stories and case studies to make the benefits more relatable and concrete. This communication should emphasize how the quick wins are building blocks toward the larger strategic goals, reinforcing the value of continued investment in data stewardship.

- **Monitor and adjust**: Continuously monitor the progress of both quick wins and delayed benefits, and be prepared to adjust strategies as needed. This adaptability ensures that the data stewardship program remains aligned with business objectives and can respond to changing market conditions or internal priorities.

By addressing quick wins and delayed benefits, data stewards can provide a comprehensive view of the value generated by their efforts. This approach helps to maintain momentum and support for data stewardship initiatives by clearly illustrating how they contribute to the organization's success, both now and in the future.

Summary

This chapter provides best practices for data stewardship, including how to align the mindset of employees, create a culture of accountability and ownership, and use tools and technologies to support data stewardship. It discusses the importance of data mapping and metadata management, as well as challenges and best practices for addressing them.

Data stewards should take responsibility for ensuring that data is managed and used as per both internal and external rules. They must take into account industry guidelines as well as federal and even international regulations when overseeing how data is used and should raise an alarm if they identify an issue. Data stewards should also evangelize safe – and creative – uses of data, maintain a positive attitude as the ambassadors of the data group's governance function, and inspire users to see data as a valued and strategic enterprise asset capable of driving business competitiveness.

Lastly, let's not forget the importance of fostering a data culture and realizing business value from data.

In the next chapter, we will examine the discrepancy that often exists between theoretical concepts and real-world scenarios. So, fasten your seat belt as we embark on this journey from the classrooms of data stewardship theory to the boardrooms of real-world application.

11

Theory versus Real Life

In the space of data stewardship, while theory provides guidance star for the principles and practices that should ideally govern our data management efforts, reality often presents a web of unexpected challenges, organizational constraints, and practical considerations that can derail even the most well-conceived strategies.

This chapter delves into the reasons for this discrepancy, exploring the nuances that separate the ideal from the attainable in the world of data stewardship. We will examine how to navigate this divide, employing strategies to bridge the gap and align real-world actions with theoretical best practices. Furthermore, we will look at how benchmarking against industry standards can provide valuable insights and direction in our pursuit of effective data stewardship in the context of everyday business operations.

Let's check out some lessons learned from real life:

- Understanding why there is a gap between theory and reality
- Bridging the gap between theory and reality
- Future-proofing your data stewardship program

Understanding why there is a gap between theory and reality

At a recent data stewardship conference, the keynote speaker, a renowned theorist named Dr. X, quipped:

"In theory, there's no difference between theory and practice. But in practice, there is."

The crowd laughed, familiar with handling unruly datasets that were more chaotic than the orderly ones suggested by textbooks.

After the talk, a seasoned data steward named Larry approached Dr. X. "You know, I tried to implement your theoretical model once," Larry said with a grin. "But my data had other plans. It's like throwing a party and telling everyone to wear black tie, but the data shows up in Hawaiian shirts and flip-flops."

Dr. X, intrigued, asked, "So, what did you do?"

Larry winked and replied, "What any good host would do. I put on a lei, served up some piña coladas, and turned the chaos into a luau. Sometimes, you just have to roll with the reality and make the most of the data party!"

As Larry's interaction with Dr. X humorously illustrates, there often exists a substantial gap between the theoretical models we construct and the reality we encounter when dealing with data. In theory, data should adhere to predefined rules, exist in harmony, and be ready for analysis and interpretation. However, the reality of data stewardship can be vastly different and more complex. This disparity between theory and practice is not due to a flaw in the theory itself, but instead, it arises from the unpredictable and dynamic nature of data. The challenge lies in understanding why this gap exists and how we, as data stewards, can effectively navigate this divide. In this section, we will delve into the reasons behind this gap and discuss practical solutions to bridge it. Understanding this gap is not just an academic exercise; it is a crucial step for any data professional who aims to navigate the intricacies of this field successfully, turning potential pitfalls into stepping stones toward effective data stewardship.

Discovering the gaps

In both theory and practice, data stewardship is of paramount importance. Theoretically, it provides a structured framework for managing and maximizing the value of the data. It dictates how data should be collected, stored, processed, and protected.

In practice, however, data stewardship is vital not just for managing data but also for dealing with the unexpected. The reality of data is messy and unpredictable. Inconsistent data formats, errors, missing data, and changing business requirements are just a few of the real-world challenges that data stewards face. Successful data stewardship in practice requires flexibility, problem-solving skills, and a deep understanding of both the organization's needs and the data itself. Despite the gap between theory and practice, data stewardship remains the key to unlocking the true potential of data in any organization.

The gap between theory and practice in data stewardship can be attributed to several factors. Let's delve into each reason by contrasting the ideal scenarios with the real-world application:

- **Data quality**: Theoretical data stewardship assumes high-quality data—complete, accurate, consistent, and up to date. In the real world, data stewards often grapple with incomplete, inaccurate, inconsistent, or outdated data. The effort required to clean, validate, and update data can be substantial, widening the gap between theory and practice. Consider a multinational corporation with branches worldwide. Each branch may use different systems to record customer data, resulting in variations in data format and structure. For instance, one branch might record dates in *MM/DD/YYYY* format, while another uses *DD/MM/YYYY*. These inconsistencies pose real challenges when trying to consolidate and analyze the data.

- **Data volume**: Theoretical models often do not account for the sheer volume of data that organizations generate and collect. In real-world scenarios, data stewards deal with massive data sets that can be overwhelming and time-consuming to manage, analyze, and interpret. The growing use of real-time data adds further complexity to the gap. Consider a large e-commerce platform that collects clickstream data from millions of users daily. The sheer volume of data generated can overwhelm traditional data management systems and pose significant challenges in data processing and analysis.

- **Change management**: Theoretical models of data stewardship are typically static, assuming a stable business environment. In contrast, real-world business environments are dynamic, with constantly changing requirements, regulations, and technologies. Data stewards must adapt to these changes, which can disrupt established data stewardship processes. Imagine a financial institution adapting to a new regulation that requires stricter data privacy measures. This change would require modifications to the existing data stewardship processes, including how data is collected, stored, and shared.

- **Human factor**: In theory, data stewardship processes are automated and free from human error. However, in practice, humans are involved at every step, from data entry to interpretation. This introduces the potential for errors and bias that can significantly impact data quality and reliability. Consider a large manufacturing firm where employees manually enter data about raw material usage into a system. Despite the best efforts, human errors can occur, such as typos or incorrect entries, which can impact the overall data quality and subsequent analyses.

By understanding these reasons for the gap between theory and practice, data stewards can better anticipate challenges, adapt their strategies, and bridge the gap to achieve successful data stewardship.

Identifying the gaps

Identifying gaps between theory and reality as a data steward involves several steps:

1. **Evaluate current practices**: Start by thoroughly assessing your current data stewardship practices. This involves examining how data is collected, stored, processed, and utilized in your organization.

2. **Compare with theoretical models**: Next, compare your current practices with the theoretical models and best practices in data stewardship. This could involve reviewing academic literature, industry guidelines, or widely accepted standards.

3. **Identify discrepancies**: Look for discrepancies between your current practices and the theoretical models. These discrepancies could range from minor variations in procedure to major deviations in policy.

4. **Understand underlying causes**: Once you have identified the gaps, try to understand their underlying causes. These could be due to organizational culture, resource constraints, lack of awareness, or other factors.

5. **Prioritize gaps**: Not all gaps will have the same impact on your data stewardship efforts. Prioritize them based on factors such as their potential impact on data quality, compliance risks, and strategic importance.

Following these steps, a data steward can identify, understand, and prioritize the gaps between theory and reality in their data stewardship practices. This is a crucial first step towards bridging these gaps and improving data management in the organization.

Let's take a healthcare company as an example:

1. **Evaluate current practices**: This healthcare company began by conducting a thorough review of its data stewardship practices, which involved assessing the handling of patient data, from collection at the point of care to storage in **electronic health records** (EHR) and utilization for clinical decision-making.

2. **Compare with theoretical models**: The company compared their practices with standard models such as the EDM Council's **Cloud Data Management Capabilities** (CDMC), or DAMA's **Data Management Body of Knowledge** (DMBOK), and best practices outlined by healthcare data regulations such as HIPAA and GDPR.

3. **Identify discrepancies**: In doing so, they found discrepancies in their practices related to patient consent for data usage, data encryption standards, and data quality checks that did not fully align with the theoretical models and regulatory guidelines.

4. **Understand underlying causes**: Upon further investigation, they found that these gaps were due to a mix of outdated technology, a lack of awareness among staff about best practices, and an organizational culture that undervalued data privacy and security.

5. **Prioritize gaps**: The company then prioritized these gaps based on their potential impact on patient trust, compliance risks, and the strategic importance of data in improving patient care. The top priority was addressing data encryption standards to secure patient data and reduce compliance risks.

Now let's look into the common gaps in the world of data stewardship.

Bridging the gap between theory and reality

Bridging the gap between theory and reality in data stewardship involves transforming theoretical concepts into actionable strategies that can be implemented in everyday operations. This is not a straightforward task as it requires adapting ideal models to the unpredictable and dynamic nature of real-world data. It involves making necessary adjustments and compromises to fit the theory into the real-life context while still upholding the principles of data stewardship. This section will explore various strategies to overcome the disconnect between theory and practice. We will discuss how to manage data consistency, improve data quality, handle large data volumes, adapt to changes, and mitigate human errors. The objective is to provide practical solutions that can be tailored to your organization's specific needs and challenges in data stewardship.

Critical thinking in bridging theory and reality

Critical thinking is essential when navigating the complexities of data stewardship in practice. As we bridge the gap between theory and reality, we must not only identify and understand these discrepancies but also develop a nuanced perspective that questions assumptions, considers context, and evaluates the practical implications of theoretical models.

Cultivating a critical mindset can help in dissecting the intricacies of applying theory to real-life data scenarios. This includes the following:

- **Questioning assumptions**: Challenge the assumptions underlying theoretical models. Are these assumptions valid in your organization's context? For instance, the assumption that all data can be standardized may not hold true for a company with diverse international operations.

- **Contextual analysis**: Consider the specific context in which your data stewardship practices operate. What works for one industry or organization size may not be suitable for another. Reflect on how organizational culture, technological infrastructure, and business objectives might influence the applicability of theoretical best practices.

- **Evaluating trade-offs**: Recognize the trade-offs that may come with applying theory to practice. For example, the ideal of real-time data quality checks may need to be balanced against the practicalities of system performance and resource availability.

- **Incremental implementation**: Think critically about how to implement changes incrementally. This allows for the assessment of each step's impact and the flexibility to adjust the approach as needed, rather than a wholesale, theory-driven overhaul that could disrupt operations.

- **Learning from outliers**: Pay attention to data outliers or exceptions as they can provide critical insights. These anomalies often highlight where theory and reality diverge, offering opportunities for refining data stewardship practices.

Integrating data stewardship into daily operations

A common pitfall in the establishment of data stewardship programs is the segregation of data stewards from the organization's core activities. When data stewardship is treated as an isolated function, data stewards may find themselves working in silos, disconnected from the business processes and decision-making they are meant to support. This can lead to a lack of recognition for their contributions and insufficient commitment from other stakeholders. To overcome this challenge, we must embed data stewardship into the daily operations of the organization.

- **Alignment with business processes**: Data stewards should have a clear understanding of the business processes and workflows they are supporting. By aligning data stewardship activities with these processes, data stewards can ensure that data management practices are directly contributing to operational efficiency and strategic goals.

- **Cross-departmental involvement**: Data stewards must be involved in cross-departmental initiatives and projects. This involvement ensures that data considerations are included in decision-making and that the value of good data management is communicated across the organization.

- **Recognition and incentivization**: Organizations should recognize and reward the contributions of data stewards. This could take the form of formal recognition programs, inclusion in strategic planning sessions, or incentives tied to data quality improvements.

- **Communication and advocacy**: Data stewards should be empowered to advocate for the importance of data management. Regular communication with stakeholders about the successes and challenges of data stewardship can elevate its profile and integrate it into the organizational culture.

- **Embedding data stewardship roles**: Consider embedding data stewardship roles within business units or teams. This proximity allows data stewards to work side by side with colleagues, increasing their visibility and enabling them to directly influence everyday data practices.

By addressing these elements, organizations can ensure that data stewardship is not seen as a peripheral function but as an integral part of the daily operation, driving the organization towards data excellence.

Next, let's walk through the common gaps in the real world and how we can address them.

Gap #1 – Standard operating procedure is written but not followed

Standard operating procedures (SOPs) are crucial for maintaining consistency and reliability in data management. However, in real-life settings, these procedures may not always be strictly followed or monitored. Here are some strategies to address this gap:

- **Training and awareness**: Conduct regular training sessions to ensure that all employees understand the SOPs and the importance of adhering to them. For instance, a healthcare organization might train its staff on the SOPs for patient data entry to ensure accuracy and consistency.

- **Monitoring and auditing**: Implement monitoring systems to ensure compliance with SOPs. For example, a financial institution could use automated systems to monitor transactions and flag any that don't comply with the established SOPs.

- **Feedback and improvement**: Encourage employees to provide feedback on the SOPs and make improvements based on this feedback. A retail company might discover through employee feedback that the SOP for inventory management is too time-consuming, prompting a revision of the procedure.

For example, we can use technology to embed data onboarding checklists into the workflow automatically. A data onboarding checklist, as illustrated in *Table 11.1*, can ensure that all necessary steps are followed when new data is brought into the system. A cloud-based data management system can be programmed to follow a specific sequence of steps every time new data is onboarded. This could include steps such as data ownership assignment, data validation, data cleansing, data transformation, and data integration. The system could also be set up to flag any errors or discrepancies that occur during the onboarding process, allowing for immediate correction. Once SOPs are configured as system workflows, everyone has to follow the same path and can be easily monitored.

Item	Description
Data owner	Confirm accountability and ownership of the new dataset
Data security classification	Classification could be public, internal, or confidential. Different workflows and approval processes as per classification.
Metadata	Ideally, this should be auto-captured by the data catalog software. Example metadata includes database table names, field names, and field style.
Business use case description, keyword tagging	Facilitate data discovery among all users
Critical Data Element (CDE)	Uphold the data quality of CDE; for example, the data steward and the data owner will get notified when there is any empty value for the CDE
Data access control	Define which user group can access this new dataset
Personally identifiable information (PII)	Indicate if the dataset contains any PII. This can aid the workflow of data encryption or masking and also auditing

Table 11.1 – An example checklist for new data set onboarding

In real-life settings, adjustments and compromises may be needed to fit the theory into practice. For example, while the theory might suggest that all data should be validated automatically via predefined business logic by the system to ensure accuracy, in practice, this may not be feasible due to unforeseeable data formats and new data sources. As a compromise, organizations might decide to use automated validation for most data (e.g., 80%) and manual validation for high-risk or high-value data (e.g., 20%). Another adjustment might involve the frequency of monitoring and auditing. While continuous monitoring might be the theoretical ideal, in practice, it might be more feasible to conduct periodic audits due to resource limitations.

Gap #2 – Insufficient commitment from stakeholders

Insufficient commitment from stakeholders is a common challenge in implementing data stewardship and governance in real life. Everyone knows it is the right thing to do, but not many of them are committed.

This usually happens when stakeholders do not fully understand the value of data management or see it as a low priority compared to other business concerns. You may refer to *Chapter 2, How Data Stewardship Can Help Your Organization*, to understand value realization. Revisit *Chapter 3, Getting Started with the Data Stewardship Program*, to quickly brush up on the concepts of prioritization of your data stewardship goals.

The table shown in *Figure 11.1* can be a powerful tool for addressing this gap. This table visualizes the relationships between different datasets and the business use cases they support. It can highlight how data impacts various aspects of the business and the potential risks of poor data management, thereby showing the business value to stakeholders. With that, we can convey the message *"Your business is only as good as your data."*

Data Set	Priority use case	Mid priority use case		Low priority use case
	Personalized recommendation	Inventory warehouse optimization	Cash flow project	Social media marketing
Product	*	*		*
Customer	*			*
Inventory		*	*	*
Sales	*	*	*	
Finance		*	*	

Figure 11.1 – A table for datasets and use case

For instance, if a table shows that a particular dataset is crucial for several high-value use cases, stakeholders may realize the importance of managing that data effectively. As per the table in *Figure 11.1*, the sales dataset is the most critical one as it serves all high and mid-priority use cases. Similarly, if the heatmap highlights the risks associated with a specific dataset, stakeholders might be more willing to invest in data security measures. You can also have a bird-eye's view of the impact of business if one particular dataset is disabled. This will be a big plus when it comes to decision-making, severity analysis, and escalation analysis.

Engaging stakeholders and demonstrating the business value of data management can help overcome the disconnect between ideal models and everyday operations. Here are some strategies:

- **Clear communication**: Communicate the benefits of data stewardship in terms stakeholders understand. This might involve showing how it improves operational efficiency, reduces risk, or supports strategic goals.

- **Stakeholder involvement**: Involve stakeholders in data governance activities. This might include including them in decision-making processes or soliciting their input on data management strategies.

- **Regular updates**: Provide regular updates on the progress and impact of data stewardship initiatives. This can help maintain stakeholder interest and commitment.

Again, adjustments and compromises may be necessary to fit the theory into the real-life context. For instance, while the theory might advocate for a comprehensive data governance model involving all stakeholders. In practice, it might be more feasible to start with a smaller group of key stakeholders. Remember, you should not boil the ocean, and you have to accept the fact that not all data is born equal.

Gap #3 – Data governance operating model cannot keep up with ever-changing regulatory requirements

Data governance operating models provide a framework for how an organization manages and uses its data. However, these models can struggle to keep pace with rapidly changing regulatory requirements, particularly in areas like cross-border data transfer and data privacy. As companies become more global and data increasingly crosses national boundaries, compliance with different countries' data protection regulations becomes more complex.

For instance, the European Union's **General Data Protection Regulation** (**GDPR**) imposes strict rules on transferring personal data outside the EU. At the same time, other jurisdictions, such as the United States, Singapore, HKSAR, and mainland China may have differing data protection laws. Navigating these different regulations and ensuring compliance can be a challenge for any data governance model.

To address this gap, organizations can take several steps:

- **Stay informed**: First, it is crucial to stay informed about regulatory changes in all jurisdictions where the company operates or transfers data. This may involve subscribing to regulatory updates, attending industry conferences, or hiring legal experts.

- **Agile governance models**: Create flexible data governance models that can be adjusted as regulations change. For instance, an organization might have a standard procedure for data transfer but alter specific steps based on the destination country's regulations.

- **Technology solutions**: Leverage technology solutions that can help manage regulatory compliance. For example, some data management software provides features that automatically apply rules based on the data's origin and destination, ensuring compliance with different regulations.

Adjustments and compromises may be necessary to fit the theory into a real-life context. In theory, a rigid data governance model with stringent controls might seem ideal. But in practice, this might be too inflexible to cope with changing regulations. As a compromise, an organization might opt for a more flexible model that can accommodate changes. This might involve fewer controls but more frequent monitoring and adjustment. While this approach might require more effort to manage, it could offer a better balance between regulatory compliance and operational efficiency.

As we all know, there is no one-size-fits-all solution, we have to strike a balance based on our organization's risk appetite and resources.

Gap #4 – Technical debt

This gap is one of the biggest blockers of all. **Technical debt** refers to the future costs associated with shortcuts or quick fixes in software development. These shortcuts might solve immediate issues, but they often lead to more complex problems down the line, requiring more time and resources to fix.

As you can imagine, we are suffering technical debt from all the legacy systems and designs from decades ago. This in turn creates the bottlenecks in technology integration for your organization. Technology integration bottlenecks occur when different systems or technologies cannot effectively communicate or work together due to compatibility issues. This can slow down data processes, create inefficiencies, and lead to inaccurate data.

To effectively address this gap, we need to realize dynamic business model requires a dynamic data governance platform and architecture. It refers to the need for flexible, adaptable data governance systems that can keep pace with evolving business requirements against the backdrop of technical debt. Let's admit that not all technical debts can be tackled in a short period of time. However, we can still have a decentralized data architecture on top of all these legacy systems in order to cope with the agile business needs.

Figure 11.2 introduces a **data mesh**. Data mesh is a decentralized data architecture that can help overcome the disconnect between ideal models and everyday operations. Instead of having a central data team responsible for all data governance tasks, data mesh distributes these responsibilities across various domain-oriented teams.

Some principles of a data mesh (`https://en.wikipedia.org/wiki/Data_mesh`) architecture include the following:

- **Domain ownership**: In traditional data management, data ownership is often centralized. However, the data mesh approach proposes that data should be owned and managed by the domain teams that produce and use it. This principle encourages a decentralized approach where each team has full ownership and responsibility for their domain's data, including its quality, governance, and life cycle management.

- **Data as a product**: This principle transforms the perception of data from being a byproduct of operations to being a valuable product in its own right. Each data domain should be treated as a product with a dedicated product owner, who is responsible for its quality, usability, and value generation. This shift allows organizations to realize the true value of their data and prioritize its management.

- **Self-serve data platform**: In the data mesh approach, the role of a centralized data team shifts from being the owners and providers of data to becoming the enablers of a self-serve data infrastructure. This principle promotes the development of a platform that allows teams to discover, understand, and use data independently. A self-serve data platform improves agility and reduces bottlenecks in data access and usage.

- **Federated computational governance**: This principle advocates for a decentralized model of data governance. Governance rules and policies are defined and enforced locally by the teams that own the data. However, there is also a federated layer of governance to ensure organization-wide compliance and coordination. This approach balances the autonomy of teams with the need for overall consistency and control. For example, in a retail company, there might be separate teams for online sales, in-store sales, customer relations, and supply chain management. Each of these teams would be responsible for the governance of their own data, including quality, security, and compliance as illustrated in *Figure 11.2*. They would use common standards and tools to ensure consistency, but the day-to-day management would be decentralized.

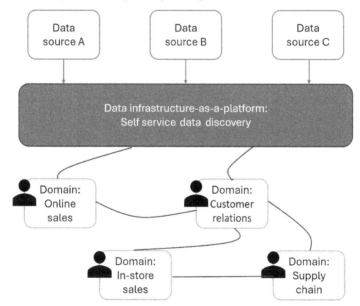

Figure 11.2 – A sample data mesh architecture

This approach can help overcome technology integration bottlenecks and reduce technical debt by distributing the load and allowing more specialized, efficient data management. It also aligns well with the concept of a dynamic data governance platform, as it allows more flexibility and adaptability to changing business requirements.

Adjustments and compromises might be necessary to implement data mesh in a real-life context. For instance, while the theory advocates for full decentralization, some central oversight might still be needed to ensure consistency and compliance. Additionally, while data mesh encourages each team to manage its own data, some companies might find it more practical to have certain central resources, such as a data quality team or a data security team, to support the domain-oriented teams. Implementing data mesh also requires a shift in culture and mindset, which might take time and face resistance. As a compromise, companies might implement data mesh gradually, starting with a few teams and expanding over time.

Let's switch gears to discuss how to make your data stewardship program future-proof.

Future-proofing your data stewardship program

In this increasingly data-driven world, it is essential for organizations to stay ahead of the curve in managing their data assets. As such, the final section of this chapter focuses on preparing your data stewardship initiatives to be resilient and adaptable to future changes and challenges. The goal is not only to safeguard your current data management efforts but also to ensure their relevancy and effectiveness in the long run. In this section, we will explore strategies and best practices to help you build a robust, flexible, and forward-thinking data stewardship program that can withstand the test of time and technological advancements.

Benchmarking with DAMA and EDMC surveys

The **Data Management Association (DAMA)** and the **Enterprise Data Management Council (EDMC)** provide valuable resources for benchmarking an organization's data maturity and literacy. These include surveys that assess various aspects of data management, from data quality and governance to data architecture and integration. You may refer to `https://edmcouncil.org/innovation/research/benchmarks` and `https://www.dama-uk.org/resources/Documents/DAMA%20UK%20Membership%20Survey%20Results%202023.pdf` for details about these surveys.

By participating in these surveys, organizations can gain insights into their current state of data maturity and literacy compared to peers in the industry. This can highlight areas of strength and areas for improvement, helping to shape future data stewardship strategies.

To further delve into benchmarking for data stewardship, you should define the benchmarking strategy for your organization. Here are some of the options:

- **Peer benchmarking**: Compare data stewardship practices with similar organizations to identify areas of improvement and innovation. This involves not just comparing metrics, but also strategies, technologies, and processes.

- **Industry trend analysis**: Stay abreast of trends by participating in industry forums, workshops, and publications. Use these insights to benchmark your practices against emerging standards and anticipate future developments.

- **Performance metrics**: Develop a comprehensive set of performance metrics that align with business goals. Benchmarking these metrics over time can help track progress and identify areas for strategic improvement.

Enhancing data stewards' skills with skillset matrix

A **skillset matrix** can be used to identify and enhance the critical skills of data stewards. This matrix can list the key skills needed for effective data stewardship – such as data operation, data quality, compliance, and leadership – and rate each data steward's proficiency in these skills.

This can help identify gaps in skills and inform targeted training and development programs. For instance, if a data steward has strong data management skills but lacks proficiency in data governance, they might benefit from training in data governance principles and best practices.

Role	Data operation	Data quality	Compliance	Technical skill	Communication
Data steward lead	4	5	8	1	9
Data steward A	6	4	5	9	2
Data steward B	7	9	2	4	5

On a scale of 1-9:

Table 11.2 – Sample skillset matrix for data steward

As illustrated in *Table 11.2*, take data steward B as an example. They have a high proficiency in data operation and data quality, moderate proficiency in technical skills and communication, and low proficiency in compliance.

Based on the skillset matrix, data steward B would need targeted training in the areas of compliance. Compliance training could cover a detailed understanding of applicable data laws, regulations, and standards. This could include practical sessions on how to ensure data practices align with these requirements and the implications of non-compliance. The training could also cover how to stay abreast of evolving data privacy and security regulations. On the other hand, the data steward could share their expertise in areas where they have high proficiency – data operation and data quality. They could lead workshops or training sessions on best practices in data operation, including data collection, processing, storage, and usage.

For their moderate proficiency areas – technical skills and communication – the data steward could both learn from others and share their knowledge. They could attend advanced technical training to improve their skills while also mentoring junior team members. In terms of communication, they could work with a mentor to improve their ability to articulate complex data concepts and insights, while also sharing their existing knowledge with others.

Yes, the priority Do is to buy this book. You got this right already.

What's next?

The following Dos and Don'ts guidelines serve as a compass, guiding you towards effective data management while cautioning against potential pitfalls. From staying current with evolving regulations to recognizing the importance of human elements in data stewardship, these pointers will help you master the art of data governance.

The Dos of data stewardship are as follows:

- Do keep up to date with changing regulations and technologies.

    - **Real-life example**: A global e-commerce company needs to stay updated about changing data privacy regulations in different countries to ensure it remains compliant. Similarly, it should embrace new technologies, such as AI and machine learning, to improve data analysis and decision-making.

- Do maintain clear, consistent communication with all stakeholders.

    - **Real-life example**: A healthcare organization implementing a new electronic health record system should maintain open lines of communication with clinicians, administrators, and IT staff to ensure everyone understands their roles and responsibilities in managing patient data.

- Do invest in training and development for data stewards.

    - **Real-life example**: A financial institution might offer regular training sessions on data governance practices and data privacy laws to ensure its data stewards are equipped to manage the organization's data effectively.

- Do regularly monitor and audit data processes for compliance and quality.

  - **Real-life example**: A manufacturing company might regularly audit its data on product defects and returns to ensure the data is accurate and reliable, and the company is compliant with quality standards.

- Do continuously review and adjust your data strategy based on business needs and changes in the data environment.

  - **Real-life example**: A retail company might adjust its data strategy to focus more on online sales data after observing a significant shift towards online shopping among its customers.

Some of the Don'ts of data stewardship are as follows:

- Don't neglect the human element of data stewardship – people's skills, attitudes, and behaviors are just as important as technology.

  - **Real-life example**: An IT company that implements a new data management system without adequately training its staff might find that employees continue to use old, inefficient data practices, undermining the benefits of the new system.

- Don't assume that once a data strategy is in place, it doesn't need to be reviewed or updated.

  - **Real-life example**: A marketing agency that fails to update its data strategy to incorporate social media data might miss out on valuable insights into customer behavior and preferences.

- Don't overlook the importance of data quality – poor quality data can undermine even the best data strategy.

  - **Real-life example**: A logistics company that relies on inaccurate or outdated inventory data might face problems like stockouts or overstocks, even if it has a well-planned supply chain strategy.

- Don't underestimate the value of data literacy – everyone in the organization should understand the basics of data management.

  - **Real-life example**: A hospital where clinicians don't understand the importance of accurately recording patient information might struggle with issues like duplicate patient records or inaccurate diagnoses.

- Don't ignore feedback from stakeholders – their insights can help improve your data strategy and stewardship practices.

  - **Real-life example**: A university that ignores feedback from students and faculty about difficulties accessing and using its online learning platform might fail to make necessary improvements, leading to lower user satisfaction and engagement.

Cultivating resilience and adaptability in data stewardship

In the fast-paced, ever-evolving world of data management, resilience and adaptability are not just desirable traits but essential ones for any data stewardship program. A resilient data stewardship program is one that can withstand setbacks and continue to operate effectively, while an adaptable program can pivot and evolve in response to new challenges and opportunities. In this subsection, we will explore strategies to foster these qualities within your data stewardship efforts:

- **Embrace a culture of continuous learning**: To stay resilient and adaptable, organizations must foster a culture where continuous learning is encouraged and supported. This means providing opportunities for data stewards to update their skills, learn about new technologies, and understand emerging trends in data management. Regular training sessions, workshops, and conferences can help keep the data team informed and prepared for changes.

- **Implement scalable and flexible data architectures**: Scalability and flexibility should be at the core of your data architecture to ensure resilience. This might involve adopting cloud-based solutions that can easily scale up or down as needed, or designing systems with modularity, allowing for parts to be updated or replaced without disrupting the whole.

- **Invest in robust data recovery and backup solutions**: A resilient data stewardship program is prepared for data loss or corruption. This requires investing in reliable data recovery and backup solutions. Regularly testing these systems is also crucial to ensure they work effectively when needed.

- **Develop a proactive risk management strategy**: Identifying potential risks before they become issues is key to maintaining an adaptable data stewardship program. This involves conducting regular risk assessments, monitoring for new threats, and developing contingency plans for different scenarios.

- **Encourage cross-functional collaboration**: Adaptability is often a result of diverse perspectives coming together to solve a problem. Encouraging collaboration between data stewards and other departments can lead to more innovative solutions and a more agile response to changing business needs.

- **Stay agile with project management methodologies**: Adopting agile project management methodologies can help data stewardship programs be more responsive to change. This might include implementing sprints for quick wins or continuous improvement cycles to iteratively enhance data practices.

By focusing on these areas, organizations can build data stewardship programs that are not only aligned with current best practices but are also robust enough to adapt to future demands. This forward-thinking approach will ensure that data stewardship remains a key driver of business success in the years to come.

Evolving theoretical models with real-life experiences

Real-life experiences can bring unforeseen challenges but also provide valuable insights that can evolve theoretical models of data stewardship. As data stewards navigate through these real-life experiences, they gain valuable insights that can help refine and evolve the theoretical models. For instance, they might discover that a certain data governance strategy is not effective in their organization due to unique cultural or operational factors. This could lead to adjustments in the theoretical model to better fit the organization's context.

Let's look at some techniques for future-proofing data stewardship:

- **Adaptive data governance frameworks**: Discuss the importance of creating data governance frameworks that are not only robust but also adaptable to accommodate new data types, sources, and technologies

- **Proactive data quality initiatives**: Explore the role of proactive data quality management in future-proofing, such as implementing machine learning algorithms that can predict and rectify data quality issues before they escalate

- **Emerging technology adoption**: Guide readers on staying informed and prepared to adopt emerging technologies such as blockchain for data integrity, or advanced analytics for deeper data insights

- **Scenario planning**: Encourage readers to engage in scenario planning exercises to anticipate potential future challenges in data stewardship and develop contingency plans

- **Sustainability practices**: Emphasize the importance of sustainable data management practices that ensure data remains accurate, usable, and valuable over time, despite changing business landscapes

Data stewards play a crucial role in this evolution process. They are at the frontline of data management, interacting with the data, systems, and stakeholders on a daily basis. Their experiences, observations, and feedback can identify gaps or opportunities for improvement in the theoretical models. They can contribute by sharing their insights, participating in the development of new strategies, and helping to implement and test these strategies in real-world settings.

Looking to the future, this iterative process of learning from real-life experiences and evolving theoretical models is likely to continue. The field of data stewardship is rapidly evolving, with new technologies, regulations, and business needs constantly emerging. Data stewards will need to stay adaptable and continuously learn from their experiences to keep their data governance strategies effective and relevant.

Moreover, the trend towards more decentralized and dynamic data governance approaches, such as data mesh, suggests that data stewards will have more autonomy and responsibility in managing their data domains. This will likely make their real-life experiences even more critical in shaping and evolving the theoretical models of data stewardship.

By continuously learning from real-life experiences and adjusting theoretical models accordingly, organizations can enhance the effectiveness of their data stewardship efforts and better meet their business needs.

Summary

In this chapter, we discussed why the gaps between theory and reality exist, strategies to bridge them, and how to future-proof data stewardship programs.

The reality of data stewardship often diverges from theory due to various factors, such as data quality, volume, change management, and human errors. Bridging these gaps requires transforming theoretical concepts into actionable strategies. This chapter presented various strategies to manage data consistency, improve data quality, handle large data volumes, adapt to changes, and mitigate human errors. It also introduced the concept of data mesh, a decentralized data architecture that can help overcome the challenges of technical debt and technology integration bottlenecks. We then concluded by emphasizing the need to future-proof data stewardship programs. The chapter also provided practical dos and don'ts for data stewardship.

Let's go to the last chapter together to deep dive into real-life case studies.

12

Case Studies

In this final chapter, we will delve into the practical aspects of data stewardship, governance, and management by exploring two compelling case studies. These real-world examples will bring to life the theories and practices we discussed in the previous chapters. The first case, *Nurturing a data culture with a data mindset*, will highlight the importance of fostering a data-driven culture within an organization, using The Bank of East Asia, Limited as a role model. In the second case, *Streamlining fund performance and reporting*, we will discuss Fencore's next-generation data management solution to showcase how deploying data strategy as a day-to-day automated operation can streamline complex processes and improve efficiency. These case studies serve as valuable learning tools, offering concrete examples of how data stewardship can unlock significant value for organizations and help them thrive in today's data-driven business landscape.

Let's learn how industry leaders stay ahead of the curve via two real-life cases:

- Nurturing data culture with a data mindset
- Streamlining fund performance and reporting

Nurturing a data culture with a data mindset – case study #1

The aim of this chapter is to showcase real-world examples of the principles and practices we've discussed throughout the book. In this case, we will look at **The Bank of East Asia (BEA)**, Limited (`https://www.hkbea.com`), a financial institution committed to fintech and digital transformation as a competitive edge. The BEA recognized the importance of data literacy across its organization and sought to instill a culture of data utilization among its staff.

The BEA faced several major *pain points* that needed to be addressed:

- The primary challenge was to shift the mindset of employees at all levels toward embracing a data-driven approach in their roles

- The bank also lacked a unified data language, which was critical in fostering effective communication and collaboration among the staff

- Finally, the bank needed to ensure that it had the right tools and standardized data processes in place to successfully implement its data strategy and fintech initiatives

Here is what the BEA did to address these pain points.

A plan of action

To tackle these challenges, the BEA formed a dedicated project team, which included the Data Science and Governance department, Fintech Development department, and Training and Development department. They collaborated with a consultancy firm that specialized in data literacy and culture empowerment.

Together, they initiated the **Data Literacy Empowerment Program** (**DLEP**) with the objective of educating three groups of staff on how to effectively speak, think, and act with data:

- **Data leaders**: Senior management and department heads who lead, nurture, and sustain a data culture and mindset

- **Citizen data scientists**: Nominated advocates across different business units, who were equipped with essential skills enabling them to influence other colleagues on data literacy

- **Data citizens**: This was all staff, who were given access to a series of webinars, building their capacity to speak data as their second business language

The program was designed to improve operational efficiency, optimize business decision-making, and promote business growth. It led to the formation of a data community, fostering a sense of collective responsibility toward data utilization.

Let's see the plan of actions and improvements for each pain point in *Table 12.1*:

Pain point	Action	Improvement
Reinforce a data mindset	Initiate the DLEP, which targets three groups of staff – data leaders, citizen data scientists, and data citizens. Over 40 workshops were conducted in six months. It aimed to equip all levels of staff with data literacy skills, thereby fostering a data-driven mindset.	More than 50% of the staff participated in the DLEP, leading to a significant enhancement in employees' data literacy. Employees were also able to leverage data analysis to support their propositions in meetings, thereby integrating data into their routine work processes.

Pain point	Action	Improvement
A lack of a unified data language	Host a series of training sessions and workshops that equipped the employees with the ability to effectively speak, think, and act with data at the same frequency.	The establishment of a common data language facilitated more effective communication among staff members, leading to better collaboration. Employees were able to use data as a new perspective to analyze problems and make more objective judgments.
A lack of standardized data processes	The BEA introduced data projects aimed at building relevant tools and designing data standardization. The bank also focused on employees' application of what they learned, encouraging them to use data analysis in their work.	It enabled the bank to achieve data commercialization and monetization. This has led to the identification of revenue-generating opportunities.

Table 12.1 – Action and improvement for the pain points

Let's see how this action plan maps to implementation of effective data stewardship.

Data stewardship in action

The BEA case study provides a compelling example of how an organization can successfully implement data stewardship, governance, and management. Here are the stages of its journey, as illustrated in *Figure 12.1*:

1. **Recognizing the importance of data literacy**: The BEA acknowledged the significance of a data-driven approach and made it a priority. This also demonstrated the bank's commitment to data stewardship. This echoes *Chapters 1* and *2* where we talk about the alignment of business strategy, data strategy, and data stewardship, and how the latter can further advance your organization's business performance. Meanwhile, the successful implementation of the DLEP demonstrates the BEA's effective stakeholder management, use case prioritization, and continuous feedback loop, as explained in *Chapter 3*.

2. **Collaborative approach**: The BEA's strategy of forming a dedicated project team and collaborating with external experts demonstrates effective data governance. This multidisciplinary collaboration, which is illustrated in *Chapters 3* and *6*, resulted in the DLEP that is amplified by the BEA's company DNA of data focus.

3. **Comprehensive training program**: The DLEP targeted staff at all levels and offered in-depth training to selected employees. This broad approach ensured that data literacy was not limited to a specific group but spread across the organization, demonstrating an inclusive approach to data management. Moreover, in-depth training was offered to selected employees to act as pioneers of the program according to their roles and responsibilities, which we discuss in *Chapters 7* and *10*.

4. **Implementation and adoption**: The BEA encouraged employees to apply what they had learned and use data analysis in their work. This real-life application of data literacy skills across all levels of the organization showcases effective data stewardship in practice and bridges the gap between theory and real life, as explained in *Chapter 11*.

5. **Further expand the positive impact**: The bank's commitment to promoting data literacy was recognized by the industry award, further validating their efforts. The BEA keeps the momentum and accelerates to the next level of success through further editions of the DLEP, demonstrating the successful implementation and sustained impact of a comprehensive data strategy, which is detailed in *Chapters 1*, *7*, and *8*.

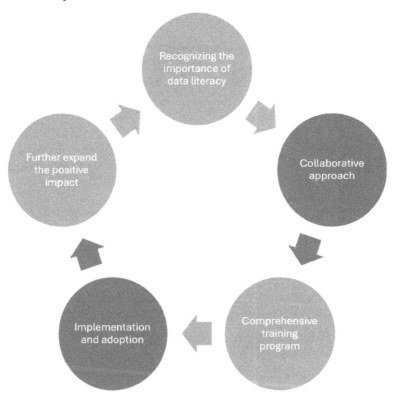

Figure 12.1 – The stages of the BEA's data literacy journey

Outcome

The BEA's DLEP initiative pioneered a unique approach to nurturing data culture – the *data mindset*. This mindset encourages individuals to use data for decision-making and innovation, fostering better collaboration among teams, which, in turn, improves business performance. With a data mindset, everyone in the organization has better ownership over data and its applications. The BEA's efforts were recognized with the *Best Data Literacy Award – Grand Prize* at the 2022 CTgoodjobs Best HR Awards, attesting to the success of their initiative (`https://dalahk.org/best-data-literacy-award-2022/` and `https://www.ctgoodjobs.hk/events/best-hr-awards-2022/winners.asp`).

The BEA's journey does not stop with the implementation of DLEP. The bank continues strengthening the overall data literacy level through the second edition of DLEP, demonstrating a commitment to continuous improvement and growth in their data strategy.

The key takeaway from this case study is the importance of creating an organization-wide culture of data literacy and usage. It demonstrates that, with a committed team, effective planning, and a strong data strategy, organizations can transform their operations and drive growth. As the BEA moves forward, it serves as an example for other organizations planning to embark on their data stewardship journey. The case study underscores the importance of continuous training, fostering a data mindset, and building a data community for sustained success.

> **Stephen Leung (the BEA's group chief information officer) on the impact of data culture in achieving operational efficiency**
>
> "The use of cloud computing, big data analysis with AI/ML technologies are important parts of our fintech strategy, assisting the bank to improve operational efficiency, optimize business decision-making and promote business growth. Improving employees' data literacy and cultivating a data culture is the foundation of the strategy and enables them to make the best use of the latest technologies."

We will now see another case study about how an investment firm with the help of data stewardship automated its data management and streamlined related processes.

Streamlining fund performance and reporting – case study #2

With the rapid advancement of technology and the rise of big data, asset managers face a myriad of challenges in managing, analyzing, and reporting data. The global failure rate of data management projects is approximately 50% (`https://www.datascience-pm.com/project-failures`), a significant statistic that has cost businesses millions of dollars in avoidable mistakes. The root of this issue lies in the outdated legacy systems prevalent in the industry that struggle to meet the evolving needs of modern businesses.

For this case, an investment firm was experiencing the following *pain points*, which are also common across the financial industry:

- **Complexity in data source landscape**: Data coming from multiple fund administrators and internal systems in different formats and standards

- **Over-reliance on manual processes**: They have to manually validate, aggregate, and visualize data with spreadsheets and PDFs (*Figure 12.2*) for portfolio monitoring and reporting

TRIAL BALANCE WITH MOVEMENTS FROM   TO

Asset Manager - Fund 1

GL Class	GL Sub Class	Counterpart	Bank Account	CCY	Op Bal Tr.ccy	Op. Bal LCY	Mov. Tr.CCy	Mov. LCY	End Bal Tr.CCy	End Bal LCY
10	A300	A Bank	A Bank - 749373948 AUD	AUD	474139.33	436208.18	3169684.63	2916109.86	3643823.96	3352318.04
10	A300	A Bank	A Bank - 464830218 GBP	GBP	1538772.11	2462035.38	1510681.49	2417090.38	3049453.6	4879125.76
10	A300	A Bank	A Bank - 957493462 USD	USD	1949209.22	2592448.26	531452.15	706831.36	2480661.37	3299279.62
10	A300	B Bank	B Bank - 3973023947 AUD	AUD	2998508.42	2758627.75	-974750.95	-896770.88	2023757.47	1861856.87
10	A300	B Bank	B Bank - 9662856271 SGD	SGD	2197981.21	2197981.21	-2012357.48	-2012357.48	185623.73	185623.73
10	A300	B Bank	B Bank - 6739567472 USD	USD	897028.45	1193047.84	773275.55	1028456.48	1670304	2221504.32
		Total for GL Subclass - Type				11640348.62		4159359.72		15799708.34
		Total for GL Class - Type				11640348.62		4159359.72		15799708.34
20	A200	Service Provider C		GBP	2869887.16	4591819.46	-2576910.73	-4123057.17	292976.43	468762.29
20	A200		A Bank - 957493462 USD	USD	1666541.38	2216500.04	2120079.22	2819705.36	3786620.6	5036205.4
20	A200	B Bank	B Bank - 6739567472 USD	USD	421626.37	560763.07	1417937.95	1885857.48	1839564.32	2446620.55
20	A200	A Bank	A Bank - 749373948 AUD	AUD	413637.43	380546.4356	2497208.15	2297431.5	2910845.58	2677977.934
20	A200	A Bank	A Bank - 957493462 USD	USD	15362.84	20432.58	436403.46	580416.6	451766.3	600849.18
20	A200	A Bank	A Bank - 957493462 USD	USD	2639466.8	3510490.84	-1065110.19	-1416996.55	1574356.61	2093894.29
		Total for GL Subclass - Type				11280552.43		2043757.22		13324309.64
20	A400	B Bank	B Bank - 6739567472 USD	USD	3986445.93	5301973.09	-1897655.6	-2523881.95	2088790.33	2778091.14
20	A400	A Bank	A Bank - 749373948 AUD	AUD	94287.02	86744.06	2762686.81	2541671.86	2856973.83	2628415.92
20	A400	A Bank	A Bank - 749373948 AUD	AUD	2272158.05	2090385.41	786293.06	723389.61	3058451.11	2813775.02
20	A400	A Bank	A Bank - 464830218 GBP	GBP	1384949	2215918.4	-146267.38	-234027.81	1238681.62	1981890.59
20	A400	A Bank	A Bank - 957493462 USD	USD	3263575.05	4340554.82	531669.67	707120.66	3795244.72	5047675.48
20	A400	A Bank	A Bank - 957493462 USD	USD	1117156.31	1485817.89	-935766.35	-1244569.24	181389.96	241248.65
		Total for GL Subclass - Type				15521393.67		-30296.87		15491096.8
		Total for GL Class - Type				26801946.1		2013460.35		28815406.44
50	400.1	Service Provider C		USD	2964195.45	3942379.95	-885324.47	-1177481.55	2078870.98	2764898.4
50	400.1	B Bank	B Bank - 6739567472 USD	USD	3291003.44	4377034.58	-1762260.67	-2343806.7	1528742.77	2033227.86
50	400.1	Service Provider C		AUD	3754438.26	3454083.2	-3177266.6	-2923085.27	577171.66	530997.93
50	400.1	Service Provider D		AUD	2392213.55	2200836.47	725312.93	667287.89	3117526.48	2868124.36
50	400.1	Service Provider D		USD	995749.01	1324346.18	-902998.36	-1200987.82	92750.65	123358.36
		Total for GL Subclass - Type				15298680.38		-6978073.45		8320606.93
		Total for GL Class - Type				15298680.38		-6978073.45		8320606.93
80	333	Fund Administrator A		USD	3137742.04	4173196.91	-2039506.01	-2712542.99	1098236.03	1460653.92
80	333	Fund Administrator A		USD	1632633.7	2171402.82	2137161.42	2842424.69	3769795.12	5013827.51
80	333	Fund Administrator A		USD	3288820.56	4374131.34	-1772039.13	-2356812.04	1516781.43	2017319.3
80	333	Fund Administrator A		USD	1201768.71	1598352.36	288182.07	383282.16	1489950.78	1981634.54
		Total for GL Subclass - Type				12317083.45		-1843648.18		10473435.27
		Total for GL Class - Type				12317083.45		-1843648.18		10473435.27

Figure 12.2 – Balance movement data of an investment provided in the PDF format, which is not machine-readable-friendly

- **Inconsistent data delivery cycles**: Data is delivered on different time cycles for different financial markets, making it challenging to achieve a unified view of fund performance

- **Currency conversion**: Multiple currencies with inconsistent exchange rates, make the reporting and decision-making difficult

- **Lack of auditable control**: It's difficult to manage the risk of human error and provide timely and accurate reports to regulators (*Figure 12.3*)

SECURITIES AND FUTURES ACT
(CHAPTER 289)

SECURITIES AND FUTURES (FINANCIAL AND MARGIN REQUIREMENTS FOR HOLDERS OF CAPITAL MARKETS SERVICES LICENCES) REGULATIONS (Rg 13)

REGULATION 27(1)(a) AND (9)(b)

STATEMENT OF ASSETS AND LIABILITIES

FORM

1

Name of the holder of a capital markets services licence: ____________________

Statement of assets and liabilities as at: (dd-mmm-yyyy)

	$	$
SHAREHOLDERS' FUNDS/ NET HEAD OFFICE FUNDS		
Paid-up capital		
(1) ordinary shares		______
(2) preference shares	______	
(a) paid-up irredeemable and cumulative	______	
(b) paid- up irredeemable and non-cumulative	______	______
Revaluation reserves[1]		______
Reserve fund		______
Unappropriated profit or loss		______
Other reserves		______
Net head office funds		______
Total Shareholders' Funds or Net Head Office Funds		______

Figure 12.3 – A partial report for the Monetary Authority of Singapore

Let's see how they tackled these pain points.

A plan of action

The investment firm approached Fencore for the solution. Fencore (`https://www.fencore.co`) is a solution provider of data management software.

Their data management solution emerged as a game-changer for this investment firm. As a platform designed with high interoperability, it could easily connect to the required third-party and internal systems for data imports and exports. The ready data models that matched popular fund administrators' data outputs streamlined the data management process. Meanwhile, the intuitive dashboards and alerts optimized workflows are a huge time saver, keeping user experience a high priority.

Pain point	Action	Improvement
Complexity in the data source landscape	Deploy a data management solution to automate the data ingest from multiple sources to form a single source of truth, irrespective of their formats and standards.	A more streamlined and efficient data management process
Over-reliance on manual processes	Deploy automated workflows and dashboards.	A significant time saving of approximately 80%, increased operational efficiency, and the reduced risk of manual errors.
Inconsistent data delivery cycles	Automate the system workflow to handle data delivered on different time cycles.	Regular and timely data updates led to more accurate monitoring and decision-making.
Currency conversion	Configure the business logic in the system to aggregate data existing in a range of national currencies into a single currency.	Simplified reporting and decision-making process, as all data could be viewed in a single currency.
A lack of auditable control	Deploy a four-eyes approval process with access controls and an audit trail capability.	Enhanced risk management with reduced chances of human error, ensuring timely and accurate reporting to regulators.

Table 12.2 – Action and improvement for pain points

The implementation process began with the creation of a security/holdings master and a fund **Net Asset Value (NAV)** master, using data management software. The platform ingested a balance sheet, Profit and Loss (P&L), trial balances, valuation detail, and holdings data, conducted quality checks, and aggregated and mapped data to data dictionaries (*Figure 12.4*), effectively creating a single source of truth. The NAV for each fund was then calculated, allowing the calculation of the overall NAV across all funds.

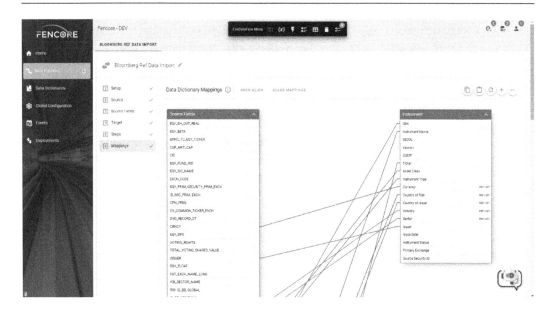

Figure 12.4 – A data mapping capability

Figure 12.5 illustrates the user interface to view and modify data. When users modify data, a four-eyes approval process is in place.

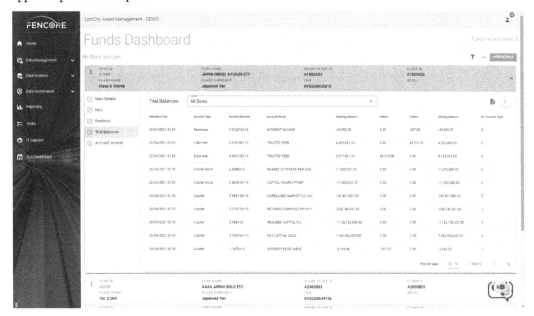

Figure 12.5 – Sample dashboards to view and modify data

The **four-eyes approval process**, also known as dual control or dual verification, is a system of checks and balances designed to ensure accuracy and prevent errors or fraudulent activities.

This process requires that any significant action, decision, or transaction must be approved by at least two individuals. In the realm of data management, these actions could include data entry, data modifications, system configuration changes, or the release of sensitive reports or information. When applied to data stewardship, the four-eyes approval process can greatly enhance data accuracy and integrity. For instance, if a data steward enters or modifies key data, a second data steward or another authorized individual would need to review and approve these changes before they are implemented, as illustrated in *Figure 12.6*.

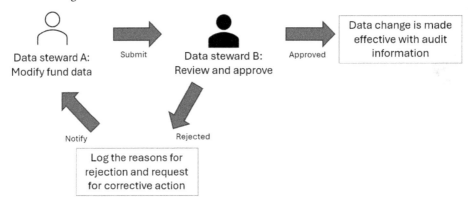

Figure 12.6 – The four-eyes approval process

This process not only reduces the risk of errors but also discourages fraudulent activities, since any action taken would need to get past two individuals. It also ensures that data stewards are accountable for their actions, promoting a culture of responsibility and trust. Moreover, the implementation of the *four-eyes approval process* in data management systems often includes an audit trail feature. This means all changes and approvals are logged and traceable, providing a clear record of who did what and when. This can be invaluable for troubleshooting, audits, or investigations.

Let's see how these changes map to the data stewardship actions we have discussed throughout this book.

Data stewardship in action

The case study presented illustrates a classic scenario in which an organization faced numerous data challenges, all of which point toward the need for an effective and automated data stewardship solution.

The alignment of business strategy with data strategy, as discussed in *Chapter 1*, was a clear starting point for the investment manager firm. The firm recognized the need to evolve its operational practices to unlock the value of data, thus moving from a traditional business strategy to a data-driven one. Let's also not forget technology should adapt to the people and processes in an organization (*Chapter 5*), not the other way around.

The implementation of Fencore's solution exemplifies the principles of data stewardship discussed throughout this book. As we explored in *Chapter 4*, developing a comprehensive data management strategy is crucial to tackling challenges such as handling data from multiple sources and delivering them according to different timelines. The data management solution addressed this by automating data ingestion from various sources to form a single source of truth. This automated process reduces manual errors and increases the reliability of data. During the solution configuration, we can refer to what we learned in *Chapters 10* and *11* to embed the best practices as standardized and reusable rules in the system.

Moreover, the deployment of automated workflows and dashboards aligns with the principles discussed in *Chapter 5, People, Process, Technology*. The solution's intuitive workflows, alongside user-friendly dashboards, empowered team members to interact with the data efficiently. This streamlined interaction between people and technology is a key element in successful data stewardship.

Regarding the data delivered at different time cycles, Fencore's automated system workflow was a crucial solution. This capability, which falls under the aspects of data stewardship discussed in *Chapters 2* and *4*, ensures consistent data management, regardless of the varying delivery schedules.

The ability to aggregate data existing in a range of national currencies into a single currency is one of the examples of a best practice, as discussed in *Chapters 8* and *10*. Through the configurable data management solution, the firm could easily consolidate financial data, a process that significantly enhanced the firm's data quality and insights.

In addition to the preceding, the four-eyes approval process deployed by the solution reinforces the data steward roles and responsibilities discussed in *Chapter 7*. This process, combined with access controls and audit trail capabilities, ensured data integrity and security, while maintaining necessary oversight.

We can observe that the next generation of data stewardship is about proactive management of data assets. Data stewardship is no longer simply about maintaining data and involves a strategic approach to using data to drive business value. As illustrated in this case study, the right technology can empower an organization to effectively navigate the complexity of data management, aligning with the principles of data stewardship to unlock the true value of data.

Outcome

The implementation of data management software led to significant improvements for the client. Operational efficiency was enhanced, as the need for manual work with PDFs or spreadsheets was eliminated. The client saved approximately 80% of their time, with fund overviews and data for reports readily available once produced by fund administrators. Data quality was also enhanced, as all data was validated, stored, and displayed in a standard format used across the company. Furthermore, the risk was significantly reduced, as manual data wrangling was replaced with automated processes, ensuring data accuracy. The built-in Kanban board for tasks in data management software also kept employees on top of required actions ahead of time, further reducing the risk of missed deadlines.

Summary

Your business is only as good as your data.

As you can see in the two case studies, the quality of your business insights, decisions, and actions is directly proportional to the quality of your data. Therefore, investing in effective data stewardship is not just a choice but also a necessity for your business's success.

A business's data culture is the union of its data mindset and data skill set. A data mindset pertains to the direction your organization takes when it comes to data management. It embodies the values, attitudes, and beliefs that your organization holds toward data. Conversely, a data skillset serves as the enabler. It comprises the practical skills, knowledge, and abilities that allow your organization to handle, analyze, and interpret data effectively.

Treating data as an asset is a fundamental shift in perspective that is essential for modern businesses. Data is not merely an operational by-product; it is a key resource that can drive your business forward. Moreover, data stewardship is everyone's business. From top-level executives to ground-level employees, everyone has a role to play in ensuring the quality, accuracy, and security of data. This collective responsibility ensures that data is treated with the respect it deserves, much like any other valuable business asset. Data stewardship is not a solitary endeavor but a team sport. It requires collaboration, communication, and a shared understanding of data's value. Every member of the team, from data stewards to data users, has a role to play in ensuring that data is properly managed, protected, and utilized.

For managers who may be hesitant about the **return on investment (ROI)** of data stewardship, you should ask them to also consider the risks of not investing in it. The costs of poor data quality, data breaches, regulatory penalties, and missed opportunities far outweigh the investment in a comprehensive data stewardship program.

Data stewardship can significantly contribute to each of these points. It ensures that your data is of high quality, thereby strengthening your business. It reinforces a positive data culture by promoting good data practices. It treats data as an asset and ensures its proper handling and protection. It fosters a collaborative environment where everyone shares responsibility for data. And finally, it mitigates risks associated with poor data management, thereby ensuring a positive ROI.

Data stewardship is not just an operational necessity; it is also a strategic choice that can unlock immense value for your business. It is the key to transforming your data from a mere by-product of operations into a valuable asset that drives your business forward. So, embrace data stewardship and unlock the full potential of your organization's data.

Now, please line up your team of data superheroes to save the world!

Index

R

S

T

Packtpub.com

Subscribe to our online digital library for full access to over 7,000 books and videos, as well as industry leading tools to help you plan your personal development and advance your career. For more information, please visit our website.

Why subscribe?

- Spend less time learning and more time coding with practical eBooks and Videos from over 4,000 industry professionals

- Improve your learning with Skill Plans built especially for you

- Get a free eBook or video every month

- Fully searchable for easy access to vital information

- Copy and paste, print, and bookmark content

Did you know that Packt offers eBook versions of every book published, with PDF and ePub files available? You can upgrade to the eBook version at Packtpub.com and as a print book customer, you are entitled to a discount on the eBook copy. Get in touch with us at customercare@packtpub.com for more details.

At www.packtpub.com, you can also read a collection of free technical articles, sign up for a range of free newsletters, and receive exclusive discounts and offers on Packt books and eBooks.

Other Books You May Enjoy

If you enjoyed this book, you may be interested in these other books by Packt:

Practical Machine Learning on Databricks

Debu Sinha

ISBN: 9781801812030

- Transition smoothly from DIY setups to databricks
- Master AutoML for quick ML experiment setup
- Automate model retraining and deployment
- Leverage databricks feature store for data prep
- Use MLflow for effective experiment tracking
- Gain practical insights for scalable ML solutions
- Find out how to handle model drifts in production environments

Machine Learning Security with Azure

Georgia Kalyva

ISBN: 9781805120483

- Explore the Azure Machine Learning project life cycle and services
- Assess the vulnerability of your ML assets using the Zero Trust model
- Explore essential controls to ensure data governance and compliance in Azure
- Understand different methods to secure your data, models, and infrastructure against attacks
- Find out how to detect and remediate past or ongoing attacks
- Explore methods to recover from a security breach
- Monitor and maintain your security posture with the right tools and best practices

Packt is searching for authors like you

If you're interested in becoming an author for Packt, please visit authors.packtpub.com and apply today. We have worked with thousands of developers and tech professionals, just like you, to help them share their insight with the global tech community. You can make a general application, apply for a specific hot topic that we are recruiting an author for, or submit your own idea.

Share Your Thoughts

Now you've finished *Data Stewardship in Action*, we'd love to hear your thoughts! Scan the QR code below to go straight to the Amazon review page for this book and share your feedback or leave a review on the site that you purchased it from.

https://packt.link/r/1-837-63659-1

Your review is important to us and the tech community and will help us make sure we're delivering excellent quality content.

Download a free PDF copy of this book

Thanks for purchasing this book!

Do you like to read on the go but are unable to carry your print books everywhere?

Is your eBook purchase not compatible with the device of your choice?

Don't worry, now with every Packt book you get a DRM-free PDF version of that book at no cost.

Read anywhere, any place, on any device. Search, copy, and paste code from your favorite technical books directly into your application.

The perks don't stop there, you can get exclusive access to discounts, newsletters, and great free content in your inbox daily

Follow these simple steps to get the benefits:

1. Scan the QR code or visit the link below

https://packt.link/free-ebook/9781837636594

2. Submit your proof of purchase
3. That's it! We'll send your free PDF and other benefits to your email directly

www.ingramcontent.com/pod-product-compliance
Lightning Source LLC
Chambersburg PA
CBHW080633060326
40690CB00021B/4914